::

Homeless in Las Vegas

Homeless

Kurt Borchard

n Las Vegas

STORIES FROM THE STREET

UNIVERSITY OF NEVADA PRESS ◢◣ Reno & Las Vegas

University of Nevada Press, Reno, Nevada 89557 USA
Copyright © 2011 by University of Nevada Press
All rights reserved
Manufactured in the United States of America
Design by Kathleen Szawiola

Library of Congress Cataloging-in-Publication Data

Borchard, Kurt, 1968–
Homeless in Las Vegas : stories from the street / Kurt Borchard.
p. cm.
Includes bibliographical references and index.
ISBN 978-0-87417-837-1 (pbk. : alk. paper)
1. Homeless persons—Nevada—Las Vegas—Case studies.
2. Las Vegas (Nev.)—Social conditions—21st century.
3. Las Vegas (Nev.)—Economic conditions—21st century. I. Title.
HV4506.L37B665 2011
362.5092′2793135—dc22   2010044884

The paper used in this book is a recycled stock made from 30 percent
post-consumer waste materials, certified by FSC, and meets the
requirements of American National Standard for Information
Sciences—Permanence of Paper for Printed Library Materials,
ANSI/NISO Z39.48-1992 (R2002). Binding materials were selected
for strength and durability.

FIRST PRINTING
20   19   18   17   16   15   14   13   12   11
5   4   3   2   1

::

"Our only hope will lie in the frail web
of understanding of one person
for the pain of another."

JOHN DOS PASSOS,
December 1940

::

Contents

::

Preface

In my first book, *The Word on the Street: Homeless Men in Las Vegas* (2005), I created a portrait of homelessness by combining interviews with homeless men with an analysis of local news articles on the topic, showing how these marginalized people shatter the carefully constructed illusion that Las Vegas is only about fun and entertainment. The words and thoughts of the forty-eight men I interviewed were central to my research and were the basis for my findings.

Words of homeless people—this time, women as well as men—also form the foundation of this book, *Homeless in Las Vegas: Stories from the Street.* Their stories offer more personal, detailed accounts of homelessness, which I now believe are needed to help effect the necessary changes in public policy that have been slow in coming to Las Vegas.

Since 2005, homelessness has increased in Las Vegas, and the conditions faced by homeless people have grown appreciably worse. In my first book, I presented a hopeful argument that the city would do right by its most vulnerable and powerless citizens and visitors. I believed Las Vegas officials might enact better policies to avoid getting a reputation for unbridled nastiness toward the poor, a reputation that might cause some people to avoid going there to spend their money. I thought that the valuable insights homeless men gave me about their lives, especially that they might be viewed as people with problems rather than as problem people, would be heard. I hoped that listening to homeless people could be a cornerstone to policies that did more than hide and persecute homeless people. These hopes were not realized.

For this book, I conducted in-depth interviews again with forty-eight homeless people in the city between 2005 and 2006. I included women among those interviewed to help counteract the stereotype that homelessness affects only men. I often conducted interviews in what is called the homeless corridor in Las Vegas, where charitable homeless services are centralized, and in public parks, public libraries, soup kitchens, and bus depots. Usually, the interviews lasted between one-half and two hours each and were unstructured. For several weeks I conversed and spent time with individual homeless people. Sometimes, only one meeting was possible. Several of these interviews along with my field notes serve as the basis for the material presented here.

Each direct participant signed an Informed Consent Statement, and participants usually allowed me to tape record the interviews for later transcription. I did not use the Informed Consent Statement in all aspects of my direct observation of homeless people. I would sometimes act as a simple observer so as not to interfere with unfolding events or conversations. In order to avoid causing any harm to anyone involved in the study, I changed all the names of homeless men and women I directly studied.

:: :: :: Many people helped me in preparing this work. My mother Elizabeth and sisters Marleyse and Susan kept in contact with me over the miles as I wrote and revised. Christopher J. Taylor collected dozens of articles on homelessness from Las Vegas newspapers. Dawn Mollenkopf gave me insights into poverty and social policy. Shawna Parker Brody, Gail Sacco, and Shannon West spoke to me in detail about their work concerning homelessness in Las Vegas. Matt Becker, acquisitions editor at the University of Nevada Press, was supportive, gentle, and encouraging when I needed it. Joanne O'Hare, director and editor-in-chief at the University of Nevada Press, helped me see this writing into print. Two anonymous reviewers of the manuscript gave me detailed comments and suggestions that improved my writing. Mariana Damon, Amanda Haymond, Katie McGinnis, Shaun Padgett, Paul Powell, and Karen Staats each read drafts of my manuscript and gave me useful feedback that enhanced the published work. Julie K. Schorfheide patiently copyedited my work. All errors are, of course, my responsibility.

The University of Nebraska at Kearney generously awarded me a Professional Development Leave from 2005 to 2006, allowing me to conduct this research. The University of Nebraska at Kearney Research Services Council provided grants, both during my leave and in reducing my course load while teaching, allowing me to write and revise.

Portions of this book appeared in *Forgotten Voice* 1(4):7, edited by Gail Sacco. Portions of chapter 3 were first published in *The Image of Violence II: Proceedings from the 2007 Society for the Interdisciplinary Study of Social Imagery*, pp. 92-99, edited by Will Wright and Steven Kaplan. Portions of this book also appeared in the *Journal of Contemporary Ethnography* 39(4):441-66, edited by Kent Sandstrom and Marybeth C. Stalp. Thank you to the editors for permission to republish the material.

In 2005-2006, dozens of anonymous homeless men and women allowed me to talk to and spend time with them. When I reread sections of this work, I can still see your faces and hear your voices. You shared your lives with me, telling me things where I knew all I could do was listen. This work is dedicated to you.

::

Homeless in Las Vegas

::

Introduction

I am reading in the Mandalay Bay resort around midnight in mid-September 2005 when I notice a man has fallen asleep nearby. We are both seated at tables in oversized stuffed chairs. He has a betting paper in front of him. I see the security guard come around the first time, wake him softly, and pat him on the back. The second time, about forty minutes later, the same guard comes and calls on his radio for assistance. He then calls "Sir!" to the sleeping man in a loud voice and shakes the chair while stepping back. Two other security guards approach from different directions.

"Sir, you fell asleep. Where are you staying tonight, sir?"

"Here," he replies.

"Are you a guest of the hotel?"

"No."

"Then you can't stay here, sir. You need to get up and move around."

The man shakes himself and begins collecting plastic plates and a cigarette butt.

"You don't have to do that, sir, housekeeping will get that," says the guard.

The man leaves the items and slowly walks away.

I tell the guard I study homelessness and ask him how often incidents such as this one happen. A few times a night, he answers, but then tells me, "He wasn't homeless, sir. He had a gold ring on," while pointing to his ring finger. "The first thing they'll pawn is their jewelry. He also had a nice bag." Suddenly, he contradicts himself: "His clothes were a bit tattered, so maybe he just became homeless. But the funny thing is, you never can tell. That's why we treat them all equally here. You never know who has money. They can come in looking terrible, but if they have money . . . ," he trails off and shrugs.

It is not entirely clear simply from appearance who is or isn't homeless today. When the security guard suggested that he could not tell for sure if the man was homeless, he presented an opportunity to think of homelessness as a temporary, cyclical condition (something a person goes in and out of over time) or *as one of many survival strategies for poor people.* That homeless people might have some objects of value (like a gold ring and a nice bag) suggests a range of identities and material resources available to homeless people who experience the condition for varied reasons and over time. For example, a homeless person might well own a car, and possibly sleep in it, or perhaps have a gym membership so he or she can shower and store personal items in a locker.

Homeless people who make use of highly portable items or temporary services (like cell phones or gym memberships around the city) also might correspond with Snow and Anderson's notion of "homeless career paths" (1993, 273). Perhaps homelessness is best thought of as a strategy for dealing with poverty, but a strategy that, over time, becomes like quicksand. Although many people who become homeless stay so only for brief periods, the end stage of this strategy would appear to be the widely held image of an obviously disheveled person sleeping outdoors who has "chosen" homelessness. But perhaps becoming homeless is, at least initially, a decision that allows an individual to survive when he or she is outside the traditional economy and when he or she cannot find a reasonable foothold into it.

Las Vegas in the middle of the twenty-first century's first decade was a particularly useful place to study how different types of homeless people live among excess within the United States. More than thirty-five million tourists visited Las Vegas in 2003 (Schumacher 2004). More than a dozen of the world's largest hotels are located there. For fifteen years, it was one of the fastest growing metropolitan areas in the United States, and nearly two million people today call the greater metropolitan area of Clark County home. Yet poverty continues to haunt modern cities such as Las Vegas. Frederick Preston of the University of Nevada, Las Vegas, sociology department found that by 2004, Las Vegas's homeless population had increased to 7,877 people, or by 18 percent, in five years (Casey 2005). Such an increase occurred despite Las Vegas's reputation for intolerance of homelessness. In 2003, the National Coalition for the Homeless listed Las Vegas as the "meanest" city in the United States for homeless people. This ranking was based on qualitative and quantitative data drawn from more than 150 cities and counties in the country (National Coalition for the Homeless 2008).

Clearly, homeless people, in Las Vegas and across the United States, are *objects* of concern and study. People who have housing, like the security guard, theorize about them. Homeless people are counted in various census efforts in Las Vegas and in regions across the United States. Agencies like the National Coalition for Homelessness track the development of city ordinances against homeless people. Yet despite such concern, the *individual lives and voices* of homeless people in the United States rarely receive attention. Celebrities, politicians, pundits, and the wealthy are frequently heard today, but the voices of disempowered members of society are muted.

I believe a key to solving many contemporary social problems lies in listening to others and, in particular, to people who are marginal and in pain. The simple act of listening allows people the immediate relief of being heard. Listening also provides a way to obtain information and suggestions about who people are and what individuals might want or need. It is a remarkable irony that homeless people are systematically left out of discussions, particularly discussions of policy, about what homeless people are like and how homelessness can be addressed.

Here I argue that it is crucial to pay close attention to the stories homeless people tell about their lives and about homelessness. Their stories reveal two central themes. First, their stories give clues to how they became homeless and how they survive, providing a testament to the causes of homelessness, to how socially isolated many individuals can be today when facing problems, and to what might well have helped or would now help them. Homeless people's stories are both a testament to their humanity and to how we might help others avoid and/or escape such conditions. Second, their stories indicate a key failure in many bureaucracies designed to help them. As state support for the poor has been reduced in recent years, charities have filled the void. These charities often provide important services that allow homeless people to subsist. However, many charitable assistance programs withhold more substantial services until a person agrees to change behaviors. Many programs follow the logic that "if you shape up, we will help you." Homeless people's stories suggest that homeless people need help first. The help needs to be true material and social support, more than simply a minimum amount necessary to keep a person alive from day to day. Their stories suggest the importance of providing housing first, harm reduction, and nonjudgmental social support programs to homeless persons.[1] Such approaches are likely to be more useful and more cost-effective methods of addressing chronic and episodic homelessness.

:: :: :: The stories of homeless people that are told here are also a corrective to some highly visual, popular representations of homelessness in Las Vegas and the United States. In 2001, the video *Bumfights: Cause for Concern, Volume 1*, co-directed by Ray Laticia and Ty Beeson, was released by Indecline Films. The documentary-styled video featured fights between, assaults on, and stunts by homeless men in Las Vegas and San Diego. Several of the men in the video were given food, clothing, money, and/or alcohol in exchange for their participation. The popularity and profitability of the video series was remarkable. According to the National Coalition for the Homeless, the first *Bumfights* video earned more than six million dollars in one month. Five other videos with similar titles were subsequently produced. Together, the *Bumfights* films have reportedly sold 6.8 million copies since their release (National Coalition for the Homeless 2007).

How did *Bumfights* represent homeless people? In the first installment (shown through handheld camera footage), a man punches, kicks, and body-slams a homeless man near the Stratosphere Tower. Another man hits himself in the head because his hair is on fire. Another man smokes crack cocaine and defecates on a sidewalk. Yet another breaks his ankle after a street fight. One man pulls out his own tooth using a pair of pliers. Another man has the word *Bumfights* tattooed on his forehead. A man referred to as "Rufus the Stunt Bum" rides outside, uncontrolled, in a shopping cart and slams his unprotected head into walls and signs (Squires and Casey 2002).

Why was such a video produced? It isn't surprising that there was (and probably always will be) an audience for shocking, violent footage of human debasement. As Allen Lichtenstein, general counsel for the American Civil Liberties Union of Nevada, noted in a 2002 interview, the First Amendment allows such expressions (Squires and Casey 2002). The producers of the video argued that the homeless men they filmed were either going to do these things on their own or were compensated for their participation—that they either *chose* to participate or would have engaged in the same actions had they not been filmed. As producer Ray Laticia put it in a 2002 interview,

> We have a few bums that we've been working with for a while, and they are willing to partake in different nefarious activities for the camera.... And when they do, we either provide them with cash or food or clothing. We don't force anyone. (Squires and Casey 2002)

Its producers thus frame *Bumfights* as a shocking but highly entertaining exposé of a subculture, as video about an odd group of people who, like everyone in the United States, have made a *lifestyle choice*.

The frequent use of video shot with hand-held cameras makes it appear that the filmmakers simply saw and recorded these homeless people instead of carefully selecting and editing video segments to construct a specific portrayal. As these films are of specific people and specific incidences, they are noncontextual: through an immediate visual focus on individuals engaged in self-harming, dangerous, and/or antisocial acts, the larger social context of those people's life histories, and the context of competitive opportunity structures within the United States and the city itself, is lost. Emphasizing the notion that they just observed and filmed participants who received small compensation, *Bumfight's* producers managed to avoid a larger question: Why might people agree to do such things for immediate cash, food, or clothes? *Bumfight's* producers wanted to sell videotapes and DVDs; they had no intention of developing a "sociological imagination" to better understand why some individuals might behave this way (Mills 1959).

Such distorted views of homeless people, according to criminologist Brian Levin, can well lead to hate crimes. Levin believes that the *Bumfights* videos might have helped inspire other attacks nationwide against homeless people. He argues that in contemporary America, openly hating the visibly homeless has become the last acceptable form of discrimination: "It used to be gays, it used to be African-Americans. But now the vogue target in many ways are the homeless," says Levin (CBS News 2006). As homeless people generally have less of a sense of collective identity than the other minority groups Levin mentions, they are perhaps seen as easier targets for attacks.

Although *Bumfights* is an extreme example, it is worth considering how the video series is suggestive of more general processes and trends that stigmatize homeless people. Expressions of contempt, indifference, revulsion, and/or blame directed at the poor—forms of expression found so commonly among housed citizens in the United States—seem to represent frustration about a problem that will not go away. Viewing poor people as lazy, crazy, addicted, and/or stupid also helps those who are not homeless, who are materially secure and successful, to feel morally righteous and superior. Co-director Ray Laticia even argued in a 2002 interview that individuals who were openly critical of his video series were themselves part of the problem for their own lack of ameliorative action: "To people who are going to take offense, I'd say, 'What have they done for the homeless?'" (Squires and Casey 2002).

Expressions of hate or distain toward homeless people allow the focus to be taken off another likely source of the problem of homelessness: that is, in cities and states across the nation, a limited pool of material resources will never be equitably distributed. The *Bumfights* videos seem to more generally suggest the stigmatized, outsider status homeless people have in contemporary urban economies. As homeless people's only value in the videos seemed to be their annoying worthlessness, homeless people could paradoxically provide either a riveting example of what happens to those who fail in this economy or a form of entertainment through videos showing the worthlessness of their bodies, personalities, and lives.

:: :: :: It is important to note that the popularity of *Bumfights* was limited and seemed to engage the prurient interests and potential hatred of only a certain number of people at a particular period in time. There was enough outrage over *Bumfights* among members of the general public that its producers, Ryan McPherson, Zachary Bubeck, Daniel J. Tanner, and Michael Slyman, faced felony and misdemeanor charges related to the film. In 2005,

McPherson and Bubeck faced jail time for possibly providing "phony documentation to prove they performed. . . . required work at a San Diego day center for the homeless" (Huard 2005, B-1). The producers also faced civil suits from the video's participants. Yet despite such charges and law suits, *Bumfights* represents a uniquely American response about the preeminence of the market. The videos strongly suggest that homeless people are outside the market, people whose images can be freely exploited for profit.

Other stories of homelessness and extreme marginality, especially stories that contextualize such conditions, need to be told. This book provides counterexamples of homeless people in Las Vegas. Homelessness is the result of myriad factors and continues for a range of reasons. Homeless people's stories are a testament to how people can survive, even under humiliating, inhumane conditions. Homeless people rarely have the wherewithal to both live in poverty *and* document their experience; my retelling such stories serves as a form of testimony for those whose stories might otherwise be hijacked for profit, mocked, or ignored. Stories that emphasize survival in the face of inhumane conditions reaffirm the human spirit, as well as the idea that such conditions can be changed if we want them to change.

This book documents the effects of being in a marginalized population, one whose survival practices have been made illegal and whose members believe they are being targeted for removal from or elimination by the city. Las Vegas Mayor Oscar Goodman's campaigns against homeless people's rights arguably represent a variation of the hateful, disparaging view of homeless people presented in *Bumfights*. The City of Las Vegas has worked to criminalize homeless living practices in Las Vegas and even to create ordinances making it illegal to distribute food to homeless persons in public parks there (Archibold 2006; Pratt 2006).

Some commentators have interpreted Mayor Goodman's actions as hateful toward homeless persons and those who want to help them (Bristol 2006). Goodman, though, downplays his attempts to deny homeless individuals of their rights by instead emphasizing their lack of *responsibility*. He claims he only wants to help homeless individuals become responsible citizens, integrated within the community. He often says that he offers a chance for meaningful employment to those homeless people who want to work, or else a free bus ticket back to their home community. In effect, Goodman's response and the increasing criminalization of homeless practices nationwide seem designed to reduce homelessness, not through help, but by *denying homeless people the right to live while homeless in these communities.*

The pain of homelessness in the United States is therefore not simply the pain of poverty: It is also the pain of being ashamed, hated, disdained, or ignored. In the United States, homeless people feel a stinging rebuke in the eyes and actions of many housed citizens, because in the United States, housing defines citizenship. But although many Americans frame homelessness as a choice, obviously no one aspires to become homeless when he or she grows up.

People in the United States who have not experienced homelessness often want simple explanations for this persistent problem, because they are hoping either for a simple solution or for an easy way to blame individuals for their poverty and thus be relieved of thinking about it. Homeless people often encounter the attitude that if they cannot escape poverty, then they deserve whatever horrors they face, including life-threatening conditions, incarceration for their survival practices, and even death. In the United States, poverty is seen as something an *individual* can surmount, but people rarely consider that the *category* of poor people cannot be eliminated: Because of the finite amount of wealth in the United States and the extreme concentration of that wealth among a relative few, others will have far less.

These stories of homeless people's lives in Las Vegas also involve their response to a discourse that rejects their lifestyles as well as them as individuals. Many homeless people I spoke to spent a lot of time fighting feelings of worthlessness and shame. Many had appalling stories of obstacles they had faced growing up, never mind in trying to achieve the American dream, stories they at times used to emphasize that their homelessness was not fully their fault or that they did not aspire to be poor. Some individual stories left me shaken, unable to imagine what it took for a particular person to have survived his or her past. Such stories testify that many people in this country suffer through childhoods so horrific that it is a wonder they can function as adults today, let alone contend in a competitive society requiring skills and emotional stability. Managing everyday material survival and the emotions that come with such marginalization is such a challenge for some individuals that vying for the American dream becomes an afterthought.

While this book serves as a form of testimony, it also serves as a form of witnessing. The vast majority of homeless people in the city (indeed, anywhere) will never have their stories told. Someone without regular food, housing, and medical care has trouble surviving and is rarely able to consider documenting his or her life. Witnessing is a form of representation rooted in legal discourse, a subjective telling of what happened. The primary research method I used to understand the lives and context of particular homeless people was talking to and "hanging around" those people. I chose this approach because I believe that the closest I can come to understanding homelessness is by talking to someone experiencing homelessness and seeing that person's everyday life. Those individuals often require an intermediary, not to tell their story, but to re-tell it in forums available to the general public, such as books and articles that become disseminated, discussed, and referenced.

The goal of re-telling these stories is to move people. We first hear stories as children, and stories become templates for a lifetime of trying to understand our world, others, and ourselves. Humans create their mental world through stories, through narrative. By re-telling stories, people gain a feeling of another person's subjective experience. If enough people hear stories of human suffering and loss, it can create, in John Dos Passos's words, a "frail web of understanding of one person for the pain of another." It is a frail web indeed, but creating it is a crucial step toward helping others through social action.

Another part of these stories is witnessing my own inability to capture the condition of homelessness, and the limits of language in conveying another person's subjective experience. As the narrator of these stories, I have to edit them, to make them readable, and to make sense of them. Such stories are therefore never "neutral": I am also aware that I too am constructing representations of homeless people. What I present is accurate inasmuch as it is faithful to the record of what was said in an interview, and it faithfully represents my interactions and observations from my perspective. People often ask me, How can I know if what a homeless interviewee told me was true? I cannot ensure that what homeless people said to me was factually accurate; I only asked for their story from their perspective. I believe that most of the homeless people I spoke to were, as one homeless person I interviewed said, "basically honest." In a number of the cases presented here, I spoke to an individual on several occasions. I was also able to observe the behavior of some of those individuals over time and could note contradictions between a person's words and his or her actions.

People want to "get to the bottom" of homelessness, to completely understand the condition in order to properly address it. Often, this form of listening is rooted in judgment. I suggest instead that the reader withhold judgment to better hear these accounts. I argue that judging and assigning blame is a largely counterproductive response to people with dire problems who need help with those problems *now*. The stories in this book, therefore, cannot get to the bottom of homelessness. Additionally, the stories represent the inadequacy of language to fully explain our world and the inability of our individual minds to fully empathize with the plight of another. I generally try to avoid speaking for others, but here I emphasize my own sense of responsibility in writing and analyzing these stories instead of the impossibility of bridging real life and representations.

It is one thing to grapple with such stories; it is another thing to throw them out altogether. All people need to talk and be heard. Like Dos Passos, I believe it is crucial that we individually attempt to understand the pain of other people, lest we destroy ourselves. It is simply too important not to try.

ONE

Operating in the Space Between
Homelessness and Tourism

RON AND RICKY

I met Ron and Ricky in Las Vegas in late August 2005. Both African American men were new to the city and recently homeless. They revealed to me the difficulties faced by many new Las Vegas residents who have little savings and who are trying to avoid current and future homelessness. They also showed me the importance of recent technologies being used by homeless people and how Las Vegas's promises of distraction and entertainment draw both stable and unstable people to the city.

The night we met I was walking on the Fremont Street Experience (FSE). First developed in 1991, the FSE is a four-block-long, canopy-covered pedestrian area adjoining several popular downtown hotel casinos. The seventy-million-dollar canopy, featuring millions of lights and an extensive sound system, provides spectacular shows at night and a misting system during the day (Gottdiener, Collins, and Dickens 1999, 55). This project has helped the old downtown of Las Vegas compete economically with newer "megaresorts" on Las Vegas Boulevard.

Ron and Ricky were sitting at an outdoor patio of a Starbucks coffee shop attached to the Golden Nugget casino. The patio lay in an unclear blend of public and private space: a gated metal fence enclosed the patio, but the patio itself was on the FSE. I noticed that they were the only two African American men on the patio, that they didn't have any cups with the Starbucks logo, and that they were using a laptop computer. I asked them if there was a wireless signal outside, as I wanted to use my laptop to check e-mail.

"Certainly," Ron said. I sat near them, and they asked me what I did. I said I was researching homelessness in the city.

"Wow—that's fantastic," Ricky replied. "We were homeless for two weeks when we first got out here."

Ricky was thirty-five, from Cincinnati, and had a goatee. He was casually but neatly dressed in a black Star Wars shirt and khaki pants, and he appeared to be in good physical shape. Ron was twenty-nine, clean shaven, heavyset, and dressed in khaki pants and a polo shirt. They told me they'd been in Las Vegas for three weeks and had been homeless for two. Ron said he was a video editor, explaining that their computer was essential to their website and business.

While Ron used the computer, Ricky became the more gregarious of the two. "We call this [Las Vegas] the place of geometry—everybody here has an angle," he said.

While they were homeless, Ricky and Ron said, they had protected their laptop by putting it at the bottom of a worthless-looking bag. They slept among bushes, and one of them held onto the bag all night. Even after years of research on homelessness, I had never heard anyone describe how he protected his laptop at night from potential thieves.

I asked what brought them to Las Vegas.

"We came out here for the opportunity," Ricky said. "In the Midwest, there [are] no jobs; it's all industrial. There's nothing."

I asked about their initial experiences in the city. "We were both working when we were homeless," Ron said. "Being down there inspired me to try harder."

By "down there," Ron meant the homeless corridor, where services for homeless persons in Las Vegas are centralized. The homeless corridor is downhill and about one mile north of the FSE. The popular Las Vegas Boulevard south, or the tourist corridor, is about five miles away from the homeless corridor. In recent years resort development has increased on Las Vegas Boulevard south (often called the Las Vegas Strip). It is home to twelve of the world's fifteen largest hotels. Images of these gargantuan hotels and megaresorts are regularly seen in popular U.S. television programs and films. Most of the thirty-five million annual visitors to Las Vegas stay on this part of the Strip. The homeless corridor, by contrast, is in an economically marginal part of the city, has far higher crime rates, and is rarely seen by tourists (Borchard 2000; 2005).

Ron explained that they eventually had found a shelter in the homeless corridor. They could stay there for free from 11 A.M. to 6 P.M., but had paid five dollars apiece to stay at the shelter at night. Ricky discussed how badly both men wanted to get out of there, away from the bleak, hopeless conditions they found in the homeless corridor.

"I didn't want to succumb to that, that spell of 'I don't see a way out,'" he said.

I asked how they had ended their homelessness. Ron said they each had received a housing assistance voucher, combined them, and were staying for a month at the Budget Motel on Eighth Street next to a Section 8 housing complex. They now lived nearby, in a much seedier part of Fremont Street, an area frequented by panhandlers, drug dealers, and prostitutes.

Ricky said that the price of apartment rentals in Las Vegas was much higher than in the Midwest. "Housing is really bad out here. They charge six hundred dollars for five hundred square feet."

"We were just hungry a few nights," Ricky continued, explaining that soup kitchens in the homeless corridor served food at odd times, if at all. "We got lunch at ten o'clock in the morning. We never found a place where we could eat at night."

Ricky mentioned many barriers to employment in Las Vegas that he had not found in other cities. "I spent a lot of my time searching for a job. It's crazy the hoops you have to go through to get a job [in Las Vegas]. You know about the cards? TAM card, Sheriff's Card, health card."

The cards he mentioned were prerequisites for applying for almost any job in the resort casino industry. Like most people who end up homeless in Las Vegas, Ron and Ricky had not known that they would need proof of criminal background checks and health status to be hired locally and that they would have to pay for and then wait to acquire such documentation. Once they had become homeless, Ricky and Ron had to make difficult decisions, such as trying to save money to afford the cards by walking or taking the bus. Ricky said that the agencies where he went for assistance were of little help.

"I walked twenty-five miles one day," Ricky said. "I had to walk to Shadow Lane to get my health card. I asked [an agency] for [bus] tokens, and it was like trying to part the Red Sea."

Ricky describes the minimal assistance programs he used and the difficulties he faced in trying to establish himself in Las Vegas. He saw the

Sheriff's Card and health card as barriers to employment, preventing him from getting a job he needed to have a stable existence. He wanted to work, but help toward achieving that end was hard to find.

Despite these troubles, both men now said that things were looking up. They had a place to live, and Ricky had a job at a nearby 7-Eleven, working the graveyard shift. The new life they had anticipated in Las Vegas, Ricky believed, would now come about. Both men now hoped that intelligence, determination, honest hard work, and some luck would be a means for material success. Ricky didn't see their start in Las Vegas in negative terms.

"It was a great experience," he said toward the end of our first meeting. "I feel like we're conquering."

:: :: :: A week later, I give Ricky and Ron a call. Ron answers—he's watching a History Channel program on ancient Rome, and he says, "I'm in heaven right now." Ron is not as happy with his job. He says he's only working two nights a week at a nearby bar as a bouncer, a job that includes doing menial tasks.

"When I used to work as a bouncer, I worked behind a desk and got to interact with people," says Ron. "I'm a social guy. Now I just stand in a corner all night, looking mean at people. And then, I don't get this—bouncers are the lowest men on the totem pole in this place. I have to take out the garbage. I have to go around and pick up forty bags of trash at the end of the night, stuff that's wet and dripping everywhere, and wheel it out to the compactor. It's like, I don't know how long I'm going to be there. I can't believe I'm saying that, since I was sleeping on the streets only a few weeks ago. But it's bad. I don't know how much longer I can do this."

Ricky and Ron, like other pairs of homeless friends I have known, seem to be alternating between periods of employment and unemployment, but they survive by pooling their resources. Since they have not had a run of bad luck at the same time, they seem to be making it.

Ron tells me he went to interview for a job in print advertising but says he probably "screwed that up" because he showed up three hours late. He says he could blame his tardiness on the bus system but that it was ultimately his fault. He says he got to the downtown bus depot at 11:40 A.M. for a noon interview. The bus was slow and was redirected because of an accident on the Strip, so he ended up stuck in south Las Vegas, at Mandalay Bay. He says he told the company about the problems with the bus but didn't get much sympathy. He also says that the job he interviewed for and his specialty in web-based design are "compatible and overlap somewhat" but that the job in print advertising might be specialized enough so that he wouldn't be competitive if someone more experienced were to apply. I imagine he is competing against a strong pool of candidates in a city like Las Vegas.

I leave him my phone number and say I'd be happy to meet them at the Golden Nugget on the FSE sometime. Ron says that they're usually off around 3 A.M. and that they'll give me a call.

:: :: :: I ran into Ricky at the Starbucks patio again a few nights later. He had brought his laptop and was trying to log on to a website to play Texas Hold 'Em. We talked for about two hours. I left for a half-hour, and when I returned he was finally playing online. We talked as he played and explained the game to me.

We started taking turns commenting on the women who passed us on the FSE, noting what we each liked about them. He said he was dating a twenty-two-year-old black woman with whom he had traveled to Las Vegas on a Greyhound bus. I was surprised and asked him how he could be out here eyeing women while he also had a girlfriend in Las Vegas. He said she was staying at Shade Tree, a shelter for women located in the homeless corridor. "She's not gonna be out at night," he explained. Ricky also said he didn't want her to live with him and Ron right now—that would be too hard on her. He said that eventually they would all get a large place.

Ricky talked more about himself. He was originally from Washington, D.C. When I asked him about his plans for the upcoming holiday, he said, "I have to find another job. I have to get more work." He explained that they were not giving him enough hours at the 7-Eleven.

Ricky says he's a self-taught poker player from months of playing in virtual poker rooms. While we talk, we look at his virtual poker table from above. He shows me how the other players give away their hand strength through their betting patterns. He predicts how the other players will act, assessing if they know what they are doing.

During his games, Ricky would look up from the computer screen, sizing up women as they walked by. After I saw two attractive women, he told me, "They're too young. Probably only have a hundred and fifty dollars between them, and that's from their dad." After spotting an older, attractive woman, Ricky said, "She probably has five thousand in the bank."

Ricky then saw a group of women and girls walking with a man. Referring to the one man with the women, he said, "Here is the problem—how do you know who he's with? Is he with this one, or that one? Is he a brother, a friend, a husband? How do you know?"

I was interested in how Ricky thought about passersby, sizing them up in the same way he figured out his virtual poker opponents. He seemed to be trying to read them, concerned about what they had and didn't have, perhaps about what he could get from them and what obstacles he might face in accessing those people or things.

:: :: :: I later thought hard about the unusual niche we occupied that night on the FSE. We were loitering, freely using electronic and other resources of the resort without its management asking us to leave. We weren't drinking any Starbucks drinks, though we used the coffee shop's wireless Internet for hours and even drew electricity from its outside outlet. Ricky explained the unspoken rules enforced by security guards on the FSE: "As long as you're sitting upright, you can sleep occasionally, but if you lay down, you have to go."

We would watch as the security personnel for the Golden Nugget wandered out into the enclosed area and seemed to stare at us, but they ultimately went away. The scarcity of chairs, tables, and benches on the FSE discourages lingering. When people sit for too long against the buildings or, as Ricky said, fall asleep, security guards tell them to move. Maybe it helps that Ricky, Ron, and I all look like casually dressed tourists, aren't visibly drunk, and don't smell. When I tell Ricky I'm surprised we can simply sit here without buying coffee, he acts indignant, saying, "Why do I have to buy their drinks? Just to sit here?" For the time being, Ricky and Ron have found a way to play free poker and surf the net in the warm night air of August while relaxing and people-watching on one of the most vibrant tourist walkways in the world.

In *Sidewalk,* Mitchell Duneier wrote about African American men in New York City selling found books and magazines on tables set up on sidewalks, making innovative use of the city's street vendor rules to carve out a subsistence living (1999). Duneier's interviewees usually became street entrepreneurs because prison records and/or periods of drug addiction made traditional employment impossible. Ron and Ricky's use of the pedestrian walkway and the rules of the FSE were more postmodern, more virtual. They are both African American men who were technologically savvy, who complained about a lack of opportunity in the East and the Midwest, and who came to Las Vegas by Greyhound Bus for a fresh start. What they were doing on this "sidewalk," though, was engaging in an *experience*, a largely tourist experience, otherwise difficult for poor people to have.

Ricky and Ron's everyday use of technology also makes them different from Duneier's subjects, causing me to think further about the link between homelessness, technology, and entertainment in Las Vegas. I revisited these ideas again in late September when I spoke with Morrie, the director of a newly remodeled, multimillion-dollar shelter in the homeless corridor. We talked as we walked through the shelter bunkroom, a quiet and cool space that was completely dark except for ambient red light from the exit sign over the door. Morrie told me about life for those the shelter served:

MORRIE: This is home for like 384 people—these people here know each other very well, they respect each other's privacy. They know who's all around them. This is where all their belongings are—this is their life here.

KURT: Some men have beds with bags and clothes hanging around the exterior of the bunk bed, [and hanging towels] maybe as a way of creating privacy.

MORRIE: Uh-huh. This is the shower complex.

KURT: Very large shower room, yeah.

MORRIE: And then more lockers all back here. So this area that we're back in here, what we do periodically, probably every two or three months, we go through and we fumigate. We take an exterminator in and we bomb an area to make sure that there's no bugs. This area is being prepped right now for Monday. We'd rather be safe than have problems.

KURT: I just noticed that there's electrical plug-ins. Are they over each bed?

MORRIE: Over there, over each bed. For cell phones. Whether it be DVD players, some people can put [on] things to listen to at night. Some people have TVs.

KURT: Do guys bring in cell phones and DVDs?

MORRIE: Oh, absolutely, absolutely.

KURT: Wow.

MORRIE: This is their home. This is where they live . . .

KURT: In that area.

MORRIE: In that area over there. Some people that's—that has been their home for the last two to three years.

KURT: Oh.

MORRIE: Yeah. It's something that's—we're really working on trying to find out why. Some people get very comfortable there. And you find out in dealing with case management that they don't really want to move. They get used to having that person underneath them, or the person above them; that's a comfort level to them.

Morrie's shelter is a basic prototype of shelter spaces and practices across the United States: a large dormitory with bunk-style beds, lockers, a schedule for turning the lights on and off, a shared shower facility, and regular fumigation of the area. But at this shelter, the traditional, sparse design includes an important addition: electrical outlets by each bunk bed so that men can recharge their cell phones and computers, listen to radios, CD players, or iPods, watch televisions, and use DVD players. As the prices for such devices continue dropping (and because recently outdated technology becomes even cheaper), these technologies are perfectly suited to the nomadic life of homeless people, who are forced to spend significant time in public space. They also can help redefine semi-public spaces, like a shelter bunk bed, as more private.

Stories about the increasing use of such electronic devices among homeless people are also, in significant respects, diametrically opposed to the caricature of homeless people as visibly poor, unintelligent, easily spotted derelicts. Ricky and Ron worked at blending in, at being the invisible poor, by dressing neatly, like tourists, and by using a laptop. Their secret near-homelessness, while helping them avoid stigma, also helps the general public maintain a false belief that homeless people match a stereotype of a visibly disturbed and disheveled street person. Dressing and acting like *tourists* rather than like a stereotype of a homeless person allowed them to *blend in* and partake in a tourist lifestyle and leisure activities.

Ron and Ricky had been homeless only days earlier. By some measures, they would still be defined as homeless, "doubling up" while marginally housed on a government voucher (Hopper and Baumohl 1994, 532). They typified what Snow and Anderson called a "recently dislocated" homeless person (Snow and Anderson 1993, 46–47): new to homelessness, having plans to get off the street, often interested in finding and using services for homeless persons, and tending not to identify with other homeless people (as when Ricky said he felt that now he and Ron were "conquering," or ending their time as homeless). They also might be examples of what Marcus called the "good" homeless—African American men trying to appear presentable to a Caucasian-dominated society to access opportunity and escape homelessness (2006, 23).

Morrie was concerned that some homeless men in his shelter were "settling in" for long periods, making their shelter bunks their home, sometimes for years. Snow and Anderson might categorize this type of homeless person as an "institutionally adapted straddler" (Snow and Anderson 1993, 55–57). These people have been homeless longer than the recently dislocated, are unsure if they will ever be able to fully end their homelessness, and identify more with homeless people. By living and working for long periods in homeless shelters, institutionally adapted straddlers have found a safe niche between homelessness and regular housing. These straddlers also appear to embody a "lifestyle"; they have apparently accepted their homelessness. Marcus similarly classified African American men who passively accepted their homelessness as playing the role of the "ugly" homeless, actively reproducing the stereotyped role of a homeless person to access social services and shelter life (Marcus 2006, 32).

Similarly, Morrie noted some men in his shelter becoming comfortable with their bunkmates, implying that this was why they stayed. Different types of homeless men necessarily access the same shelter for different purposes, a fact evidenced by the shelter's providing both electricity for advanced technology and chemical pesticides for bedbugs. By providing a safe, comfortable environment complete with electricity, the institutionally adapted straddlers and perhaps the "ugly" homeless in his shelter now could charge several key electronic gadgets, providing distractions many people today associate with "home," "lifestyles," and "leisure." For recently dislocated men like Ricky and Ron, the use of electronic technologies could provide another tool either to leave shelter life or to temporarily make it more tolerable through entertainment and escapism.

:: :: :: What role does distraction play in contemporary homelessness and in an individual's pursuit of happiness and well-being? Distraction can be understood in both everyday terms and in larger, social-structural terms. On the everyday level, we individually experience distraction in our daily lives, both as desired distractions (entertainment) and undesired distractions (annoyances, noise). On the larger level, our culture is increasingly defined as distracting: a carnival culture (Twitchell 1991), one in which we are amusing ourselves to death (Postman 1985), in which our goal is to live a life like those we see in the movies (Gabler 1998) and our self is saturated by the constant inflow of media (Gergen 2000).

Distraction is also a defining feature of tourist Las Vegas. So, to what extent do homeless people of various types come to Las Vegas to experience tourist distractions, to have relatively easy access to entertainment, alcohol, gambling, sunshine, and tasty, cheap food? Conversely, to what extent do people who *become* homeless in Las Vegas intermittently enjoy the same escapism while trying to escape their homelessness? A man who had been homeless for years once told me, "If I was gonna be homeless, I might as well be homeless here." If Las Vegas is attracting thirty-five million people from around the world who want to escape from their everyday lives, why wouldn't that also explain its appeal for some homeless people, who at least there can regularly escape from the misery of their poverty?

During periods of economic prosperity in the United States, homelessness has often been considered a failure or an unwillingness to achieve the American dream. In recent years, as economic opportunities have stagnated or diminished for many Americans, Las Vegas has become synonymous with entertainment, luck, and distraction; it perhaps embodies a new American dream. Stories of homelessness in Las Vegas reveal a rupture in the life narrative of homeless Americans, a rupture that these homeless men and women deal with through tending to immediate survival needs and pursuing diversions in lights, gambling, and addictions.

Homelessness today reminds us that, for many Americans, micronarratives, or perhaps anti-narratives, are replacing the grand narrative of the American dream. Long-term goals of upward mobility, or of simply having a house, a car, a modest career, and children, are increasingly fantasies. These micro-narratives for homeless people are not stories with a point but descriptions, a series of reactions to immediate trials, a concern with the details of getting a cigarette, a drink, something to eat, a place to sleep that night. For homeless people, these micro-narratives might in time become the major story of the self, eventually replacing the grand life narrative by making it irrelevant. Concern with the here-and-now replaces concern with the long-term future.

Perhaps the popularity of Las Vegas today represents a profound ambivalence about the possibility of achieving the American dream. For some, the city is "the Last Detroit," where working-class people can still attempt to get ahead materially and socially (Rothman 2003, 63). Should that plan fail, however, the city can at least become a place to pass the time through addictive distractions, through neon lights and people-watching. Las Vegas could then be seen as a place where if playing by the traditional rules of work and material accumulation doesn't pan out, there is always a backup plan: to escape into a life of immediate stimulations, distractions, and/or addictions—to be comfortably numb.

:: :: :: On September 5, I run into Ron and Ricky again at Starbucks. They call me "doc" and "professor." Ron says he has been good and has been working. Ricky, on the other hand, got fired from the 7-Eleven. He said the woman couldn't even really tell him that he'd been fired—she just kept putting him off, telling him to come back tomorrow.

"I just wish people'd be straight up with me," Ricky said.

Ron sees a man pass by on the FSE with a fancy video camera, and he goes to talk to him. The man says he's with a Bulgarian news agency and gives Ron his card. Ron wants to start doing video graphic work; he shows me his website and online promotional material on his laptop. It's a sophisticated site; and when I ask if he learned this in college, he told me that he was self-taught. Ron made some of the material while working for a TV station back home. Ron and Ricky then start talking about how much money they will make in the future and mention that they need to get business cards made. Now Ron and Ricky seem to be using the street to get ahead, this time through personal and virtual networking.

Ricky encourages me to talk to a woman in the Starbucks patio who he says is looking at me, but I'm too shy. After I fail at an attempt to say hello, the guys joke that I can no longer sit with them. We seem to have fallen into a pattern of joking about and promoting our individual masculinity. Ricky soon says hello to the woman and her friend. He reports back to us that she's twenty-one and from "some island country." While Ricky was talking with the woman, I told Ron that Ricky seems pretty confident about chatting with female strangers. "That's probably why he has five kids," Ron replies, smiling. He quickly says not to repeat that to Ricky. I nod.

After learning the woman's name and finding out that she has a boyfriend, Ricky rejoins us. He wants to play cards at Binion's, and he says that I can watch. We walk to a nonsmoking poker area in the back. He buys thirty dollars worth of chips. Ricky plays seven hands in about twenty minutes, losing gradually at first, then dramatically at the end, trying to use a pair of queens to beat a flush.

When we return to Starbucks, Ron is playing virtual poker and talking to a couple from England. We all make small talk while watching Ron play. Ricky, perhaps still mulling over his loss, wants Ron to bet more aggressively, but Ron won't. "See, this is why Ricky has problems," Ron says. "He tries to tell you what to do, in a demeaning way." I'm not sure what to make of this open disagreement, so I remain quiet.

I was learning that Ricky and Ron's relationship involved ongoing tensions and instability. Here were two African American men who, when they first met in Las Vegas, were each homeless, without local connections or resources. As one homeless service provider told me, it makes sense that homeless people gravitate toward each other as a source of mutual understanding, support, friendship, and potential roommates. The problem with such relationships, though, is that the individual problems each person already has will make it difficult for their relationship to remain stable. The housing voucher they each received allowed Ron and Ricky to rent a motel room together for a month, but each man's words expressed the stress of their unstable living situation and future.

Listening to the problems Ron and Ricky faced, along with seeing the problems they had in trying to make the best of their situation, indicated to me that they were at risk of becoming homeless again. Simply put, a one-month housing voucher for Ron and Ricky was helpful, but only as a short-term solution to their situation. Recent research on homelessness in Toronto stresses that homeless people need more than simple accommodations for brief periods to change their lives:

> While—technically—individuals in this category would be defined as "housed," there is little psychological affiliation with the term "home" for [these] people. The subjective enjoyment of "feeling at home" is almost entirely absent for many of these individuals, who report a lack of comfort, security, and stability as hallmarks of their accommodation. (Tremblay 2009)

The phrase "housed but still homeless" (Anucha 2003) seemed to best capture Ron and Ricky's current state.

I notice that Ricky's right eye looks red, and his jaw on that side is perhaps swollen. He seems reluctant to talk about it. Ricky says he's not supposed to eat sugar for a few days; later, he tells me he has diabetes. I ask him if he's seen a doctor, and he has. As it has gotten late, I soon say good night. They again give me their phone number and room number at the Budget Motel.

:: :: :: A few weeks later, in early October, I visit Frank Wright Plaza, a public park within two blocks of the FSE where many homeless people rest and socialize. During an interview, I see Ricky running by with his girlfriend to the nearby bus depot. They are going to the airport, where she is catching a plane. He briefly stops to tell me she is going back to Ohio because she is pregnant. Despite this serious piece of information, he adds, "We're gonna have to party tonight. It's Friday night—we should go gambling, hit the clubs, maybe a strip club." I laugh and say OK, I'll talk to him tonight.

At 10 P.M. I go to Ricky and Ron's place. It is tight quarters for two men—certainly under three hundred square feet. They share one double bed. It looks like a motel room. The amenities include a separate bathroom, a color TV with cable, a small refrigerator, and a microwave.

We go to a bar to bowl, shoot pool, horse around, and have fun. Because Ron works at the bar, everything for us is free except for the drinks, which cost a dollar each when you order eight. Ricky gets us eight rum and Cokes, and then eight more. I usually don't drink, and so I have a hard time keeping up. Ricky regularly chides me, "I don't see you drinking" or "I don't see a drink in your hand." I wonder if, considering his diabetes, he should be drinking. He also wanted to celebrate—he had recently begun training to be a security guard on the FSE. He has a black uniform and will ride either a bicycle or an electric cart. Ricky says he has Thursdays, Fridays, and Saturdays off, so he's thrilled.

:: :: :: About a week later, I call Ron at the motel. He's says he's staying in tonight, because going out usually means spending money. It is hard to hear him, since the pay phone I'm using at the Golden Nugget is right by the lounge act. Ron says Ricky is doing well and that he's going to work a lot this weekend at his new job as FSE security—some thirty-five thousand motorcycle enthusiasts are expected to come to the city for a weekend festival. He tells me to look for Ricky out there tonight and says that he and I should get together sometime.

I soon find Ricky working security in the area of Fremont Street near the Plaza Hotel. He's in uniform, and he carries mace instead of a gun. I ask him if he's feeling better, and he says yes, that his blood sugar is way down. When I ask him about his job, he says they that pay eight-fifty an hour but that his health benefits won't begin until after six months of work. He says, "Most people don't last that long." I ask him what would happen if he were attacked or otherwise injured out here on the job. "I'd be on my own," he says. "I have to make sure that doesn't happen."

He says his new job is good for him, since he walks all night. He carries himself well and gets several nods from other guards and workers in the area. He says "excuse me, sir" to every man he has to pass and uses the word *sir* when giving two men directions to get to the Las Vegas Strip by bus. When I ask him how he was trained to deal with homeless people he sees on the FSE, he says that if they are seated, he tells them to move on. He usually gives them several chances to be aware that he has noticed them, though, and to go voluntarily.

He tells me he is getting annoyed at Ron, in part because Ron is staying in a lot at night and is depressed. Ricky says he doesn't like Ron's self-pitying attitude, particularly about being overweight. He also says Ron is a slob, which is driving him nuts. Ricky still says he wants to get a house with Ron and his girlfriend, but they are finding houses here to be expensive, with rents starting at around eight hundred dollars per month. He says he will have to save more money in order to rent one. As our conversation ends, he expresses optimism about getting a lot of overtime work this weekend.

:: :: :: Ricky now works to reduce the number of homeless people on the FSE. The area has a more overt problem with homeless people loitering because of its proximity to the homeless corridor, which is less than a mile away. Resort casinos on the Las Vegas Strip are farther away, especially those being developed on the popular southern end of the Strip. Still, the relative openness of all casinos in Las Vegas makes the city somewhat unique among privately held, themed tourist destinations in the United States. "Compared with the completely privatized world of Orlando's theme parks, the tourist attractions of Las Vegas are more public in nature, more permeable to the larger urban environment" (Anderton and Chase 1997, 68).

Homelessness in Las Vegas also occurs in the context of a tourist economy promoting images and experiences. As Anderton and Chase note, the boundaries between public and private space in the city where those images and experiences are bought and sold are more permeable than in other tourist cities in the United States. Homeless people, therefore, attempt to use the resources of the resort casino industry, particularly as places to rest, eat, and/or clean up. Resort casinos are open all night, making them perfect for homeless people who can't or don't want to use homeless shelters in the evening. Several of the chairs are comfortable, and the atmosphere after midnight is relatively quiet; and because of surveillance and security forces, a homeless person is generally safer hanging out there than sleeping outdoors.

The stories of indigent people who use the resources of resort casinos in Las Vegas suggest that these resources sometimes provide extensions and/or alternatives to charitable and governmental assistance. Charitable assistance in Western countries is often rooted in the principle of residual social welfare: Help is provided based on documented need, is temporary and minimal, and is offered when all other alternatives for help (such as the market or the family) have been exhausted (Esping-Anderson 1990; 2002). The use of resort casinos as "public" resources and spaces by homeless people indicates the creativity of some homeless individuals in solving their problems and meeting their needs. When they want free places to use computers, or places to find drinks and food, or places to rest temporarily, homeless people can view reliance on charitable agencies in the depressing areas of the city described by Ricky as one option to be weighed against others. By looking like tourists, otherwise indigent people can try to subsist in resort spaces open to the public in Las Vegas.

Surveillance and security forces, though, also impede homeless people from using the resort casino resources as places to rest. As an example, I previously discussed the man who fell asleep in the chair at Mandalay Bay and was asked to leave. The security guard who woke him, who is paid to analyze and react to visible behavior, is not particularly interested in interpreting whether or not someone is homeless per se. He focuses on indicators that the man might have money (the gold ring) and that he might simply be someone exhausted after a long day of tourism. Because the sleeping man might be a player at the casino or a guest at the hotel, the guard first gives him a gentle wake-up. The second time, the man is awakened more forcefully, surrounded by guards, asked specific questions about where he is staying, and told that he needs to move. The guard did not seem interested in judging him indigent or not, but told me he had a procedure to follow when waking people who fall asleep more than once for extended periods. Because the guard doesn't know whether or not this man has money, he has to treat him carefully, telling him he has to "move around" instead of "leave the property." The guard has no legal right to look in the man's wallet for money—ultimately, the clearest indicator for the property owners in determining whether or not a sleeping person should be allowed to stay. Because it is unclear whether the man has any funds, he is allowed to catnap for perhaps an hour and a half.

The incident led me to ask some questions that are impossible to answer: How many different types of homeless people use the resources of resort casinos, particularly on the more upscale south end of the Strip, to meet their everyday survival needs? What use do they make of these resources (can they collect abandoned drinks, for example? Can they sleep in the bathrooms or take towels or toiletries, because bathrooms cannot be monitored by surveillance cameras as the casino floors are)? The questions can't be answered because homeless people using such survival tactics don't want to be found out. They benefit from blending in with tourists, simultaneously taking advantage of the amenities offered by resort casinos and the anonymity they offer. In Las Vegas, such people operate between the space of homelessness and tourism.

Charities for homeless people in the United States typically follow older models of charitable-based assistance developed in England. The Poor Law Amendment Act of 1834 presented the principle of "less eligibility": that is, poor people receiving charity should see it as such an unappealing option that they consider it a last resort. This principle seems at odds with the general orientation of tourist Las Vegas, where excess and evidence of a post-scarcity economy abound. Many homeless people in Las Vegas might, therefore, reject the charities that offer poor people a degraded form of assistance, particularly if they see other options. Some institutions provide the barest forms of assistance, such as stale bread and floor space, to those without resources. There is a hierarchy of shelters and soup kitchens in the city, though, and at some of the better ones (such as Morrie's, discussed above) you will find homeless people with cell phones, computers, or other objects of value.

:: :: :: Studies of homelessness in the United States have long involved arguments about how the condition involves degrees of freedom and poverty. *The Hobo* (Anderson 1961), the first book-length sociological study of homelessness published in the United States, helped frame this debate. From the 1880s to the 1920s, itinerant unskilled workingmen would go from job to job on railroad lines, developing the Western United States, and returning to areas like Chicago's "Main Stem," with its flophouses and cheap services (Anderson 1961). These men sometimes experienced prolonged unemployment, yet they were also romanticized for their freedom from the traditional male role of family breadwinner.

Though hobos were often depicted as choosing their lifestyles and the irregular employment that went with it, the Great Depression of the 1930s forced masses of people to become homeless. The economic downturn of that era promoted a view of homeless persons as generally "innocent," or deserving material assistance through government and charitable programs. During World War II and the subsequent postwar prosperity, a dominant perception developed that homelessness was increasingly a result of poverty, an inability to work because of old age, disability, and/or alcoholism. The 1950s, 1960s, and 1970s saw an academic focus on the "bum" or skid row alcoholic (Bahr 1973; Bahr and Caplow 1973; Blumberg, Shipley, and Moor 1971; Bogue 1963; Spradley 1970). Hobos and bums began to be seen as personally responsible for their homelessness. These homeless persons were often white males who were thought to have been able to achieve a "normal" life involving a family and steady work, if they had wanted one. The popular framing of "bums" as able-bodied men who chose homelessness, however, stood in contrast to others who lived in skid rows but were less frequently noticed by the public, such as women, elderly or physically disabled men, illegal workers, and the mentally ill or unstable (Bahr 1973; Bogue 1963).

The relationship between homelessness and mental illness in the United States is complex. Although deinstitutionalization of the mentally ill in the United States began in the 1950s, community mental health centers designed to provide outpatient care were slow to develop. Mentally ill homeless people began becoming more visible in urban areas. There is still debate today among academics regarding the extent and severity of mental illness among homeless persons (Borchard 2005; Marcus 2006; Shlay and Rossi 1992; Snow, Baker, and Anderson 1988; Snow, Baker, Anderson, and Martin 1986). Although in some ways mentally ill homeless people were seen as victims of poverty, such homeless people were also thought to embody freedom and a lifestyle in another way—they were considered "free" to be mentally ill and, if they so chose, homeless.

In the 1980s, with cutbacks in social programs wrought by the Reagan administrations, several academics again began emphasizing a view of homelessness rooted in poverty. Popular debates revolved around the "innocent" versus "guilty" homeless, or the extent to which homeless people deserved charitable assistance (Snow and Anderson 1993). Reagan himself was a strong proponent of personal responsibility, promoting a belief that homeless people were addicted, mentally ill, lazy, unintelligent, or simply preferred personal freedom to a structured life (Borchard 2000; 2005). In Los Angeles, such views inspired some homeless people there to attempt political action to emphasize the structural elements of homelessness (Ropers 1988). New York City was also thought to be an epicenter of a national "homeless crisis" in the 1980s, caused by a lack of federal support for social programs. The "crisis" was soon forgotten as cities increasingly gentrified their skid rows. The ongoing presence of homeless people in urban areas became normalized, while crackdowns on particular behaviors often associated with homeless living increased (Marcus 2006). Today, major American cities frequently engage in what critics call the "criminalization of homelessness" to discourage homeless living practices in cities (National Coalition for the Homeless 2008).

Homeless people in Las Vegas need survival strategies, which at times overlap with a tourist agenda. In a post-scarcity economy like that of Las Vegas, homeless people know that they usually do not risk starvation, but they have to develop short-range plans for acquiring food and perhaps places to rest. The long-range goals they had before they became homeless become replaced by shorter-range goals of immediate survival with ephemeral joys and distractions. The idea of a "homeless lifestyle" might then become a chicken-or-egg question: Which came first, the homelessness or the lifestyle?

Today in Las Vegas, the resort casino industry offers virtually anyone who enters its establishments a wealth of small items at reduced or no cost, including free promotional clothing and food, cheap rooms (which homeless people told me they use to "double up" for a night), small amounts of cash for joining frequent players clubs, cheap food, cheap alcohol for those playing slot machines in casinos, and services such as public bathrooms and places to linger. Because of such promotions by the resort casino industry, homeless people in Las Vegas have options that are not available elsewhere. The sheer enormity of most resorts and the waste produced by most of their patrons allow most homeless people access to abandoned food and drinks. As one homeless man, Jerry, once told me while he was searching a garbage can for food, many homeless people in the city benefited from the immense waste of its post-scarcity economy. He said, "There's no town like this for [finding] a quart of beer and food. That's why all these homeless people are here" (Borchard 2005, 48).

As a guard on the FSE, Ricky now is part of the security team within the area, paid in part to look for homeless people who are trying to make use of the street and connected casinos for survival purposes. Although Ricky has "switched sides," trying to earn money legitimately while asking the indigent to leave the area, he is episodically homeless and could easily become homeless again if his health problems or roommate problems continue. He has learned the angles of both the poor and those paid to manage them.

:: :: :: The next week I run into Ricky at work on the FSE. He tells me his birthday is coming up that weekend. I congratulate him. As we talk, Ricky has a prolonged, strange interaction with a muscular Hispanic man outside the FSE offices where he works. At first I thought they knew each other, but then the Hispanic man begins asking Ricky for money. When Ricky walks away, the man curses him, calls him a racist, and challenges him to a fight. Ricky tries to hand me his belt with cuffs, showing the man that he will fight if pressed.

After the would-be fighter leaves, Ricky's jaw is tight. He tells me that he meets a lot of women while he works security on Fremont but says that those encounters won't lead to a better job. He tells me he likes people and thinks he treats them well, but some people always treat him poorly in return. He finds it frustrating.

I try calling him that weekend, but there's no answer. By November, the person answering the phone says Ron and Ricky are no longer there and have left no forwarding address.

DISCUSSION

Listening to Ricky and Ron allowed me to consider four interrelated themes: the difficulties they had in attaining a steady material existence in Las Vegas; the role of technology in the lives of homeless people; the role of determination and distraction in homelessness; and how Las Vegas might facilitate episodic homelessness, which some might interpret as evidence of an individual choosing homelessness or a "homeless lifestyle."

Ron and Ricky said they came to Las Vegas to pursue opportunity. Most of our conversations touched on the difficulties they had in getting stable housing and steady, meaningful work, and the challenges of living from paycheck to paycheck. If the stereotypical image of a homeless person in the United States is that of a derelict, uneducated white male who is unwilling to work, Ron and Ricky seem the opposite. Though I never asked about their respective educations, both African American men were technologically savvy, engaging conversationalists, and cared about their appearance. Why, then, were they intermittently homeless? Ron and Ricky did not seem to have stable work histories, but presented a belief that by coming to Las Vegas, they would have better opportunities to succeed materially. In reality, however, each man had arrived in Las Vegas with very little money and, it seemed, without knowing anyone locally. As newcomers in such a competitive city, they were at a distinct disadvantage in trying to find work and housing.

Other personal factors also seem important in considering why each struggled with housing and employment. My only discussions of family with either man involved the future birth of Ricky and his girlfriend's child, and Ron's mentioning that Ricky had several other children. Both men seemed to have left whatever family and friendship networks they had had in favor of trying their luck without help. They did not think their previous networks were worth much or could help them achieve the life they wanted as quickly as they wanted it. Both men hoped to be "conquering" in Las Vegas, as Ricky put it, but were finding the city a difficult place to obtain a good-paying, stimulating job and a decent apartment. Though Ricky and Ron never discussed racism with me, it might also have affected each man's opportunities in the city. Each man also had personal problems or personality characteristics affecting his ability to achieve his material goals: Ricky might have had addictions to gambling and/or alcohol, a tendency to ignore his medical condition, and a tendency to criticize; Ron was overweight, might have experienced depression, and at times seemed withdrawn. Their personal problems could well have been exacerbated because neither man felt he had a steady, supportive environment from which to draw strength.

Structural factors also help explain their homelessness. Las Vegas is an example par excellence of a postmodern, service- and image-based tourist economy, one promoting entertainment, themed environments, and consumption promoted as defining one's "lifestyle" (Anderton and Chase 1997; Bauman 2007; Gottdiener, Collins, and Dickens 1999; Rothman 2003). The city managers, administrators, and employees must therefore manage images of the city to promote that economy. City managers, administrators, and employees work to create a fun, entertaining environment with less restrictive norms than most cities, which attract those with money as well as those without, the latter becoming a problem population that must also be managed or encouraged to leave.

The spatial arrangement of homeless services in the city can be seen as both helping homeless people and undermining their ability to attain traditional housing. Homeless people are viewed as a population that sometimes deserves sympathy, but more often requires social control (Borchard 2005). Ricky described how services for homeless people are segregated to the most economically marginal and dangerous part of the city, away from tourist and popular residential areas. Such segregation centralizes those services and also discourages their use. Like Ron and Ricky, many of the homeless people I interviewed tried to avoid the homeless corridor. To address those homeless people unwilling to use the centralized services in the homeless corridor, the city chooses to manage homelessness and the *appearance or visibility* of homelessness by creating laws restricting behavior (such as prohibitions on panhandling, drinking in parks, and sleeping in encampments) in order to maintain the image of a clean and carefree environment. In response, some homeless people attempt to control the appearance or visibility of their homelessness to better take advantage of opportunities in the city. Las Vegas police then play cat-and-mouse games with homeless people who try to live outside the corridor where their homelessness is condoned.

Las Vegas's image, therefore, creates conditions for homelessness while downplaying the existence of homelessness. Las Vegas attracts people looking for a fresh start, people who perceive the city as having lots of money, excitement, and opportunity. Most jobs in the service industry, however, are not well-paying and are repetitive or unexciting. The city requires thousands of waiters, buspersons, dealers, cashiers, security guards, janitors, and maids, jobs without much future for skill development or promotion. When Ron and Ricky tried working such jobs, they described them as dull, frustrating, demeaning, stressful, and/or threatening. They rarely spoke of enjoying their work.

So in the interim between the reality of their current lives and their dreams of better ones, Ron and Ricky did what tourists in Las Vegas do: They drank, gambled, took in the lights and sounds of casinos, and went people-watching. Contemporary life emphasizes use of credit and enjoyment of the present rather than delayed gratification and the long-term future, and people grow tired of the glacially slow process of acquiring money, education, emotional stability, and a solid network of family, friends, and acquaintances. While Las Vegas attracts thousands of more materially and personally stable tourists who come for a few days and then leave, the city also draws less materially and personally stable individuals. As the latter attempt to gain material stability, they encounter a Las Vegas that is the opposite of its popular image, an experience that is dull, frustrating, less than glamorous, and less than prosperous. Men like Ricky and Ron might then realize that they will not be able to succeed materially or personally there; but at least for the time being, they don't have to. The city provides enough opportunities to survive, as well as imagined glamour, excitement, and distraction, to compensate for unfulfilled dreams or to just dull the pain, kill time, and perpetuate denial about themselves and the city—that is, until a person becomes visibly poor, when a new set of rules applies.

TWO

In the Rough

JESSI

I met a group of homeless people, and got to know one in particular, over the course of a few months at a park in downtown Las Vegas called Frank Wright Plaza. Jessi, a middle-aged Native American woman, drinks with other minority group members in the public park. Her recent homelessness seemed connected to a tragic accident. In the park she found comfort with other members of minority groups who made fast friends while drinking and passing the time.

Frank Wright Plaza sits between the Downtown Transportation Center (DTC) and City Hall. The Gold Spike Hotel, which serves cheap food and offers penny slot and video poker machines, is only a block away. City Hall is across the street from the park. Homeless people are allowed to use the park until it closes at 7 P.M.

The park, named for a local historian, was dedicated in 2003. Before that, the area was a parking lot that people walked through on their way to the buses at the DTC. Now, small trees in the park provide shade for nearby benches and picnic tables, grass grows between concrete paths, and there is a drinking fountain and a larger, decorative water fountain. The decorative fountain has a sign on it that reads "Water Feature Closed to Comply with Drought Restrictions. Duration Unknown."

Dozens of homeless people sleep and socialize in the park every day and, like Jessi, sleep in hidden areas near the park and bus depot when the park is closed. Every day, many poor people also drink at Frank Wright Plaza, despite laws prohibiting alcohol use there. The nearby DTC provides restrooms, a few video poker machines, and an air-conditioned space that homeless people sometimes use if the park gets too hot. The DTC is also the central hub for local buses in the city. The Gold Spike also has restrooms, a water fountain, and inexpensive food, such as a half-foot-long hot dog, with condiments, and a soda in a Styrofoam cup for $1.50. Despite the Gold Spike's catering to poorer tourists and locals, several homeless people I meet in Frank Wright Plaza complain that they have been forcibly ejected from the Gold Spike. Those who aren't allowed to enter ask more recently homeless people or friends to go to the Gold Spike to bring back food. The park is also two blocks from the FSE, with its cheap eating and drinking opportunities, casinos, security force, and endless people-watching and light shows.

:: :: :: In late August, I park downtown near the Gold Spike. A woman and man walk by me on the sidewalk. The woman turns to look at me as she passes my car. She has light brown skin, a round face, dark eyes, and a friendly smile. Her straight, jet-black hair is pulled behind her ears and runs halfway down her back. She looks as if she knows me, though I have never seen her before. I smile back as I put my sun visor over the windshield. She turns and walks away with her friend, heading for the park.

A few days later, I see her again in Frank Wright Plaza. At first I didn't realize it was the same woman. She was with a group of people in the park, several of them Native Americans, drinking under the shade of a tree. I decide to sit nearby, hoping to talk to them. As she looks at me again and smiles, I approach her group.

She tells me her name is Jessi. She asks me what I am up to. I tell her that I am a researcher studying homelessness in Las Vegas. She seems surprised, not fully believing me.

"Oh, so you're gonna write a book? About the people in the park? It's a great group. I tell you, there's so many stories here. Every one of these people has a story. I'm gonna write a book about it too. I'm gonna call it 'The Park Story,'" she says, with a huge, happy grin. "You like that?"

Her smile confuses me—I can't tell if she is mocking me or is sincere, but she seems good-natured, so I smile and play along.

"It's a great title," I say.

"Yeah, it's going to be great."

I ask her how long she's been out here.

"Since March," she says. I notice she has a slight speech impediment and that she's missing some teeth along one side of her mouth. She also has two long, deep scars on her right arm, running from her wrist to her bicep.

"Wow, you've been here a long time. Half a year."

"I was on my way out to San Diego, but stopped here. I've seen a lot of good and bad out here. You see great things and really bad things."

I mention that it must have been bad being in 115-degree heat this summer.

"One seventeen! One seventeen!" she replies, correcting me. "Yeah, it broke the record. That was terrible."

As I consider the horror of being outdoors for hours in that kind of heat, I note how friendly she seems. I'm used to a certain amount of rejection from homeless people I approach for an interview. I find her openness encouraging. I ask her more questions.

"So, what's the best thing you've seen?"

"People looking out for each other. They're great people out here, so real."

"What's the worst thing, besides one seventeen?" I ask.

"I was raped," she says.

I don't know if my expression changed or if she realized how blunt her admission was, but she suddenly laughed a small laugh and nodded.

"Yeah," she said, smiling a small smile, still nodding as she looked off into the distance.

I felt uncomfortable, like the conversation had gone in a bad direction. I decide to change the topic.

"So what are your plans?"

She perks up. "Me and my friends are gonna hop a train tomorrow to San Diego, ride the rails."

"Have you done that before?" I ask.

"No," she says, smiling.

"People can lose legs or arms doing that," I add, hoping to make her rethink the decision. She doesn't say anything.

:: :: :: Our interaction seems so comfortable that after a few minutes, I ask her if she would like to be formally interviewed.

"What do you mean?" she asks. I get out my informed consent form, and she and her friend Wayne begin reading it. I then prematurely pull out my tape recorder.

"Oh no, that's OK," she says, staring at it.

Wayne, who has been sitting with her, asks me if I can give him some money for food if I interview him. I agree. After I start talking directly to Wayne, Jessi goes to sit away from me with several friends. Eventually she goes to lie in the grass, facing an African American man. I assume they are a couple. I feel her and her other friends' eyes on me occasionally, and particularly on my tape recorder.

Wayne is a middle-aged Native American man of average build, with spiky, jet-black hair. During the thirty-minute interview he becomes emotional, crying twice. He says everyone he knows on his reservation is dying. He mentions the deaths of several family and friends, including his parents, who died when he was three years old. He says he uses drugs like crack, PCP, alcohol, any drug he can get his hands on, and occasionally works as a prostitute. He is bisexual. He keeps saying, "I'm not gonna kill myself, I can get through this." It seems as though he's trying not to see suicide as the ultimate solution to his problems but that he can't help considering it. He seems to be pouring his heart into the interview, but he also smells strongly of alcohol. I wonder what he is like when he's sober and if he would even agree to an interview if he were. He says he wants to get better, but sometimes he just has "to go out on my mission," a phrase that is street vernacular for going on a binge.

After the interview, we walk over to the Gold Spike—he wants their chili but says they've "eighty-sixed" him. I go into their restaurant to get it, and I spot Jessi there by the first table. Someone had just bought her ice cream in a Styrofoam cup, in which they serve everything at the restaurant. When I see her she returns my smile, but it seems polite, more guarded than before.

I go back out to give Wayne his chili, and he asks for a couple more bucks for later. I don't want to seem stingy, especially if I might be coming back to this group of people again. I give him a few dollars. After eating a few bites, he asks me if I have a girlfriend. I reply yes. He says huh and nods. We make small talk for a few minutes before he says goodbye.

:: :: :: A week later I make another visit to the park. Jessi is there, wearing a black Harley Davidson cap, black breakaway sports pants, and a red San Francisco 49ers jersey. She's trying to mediate a squabble over a bottle of gin. A young man took it from an older one, and several people in Jessi's group accosted the perpetrator, pulling the bottle out of his hand.

Jessi goes back to sit with a man. I walk over to say hello, and she introduces the man as Terrence, her boyfriend. He is not the same man she was lying with in the grass last week. He's a good-looking African American man, with short hair under his Yankees baseball cap. He sports a goatee, clean jeans, and a black shirt. I sit with Jessi, and she tells Terrence I am writing a book on homelessness. She explains that they are sleeping rough. He is stone-faced, looking away, and so Jessi and I carry on an awkward conversation in his presence. She asks how my book is going. "Good," I say, not sure how to respond. At one point Terrence takes out some sunglasses, and he and Jessi try them on.

"We found these in the bushes," Jessi says. "You wouldn't believe what you can find in those bushes over there by the interstate. We found a whole can of meat. There was other food, but we didn't touch it because it looked bad."

I wonder about how even canned meat would have held up in the previous week's heat that had topped 100 degrees. Eventually she seems to be focused on talking to Terrence, so I decide to leave.

"Take care," she tells me as I walk away.

:: :: :: A few days later, we meet in the park again. She casually starts introducing me to some of the people I saw during my first few days at Frank Wright Plaza. There is Sean Paul, whom everybody also calls S.P. or Pop. His dark black skin contrasts strongly with his bloodshot eyes and patchy, black and white beard. His slightly puffy face and slow, meandering manner of speech remind me of Muhammad Ali before his Parkinson's symptoms became highly noticeable. His jeans have light stains running down both legs on the front. Sean Paul and a man who introduces himself as Ebony are sitting together at the park table. They seem like good friends. Ebony is also African American and is much smaller and thinner than S.P., but he seems more alert. He wears a plaid short-sleeved shirt and jeans.

S.P. asks where I am from, and he gets excited when I say Nebraska.

Ebony says he used to drive a truck in a circuit that included Chicago, Missouri, St. Louis (where he's from), and Omaha, mentioning the numbered interstates connecting the cities. He smiles and gives a knowing nod while pulling his hand down, as if he were causing an air horn to sound. S.P. wants to talk over Ebony, though. As S.P. begins to talk about North 24th Street in Omaha and his family there, Ebony begins to look at me occasionally, making a closed-mouth smile while doing a circular head nod. I eventually realize he is mocking S.P. in front of him. I suspect S.P. has repeated his stories about Omaha and his family there a few times, or maybe Ebony is doing this just because S.P. likes to talk. Occasionally, Ebony points his thumb at S.P., and raises his eyebrows while smiling. I smile and raise my eyebrows back, but feel like this is a strange conspiracy. Then, once S.P. reveals a hidden can of beer and takes a huge drink, I realize that it is just a less-drunk person openly making fun of a drunken friend.

Near S.P. and Ebony are Michael, Sarah, Mark, and Rich. S.P. begins to lead Sarah and Michael in singing a wildly off-key version of a gospel standard. Rich seems somewhat autonomous from this group of mainly African Americans. He is a wiry, disheveled white man with a large, scraggly blond beard, wearing a long-sleeve shirt, dirty khaki shorts, knee-high socks, and tennis shoes and carrying a backpack. As everyone else is interacting and drinking, he goes off on his own, picking up cigarette butts. He begins looking through the nearby trash bin to find aluminum cans, which he then stomps on and puts into his clear plastic bag. Eventually Michael offers him a beer, which Rich drinks while doing his work. Michael offers me a beer, too. I thank him but decline.

"All right," he says nodding. "Out here we all share with each other," he says, acting as the one who will introduce me to the way things work with this group in the park. "Everybody's family out here." A few people, including Jessi, nod in agreement.

:: :: :: The following Friday afternoon at the park, Jessi, Michael, Sarah, a man called the Chief, and a few others are there, talking and taking swigs from bottles and a twelve-pack of canned beer that Michael has supplied. When I motion over to Terrence, who is sitting away from the group but facing them, Jessi says she's not with him anymore. He has told her that they are voluntarily homeless and that they don't have to be living this way. She says it pissed her off and that she doesn't need that type of person in her life anymore. The Chief, whom I first met briefly while interviewing Wayne, is asleep face-down on a blanket next to a friend.

Two Las Vegas Marshals, a man and woman, begin to walk toward the group. Jessi alerts the group of their approach from fifty yards away, and everyone begins hiding their beer.

"How are you today?" Jessi asks the marshals, smiling and nodding. They look at her, expressionless. As the female marshal walks by, she sees S.P.'s bare, swollen, cracked feet and the flies that land on and then leave them. She keeps walking. Jessi later relishes recounting the marshal's reaction.

"She smiled at you!" she says to S.P., laughing. "She knows not to mess with Sean Paul!" I don't fully understand her point until she explains that the female marshal is new and being trained. It seems that the male marshal had told her about S.P., and that he should be left alone in the park. She seems happy at this small victory, their ability to carry on partying without harassment or legal problems for another few hours or a day.

It is sometimes said that Las Vegas is a magnet for losers. People with little education or skills come to the city from across the United States in hopes of getting rich by gambling, or by stripping, or by getting a job in a casino earning great tips, or by finding someone with the right "connections." At first look, it seems that Frank Wright Plaza is a gathering place for some of the biggest losers in the city—people who have nothing, who spend time getting high or drunk, sleeping in public, having quarrels with each other, or simply killing time. Although I am interested in this type of homeless person, those who seem to avoid social services and sleep in the rough, I also realize that I am getting headaches if I spend too much time in the park. I realize I'm having a hard time being around intoxicated people for hours on end.

At 6:50 P.M., everyone notices the new female marshal coming back, and personal items are rapidly collected so we can leave before being ticketed for violating the no trespassing laws that are enforced in the park at 7 P.M. The Chief is face-down on the ground again, and Jessi is desperately trying to wake him up. As the marshal approaches, Jessi tries to buy more time.

"Hello," Jessi says to the marshal, smiling and being respectful while trying to wake her friend.

"He drunk?" the marshal states more than asks. She places her boot on top of the back of his shoe and presses down hard. Suddenly the Chief awakens, looking disoriented, and Jessi is near his face, helping him get it together quickly.

"Naw, he's all right. Just fell asleep," Jessi says to the marshal, whereupon she gets the Chief onto his feet and helps him stumble out of the park.

I had asked Jessi earlier why everyone calls him Chief.

"He's a chief, he's the leader of his tribe," she says, seeming confused by my question. "He has horses and land on his reservation. It's terrible that he's out here. I want to get him on a bus back home."

As the group now leaves the park, Jessi and another Native American man start to walk away rather quickly with the Chief, and Michael, S.P., Sarah, and Mark begin slowly moving in another direction. Although I want to follow Jessi, she and her friends manage to lose me around a corner. I decide to stick with S.P., Michael, Sarah, and Mark, who now slowly shuffle toward Fremont Street.

At the FSE, Michael begins getting upset about the way he thinks one of the kiosk vendors was looking at him.

"Who the fuck does she think she is?" he says, a menacing manner surfacing. Sarah tries to drag him away from the vendor's gaze, and we manage to get around the corner; but Michael wants to go back and eventually starts walking toward the kiosk area.

"Oh no," Sarah says, smiling and shaking her head. "I hope to God he don't get in trouble again."

As we wait, S.P. unexpectedly asks me, "How do I know you aren't the police?"

"I'm not," I say, unsure why he has made this sudden accusation.

I go to see what Michael is up to, and he comes around the corner, carrying a new baseball cap tucked under his shirt. As we walk down the street, he removes the tag and puts it on. Sarah asks to have his old hat, which he gives her. She simply lets the one she's been wearing drop on the street. Michael then turns to face me.

"You see this is what you gotta do if you're gonna hang with us. You gotta take that bag," he says, placing his hand on my black backpack, "go in that store" he says, motioning to the nearby Walgreens, "and *get stuff.* Out here, we all share. We family," he says, using the same phrasing from the other day, but now in the tone of a demand rather than as an explanation. Though Jessi had introduced me before as a writer, I later realize that Michael must have forgotten. After all, why would I be hanging out with homeless people in Frank Wright Plaza if I weren't also homeless?

I act as though I understand, but I make no move to go to the store. We shuffle on for another block, and with S.P. barely getting one foot in front of the other, we cross the street. Cars stuck in the middle of the intersection wait for us well into the red light.

I am still concerned and mulling over having been asked to shoplift to prove solidarity with a group to which I don't want to belong, when suddenly Michael begins asking S.P. if he knows me.

"I don't know him," he says. He turns to Sarah.

"I don't know him either," she says.

We inch along a few more feet, and suddenly Mark takes me aside.

"I'm sorry, man, you have to go," he says. It is abrupt, but he has also just provided the break I've been looking for.

"OK," I say cheerfully as I begin walking in the other direction. "You guys have a good night."

I have found it hard trying to meet homeless people, but it is even harder to meet and try to talk with homeless alcoholics. With Jessi gone, I had lost my gatekeeper, or the person who first accepted me and who normalized my presence at the park despite the fact that I didn't drink. Without her near me, it becomes ever clearer that the group's primary interest is in alcohol; everyone around them is usually drinking, intends to get a drink, or both. There is really no place for understanding an outside researcher's interest, and plenty of reason for the group to be suspicious of someone hanging around who seems untested and unfamiliar.

Listening to the stories and observing the behavior of homeless people in Frank Wright Plaza reveals that ongoing alcohol use is important in their lives. It is so important, in fact, that those I observed in the park chose prostitution, looking for aluminum cans to recycle, trying to find things of value in bushes, stealing things, and sleeping outside as survival strategies rather than seek assistance through social services, where sobriety is often a precondition for access. Although the homeless corridor (where services for homeless persons in Las Vegas are centralized) is only a mile away, those I observed in the park did not usually seek out those services. Instead, the people I hung out with in the park "got by" in other ways.

:: :: :: I go to dinner on Fremont Street and then walk the street after dark. I see many of the people from the park (Ebony, the Chief, and Sarah) wandering around, enjoying the free outdoor music and light shows. Later in the night I see Jessi sitting and swaying on the edge of a pillar outside the Fremont Casino. She is very intoxicated. We sit and talk for about forty minutes.

Because of the way she's sitting on the ground, I notice something peculiar jutting out of her jeans near her knee.

"I lost my leg in an accident," she tells me.

I feel embarrassed, wondering to myself how I failed to notice this before. Most of the time we have been sitting still among people in the park rather than walking around. She says the accident happened four years ago—she was crossing a street. She says she replays it over and over in her mind. Her biggest wish is for those two minutes back, the ones where she decided to cross the street and was then struck by the vehicle. I understand from her repetition and stupor how desperately she wants to mentally escape, since she cannot turn back time.

She tells me about her father. When she was fourteen he wanted her to marry a man he chose for her, but she refused. She says she embarrassed her father. She says she dishonored her parents when she left her home on the East Coast with Terrence, because he was black.

As we are talking and sitting on the ground on the FSE, I begin to worry that one of the bicycle police officers circling us every few minutes will soon ask us to move. Several people seem to look at us as they pass. Many of them are smiling at Jessi, who is loud and visibly drunk, swaying while talking through her hair, which keeps falling in front of her face. Because of the street noise I have to lean in to hear what she is saying. Her spittle hits my lips and eye while we talk. I try to wipe it off discreetly.

She is visibly distressed, wanting to talk about the past, about her falling-out with her parents, and especially about how losing her leg changed everything. She grew up in the Bronx and lived in northern New Jersey for several years—she describes tough neighborhoods. She once had a semi-stable life, but she abandoned it. Her quarrel with her dad and mom was followed by another loss—of her leg and her physical sense of self.

She speaks in a repetitive loop about how active she used to be and how fat she's gotten since the accident. She loved to surf and says she flew a lot to do it.

"I traveled all around the world, just to ride the waves. Everybody knew me on the beach in Hawaii. It was great. I loved to surf. It was who I was."

I suddenly realize she should try to sober up, or at least drink water so that her hangover won't be so awful. I offer to get her a glass of water from the casino. She says OK, and I return after five minutes of waiting at a busy bar. She's happy to see me again, and drinks the water slowly.

Jessi begins moving closer to me while we talk and as she explains her life, and she takes my hand in hers. I don't protest—I think that a sudden withdrawal from such an overt gesture would be upsetting. I rationalize that she also seems in need of human contact, and that I like her, and that holding hands with someone is an innocent gesture. She seems to want to interlace our fingers, though. I tighten my fingers so she can't intertwine them. She seems to look at me with longing, but then her eyes go out of focus. She stares at her small hand in mine, a drunken smile visible through her hair. I feel uncomfortable with what is happening and begin to think of excuses to leave.

She eventually says she needs to go to the restroom, and I tell her I'll wait. I feel unsure what to do—I want to hear her story and I like her as a friend, but I am thinking that her drunken state seems to be affecting her view of our relationship and of me. I wonder if I am taking advantage of her, if she would be this personal with me if she were sober.

After ten minutes I begin to wonder what has happened to her. After fifteen minutes, I go in to the casino, looking for her, but to no avail. She might have fallen asleep in the bathroom, I think while I stand outside the women's restroom. She also might have left. I consider asking someone to check the bathroom for Jessi but then realize that, given her options, it might not be a bad place for her to sleep. I go home.

:: :: :: On September 20, I see Jessi, S.P., Michael, and Sarah at a park bench at the plaza around 3:30 P.M. S.P., Michael, and Sarah are all drinking and singing. I notice S.P. has a new, sturdy black cane, one with a four-legged base.

"I got that for him," Jessi says, smiling triumphantly at me.

"How?" I ask, knowing that medical equipment is expensive.

"It fell into my lap," she says, smiling mischievously. "Found it in a casino. Somebody left it."

I look at her, dumbfounded.

"Yeah," she says, smiling and laughing, "it just fell into my lap."

I say that was quite a find, and think briefly about both how she got away with it and how some poor disabled person is now really missing it.

I feel a bit awkward about the other night—I think Jessi seems less enthusiastic about seeing me today than she's been in the past. She asks what I'm up to today, and I tell her I'm going to head off to the shelter. She nods, but soon sees someone and says, "Hey, there's my friend." He comes over, and she says he saved her the other night. They go off to talk, and I decide to go to the shelter.

"Hey, I hope it all works out for you," she says to me when I leave. The statement threw me off. On the bus, I wonder if she might simply remember me as someone she knows, if she has forgotten that I'm here doing research.

Twenty minutes later, the bus stops in the homeless corridor, and I walk up Owens Avenue. At the Salvation Army, a woman in a black SUV drops off three large boxes of clothes outside the day shelter and safe center, where dozens of visibly poor people wait outside. Suddenly three homeless men rush toward the packages, opening them and grabbing their contents. At least ten more people immediately follow suit, and the rush of people seems to get everyone's attention. Those in wheelchairs, too tired to move, or too out of it, simply look on.

A stern-looking black man wearing designer jeans and a denim jacket, his hair braided in cornrows, has grabbed a shirt and five pairs of jeans, which look new, and heads into the day shelter. Other people follow the logic of "grab first, try on later," and several retreat to their space in the dirt-and-concrete waiting area, where they then look over the clothes they've claimed. People with items soon begin to approach each other, and informal trade negotiations begin—"Hey, you a thirty-five? You got a thirty-one?" Some friends seem to offer each other the clothes as a repayment of past debts. One man gives a friend a pair of jeans and says, "I'll give you the rest later, OK?"

The man with the cornrows comes out of the day shelter with his tall, white girlfriend, whose dark hair is in a crew cut. She walks around smiling, showing friends her new designer jeans with orange stripes down the side. People seem to look on with envy, and I feel a surge of anger. Why didn't the woman in the suv who dropped off the boxes take them inside the building to a supervisor so that the clothes could be more equitably distributed to those who need them? Was this free-for-all, in which the strongest people claimed the lion's share of clothes (some of which still had tags on them), supposed to be charity? It seemed instead to reinforce the misery of those who can't help themselves, leaving them so close to donations that yet were still out of reach. It is a self-perpetuating system, I think. As I watch the woman now modeling her form-fitting designer pants, I think about how unfair it is. I think of how predatory and selfish people can, even in poverty (perhaps especially in poverty), use their predatory traits to improve their existence.

It also strikes me, looking around the yard, that a lot of high-end apparel labels are on display. Among them are Southpole, Ralph Lauren, Air Jordans (one man is carrying a clean pair, which perhaps are a collector's item), Abercrombie and Fitch, Guess, Perry Ellis Portfolio, and Nike. People in the yard had been wearing many of these labels even before the clothing in the boxes was dropped off. Although the fashion is wildly inconsistent (and there is no attempt at matching labels or in some cases even colors), it strikes me that hundreds of dollars in fashion clothing is being worn here. The clothes, though, had been considered outdated and worthless and thus suitable for donation. Where they once had value and fit in as someone's statement of adherence to a particular lifestyle, time and circumstance have now made the items superfluous, unwanted— something for marginal people.

:: :: :: Disheartened, I decide to take the bus back home. On the ride back I have to connect buses through the DTC. While transferring I spot Jessi alone at a picnic bench. When I was trying to figure out later why I found the scene so strange, I realized that I had never seen her by herself before. I stop to talk and see that she has a cell phone. I joke with her about it, asking her how she can afford it. She says her parents pay for it. She's been trying to call them for a ticket home, but they won't pick up—she keeps getting the answering machine. I tell her she looks depressed.

"I want to go home," she says, a tear streaking down her cheek. "I'm tired of it here. It's too hard, being homeless. Las Vegas is too hard."

I agree with her last comment. We talk for more than an hour. At first I feel awkward about the other night, but when I ask her where she went off to, she claims ignorance.

"I saw you on Fremont the other night?" she asks.

"Yeah," I tell her, smiling slightly. It disturbs me a bit that we talked for a half an hour that night and she recalls none of it, saying she simply remembers waking up at her campsite the next day. I later think that this might be a partial blackout or an excuse, her way to avoid embarrassment over her intoxication or our interaction. Perhaps it is both.

Otherwise, she wants to talk. She tells me a lot about herself, her accident, and some more about Terrence, Michael, Sarah, and the Chief. About her accident, she says, "I just wish I could replay that day over again. I wish I could change that day. I used to surf, you know? I used to ride the pipe." She loves using this last phrase over and over in describing her life before losing her leg.

Some people I have spoken to on the street seem to have worked very carefully on their life narratives, trying to come up with the clearest distillation of their life's meaning, of how their story unfolded. The people who talk usually aren't discussing success or the ways in which they became fortunate. People who are successful don't often have cause to think about their life narratives; they are busy enjoying their happiness, living their dream. I have found, however, that people who have experienced tragedy often have time to reflect on it and feel a desperate and futile need to communicate that tragedy to others, most of all to those who care. In everyday conversation, Jessi is warm and upbeat—her smile is contagious. But I wonder if, when she is alone, she repeatedly plays in her mind the tragedy of losing her leg, as she seems to do in our conversations. Maybe that's why I've never seen her alone—she wants the distraction.

Although we often complain about the pain others have caused us, nothing compares to how we can torture ourselves. She relives a trauma again and again, and in particular the central role it now takes in her new narrative about what she sees as the rest of her worthless life.

"Now I'm nothing. I don't have anything to live for. I have wanted to put a .45 in my mouth, believe me," she says, crying.

I try to point out that she seems to have a lot to live for, but I hesitate, being aware that contradicting someone in this state is dangerous—you risk being told how wrong you are because you have no idea what they're going through. It would also invalidate her real feelings of loss. On the other hand, I want to offer her alternatives to these thoughts and give her my view that her life is hardly worthless. By losing a part of her body, she lost her definition of herself, and she has replaced her view of herself as active and athletic with an identity freefall of drinking, casual sex, and homelessness.

I mention how helpful she's been to different people in the park, especially to S.P. I tell her that his story really interests me. She says she has been writing about him for her own book. She says he is sixty-six, a diabetic, a veteran who served in the Marines, and that he gets a $1,200 disability check from the government each month. He rented a house until recently, when he lost it. Jessi says he was a singer, which explains his tendency to frequently burst into song. He even had a piano in his house. Jessi says he's been in and out of homelessness for thirty years—he's been given bus or plane tickets to leave several cities, including Reno, Chicago, "even New York!" she exclaims.

She ends up telling me that she actually bought the cane for S.P. that she previously claimed to have found, the one he had in the park. It cost $250 and came from a medical supply store. I look surprised.

"How did you get the money?" I ask.

"I had my folks do a direct deposit into my account," she says. I am confused.

"But you told me you found it," I say.

"I know," she said, "I didn't want anyone to know I bought it. I told them all I stole it. They believed me. They wouldn't have accepted it if I'd bought it, so I said I stole it, and now they all love it, especially Sean Paul." I look at her, thinking about her display of compassion.

"That was really good of you," I say. She smiled to herself while looking down at the table, nodding.

"He can't walk," she said. "He needed it. And he loves it. You should have seen his face! He thanks me every day for it." I agree that he certainly needed it.

"Well, that's a great thing you did," I say.

"It's funny," she replies, "sometimes people can't give somebody else what they want, even if it's simple. Like yesterday, I was outside of the Gold Spike, and I was panhandling, asking people if they could give me 75 cents so I could get a cup of coffee. So I ask this guy, and he says, 'So you want 75 cents, huh? I'll give you $300 if you come up to my room with me.' So I joke with him and say, 'That's a lot of quarters.' He says, 'Yeah,' and begins describing all the things he's going to do to me, which I won't repeat. So I said, 'Look, I don't want $300, I just want a cup of coffee. I just want three quarters,'" she says. She repeats the last two lines, emphasizing that he wasn't offering her what she wanted. "So I stop talking to the guy. Then, next thing I know, the Gold Spike is kicking me off the property, because the guy has told them that I was soliciting him for prostitution! *He* solicited *me*! He told me his room number, which turned out to be good."

"Oh yeah," I said, catching on, "because you could say, 'How else would I know his room number?'"

"Right," she says. "He was trying to get *me* up there! But they still kicked me out."

I think about the contradiction between her buying and giving away a $250 item one day while begging for 75 cents the next. A once-homeless friend of mine told me that some homeless people just aren't cutthroat enough to survive in a competitive, free-market society—that they often come from bad backgrounds and long for better human relationships, but therefore are too idealistic and naïve. It's the idea that someone would give you the shirt off his back, but in this case it's the only shirt he has. I also think it odd that Jessi would ask her parents to send her the money but not ask for some spending money for herself.

I ask her what the relationship is between S.P., Michael, and Sarah, since they alternate between calling S.P. "pop" and "granddad." She says they aren't related and, candidly, that Michael and Sarah are using him for his money. She paints Michael out to be a bully and a thug and says Sarah is bipolar. She says S.P. "pisses himself," which explains his lightly stained pants.

I ask her where she's staying.

"Over by the Plaza [Hotel], by the tracks, with Terrence," she says, surprising me with the revelation that she is seeing Terrence again. "He gets up and goes to work at 2 A.M."

I ask if it's safe to camp there.

"Oh yeah," she says, gesturing by throwing her hand away from me, as if it was nothing. "We have cardboard and a blanket. We're fine. Nobody's out there."

She is sober and agrees to talk to me so I can fill in the details of her life. Jessi is forty, and she lost her left leg four years ago in the accident crossing a street. The two long scars on her arm were also a result of the accident.

She was a medical technician and worked for Bristol-Myers Squibb for nine years. She has a bachelor of arts degree from Rutgers. After she mentions such a prestigious job and elite education, I look at her surprised, my mouth open.

"Yeah," she says, laughing and smiling. I ask her what she did at her job, and she tells me that she was a technician, just looking at slides all day and punching information into a computer. She says she owned a home in New Jersey that was two blocks from the beach. She tries to tell me about her surgeon but can't think of a particular word, so I wait.

"Vascular!" she exclaims. "My vascular surgeon was a doc at Princeton. God, I can't believe I couldn't remember that word. I worked in medicine!" she says, shaking her head and smiling. I think about her drinking and her possible blackouts.

She tells me about her nineteen-year-old daughter. Jessi voluntarily gave up custody to the girl's father after her daughter's birth—she says she wanted her daughter to have a better life. When she more recently abandoned her fiancé and her old life, she sold everything—her house and other property—to pay for her daughter's college. Her daughter, Melissa, attends San Diego State University.

"She's a good girl. She's a virgin! She's nineteen years old," she exclaims. "I lost my virginity at fifteen."

It's as if Jessi uses this fact to project a different life course for her daughter, a different narrative of hope and a good life.

"Have you seen her?" I ask.

"I've seen pictures of her. She's so beautiful—five foot eight. Her hair is blacker than mine."

"That's pretty black," I say, smiling.

"Yeah, jet-black hair, dark eyes. I sent her a picture of me, and I asked her, 'Am I good-looking?' She said, 'You're good-looking as me, but with bags,'" whereupon Jessi roared with laughter.

When I ask how long it took her to figure out that Michael and Sarah were using S.P., she says, "About a week. I was so naïve."

She returns to the topic of her daughter.

"Melissa was raised by her father and his family," she says. When she gave Melissa to them, she was concerned about how that information would affect Melissa psychologically.

"I told them to tell her I was dead," she says plainly.

I look at her, surprised.

"I didn't want her to be messed up, you know? I didn't want her to think, 'Oh my God, my mother *abandoned* me.' That can really screw a kid up."

I nod in agreement.

"I told them, 'When she turns eighteen, you can tell her about me.' And they did," she says, smiling.

I ask her about her leg. I say it must hurt.

"It does," she says.

"Do you take anything for it, like ibuprofen?"

"No, I don't want to get on that stuff. It screws up your soul. Sometimes I drink, but . . . Right now, I've been walking around on it so much that, it's kind of gross, but I have the part that connects to my leg wrapped in socks. It's pretty gross down there."

"I imagine you must have a problem keeping your leg clean."

"Yeah," she says, looking away.

She tells me her father always told her she should live her life based on three ideas: dignity, pride, and honor. She said that he disappointed her when he didn't allow her to make her own choice about whom she should marry. She said he denied her those three things, the things on which she was told to base her life.

She told me that when I write her story I should stress that her life has been about dignity, pride, and honor. I agreed that I would.

:: :: :: Two weeks later, I see her in the park. Her nails are done, and she is wearing makeup. She hasn't been in the park lately. It rained hard for a couple days, and she and Terrence got a hotel room. She says she wanted to feel better about herself, so she got a manicure.

"There goes the love of my life," she says about a man—not Terrence—walking nearby. After talking with him for several minutes, he walks away briefly. She returns to tell me that that was Rob. I smile and am glad she is happy.

When Rob returns, I decide to leave. I ask her again if I could formally interview her, and she agrees that we should meet in the park in a few days, at 1 P.M.

When I go there a few days later at the appointed time, she is not there. No one has seen her.

I stop into the Gold Spike to use the bathroom. Jessi and Rob are there, talking while seated in front of video poker machines. I decide not to interrupt them.

:: :: :: Weeks later, on November 8, I see Jessi in the park.

"You remember I was supposed to meet you for the interview?" she asks.

"Yes," I answer, surprised she is raising the topic of the missed appointment.

"I went to jail for four days."

I am confused, knowing that in fact she stood me up. I think, though, that she might have gotten the dates wrong, or perhaps she just went to jail since I last saw her and wants to talk about it.

I say I'm sorry, and she recounts how it felt. She said it was the most humiliating experience of her life. It was dirty and it stank; she rolled her eyes while describing the smell.

I asked how she ended up there. She says the police stopped her and ran her ID, and they found a warrant for her arrest. She had been charged with assault with a deadly weapon.

She explained that, earlier in the summer, a man had attempted to drag her into a hotel room in the nearby Plaza Hotel to rape her. She got away by detaching her leg and beating him with it. That was the deadly weapon she used, she said, smiling.

A detective reviewed her case and witnesses corroborated her story. The charges were dropped. But she says she was humiliated in jail, especially by the male guards who would watch her use the bathroom. She recounts how she was kept in solitary confinement in jail because of the seriousness of the charge and that, because her leg was the weapon, it had been taken away from her during confinement.

She talks about how she will need to leave soon and says that she will have a new leg waiting for her in New Jersey in December. It's a bionic model. She really wants it.

:: :: :: In late November, I think I spot Jessi walking with Rob near the park, by City Hall. I think I recognize her long hair and slight limp. They have on winter coats, as it has been getting cold. As I round the corner to see if it really is her, though, the two are gone.

That was the last time I saw Jessi around Frank Wright Plaza.

DISCUSSION

Two main policy implications emerge from listening to Jessi's story and from observing the activities of her friends in Frank Wright Plaza. The first involves improving the opportunities available to poor Americans and to minority group members. The second involves developing stronger supportive environments in the community for people who have problems functioning as adults because they experienced traumatic childhoods, who are suffering from a traumatic loss, and/or who are homeless.

Jessi's friends in the park are largely Native American and African American and have had narrower opportunities for achieving education and wealth in comparison to the percentage of dominant racial group members who can better achieve these goals. Minority group members are by definition at a disadvantage in trying to improve their life chances or elements such as having good health, a good education, and a good job—elements of a "good life" that are often attained more readily by members of the dominant group. Minority group members see the inequality of their lives and must live with that. Their shared social status, marginalization from other friends or family, and current social conditions might have led them to seek out others in a similar position for acceptance and made those immediate friendships important—as Michael said, they were "family." As a white male university researcher who would not drink or steal, it made sense that I was a strange and distrusted presence, possibly even an undercover police officer.

Research now confirms that individuals who experience a lack of opportunity early in life are at much greater risk of developing a host of other personal problems. Geoffrey Canada, for example, suggests that without strong social support, children from poor African American families in Harlem subsequently face a far greater likelihood of experiencing lifelong problems with school attendance and performance at an earlier age, gaining job skills, getting and keeping good employment, alcohol use and other addictions, broken families, crime, and health. To test the theory that a poor and unsupportive social environment was at the root of these later individual and community problems, Canada developed the Harlem Children's Zone program that allows at-risk children there to learn in a nurturing environment that also promotes high standards (Tough 2008). The program addresses the children's home environment and provides academic and social support for the child's parents, helping them be actively involved in and encouraging of their children's efforts.

The subsequent increase in educational performance by those children once seemingly condemned to a life of poverty and problems has been hailed as remarkable. Canada promotes the goal that each child in his school will go to college. Nearly all the members of his school's first graduating class are attending college. While the lives of the members of this first cohort are still unfolding, the increased opportunity each of the Harlem Children's Zone participants now has in early adulthood suggests that each might avoid the problems that their neighborhood peers might experience—problems with unemployment, divorce, poverty, drug use, lower self-esteem, and poor health. Canada notes the costs of his charter school, but also observes that those costs are far less than the expense of paying for the myriad social problems that are likely to develop from children raised in poverty and oppressive environments. Helping at-risk children by promoting nurturing, supportive social environments in which they can grow can, I believe, goes a long way toward reducing secondary problems such as homelessness.

That said, some might argue that Jessi herself came from such a supportive environment—that she would not have had the opportunity to go to a prestigious college and have a medical career without a good home life and caring parents. I would agree. I would add, though, that sometimes a person's apparent successes can belie a deep insecurity about his or her true worth and can promote a false sense of self rooted in accomplishments and external validation (Miller 1997). In other words, material success and the appearance of social stability do not necessarily equate with emotional stability and psychological health. For individuals like Jessi who faced several major traumas, such profound losses can seriously undermine a sense of self that is already less stable.

Jessi and her friends drink in the park, I believe, partly because of their feelings of shame and failure. They are in the park because they are believed to be "losers" rather than tragic figures (de Botton 2004). A tragic figure is seen as someone who endures great pain and deserves sympathy, while losers are seen as stupid and as having brought their problems on themselves. Shelters in the homeless corridor often withhold services from alcoholics, indicating that homeless persons who choose to drink do not deserve bed space. In the last few years, other approaches, such as housing first and harm reduction, have been developed, emphasizing that chronically homeless alcoholics need help first "where they're at" (Ending Community Homeless Coalition 2009, 6). Although the long-term goal of several harm reduction programs is for the individual to stop drinking, such programs recognize that immediately imposing abstinence on an addict can be counterproductive. Harm reduction "aims to decrease the risk of dangers associated with the disease" (Ending Community Homeless Coalition 2009, 6). Housing first approaches provide housing to homeless individuals—"it assumes that housing stabilization is key in the return of the individual or family to independent living" (Ending Community Homeless Coalition 2009, 6). Judgment is withheld in favor of providing immediate housing, allowing individuals the stability to eventually change their lives.

In Frank Wright Plaza, escapism is the order of the day. Because many shelters in Las Vegas will not serve people who have been drinking, those in the park often fend for themselves. Addicts have a long road ahead of them to sobriety—they must commit to making healthier choices, to developing a supportive social environment, and to learning to live between improving the world around them and accepting that world. For some, it could be the struggle of a lifetime.

Jessi's primary leisure activities—drinking, socializing, and sharing intimacies with other discouraged homeless people in a public park—seem directly related to her identity at this point in her life. Her "lifestyle" reveals how homelessness literally involves a loss of one's place, a loss of meaningful connection to others. When this happens, misery loves company, or perhaps misery finds some relief in an immediate and nonjudgmental acceptance. Jessi, Wayne, S.P., Ebony, Michael, Sarah, and others in the park are self-medicating their physical and psychological pain and are enabling each others' escapism through alcohol or relationships.

I believe their stories suggest that we move away from blaming and condemning homeless people as drunk, unintelligent, and/or antisocial people and to instead consider what they need now. With increased individualism in our society, programs must be developed so that individuals, especially individuals in pain, can meaningfully connect with others. In tandem with housing first programs, professional mental health counselors should provide greater outreach on the streets of Las Vegas, even to those without insurance or the ability to pay. The streets are an alienating, lonely place, and homeless people's lives generally do not improve the longer they are homeless.

THREE

Confronting Aggression, Pride, and Need in Former Convicts

KEVIN

Kevin was Caucasian, about five feet seven, muscular, and wore black jeans and a checkered flannel shirt. A former convict with a history of violence, Kevin had recently been released from prison and now sought local work in construction. I met him at the DTC in late November 2005. His face and speaking voice reminded me of Harvey Keitel, but his pointed, balding head undermined the resemblance. He had an overstuffed backpack and sleeping bag by his side. His story suggests the difficulty he as a former convict faces in reintegrating into society, but it also underscored the problems brought on by his aggressive, self-defeating personality.

Kevin seemed to have had troubles but was trying to change. He was telling me a story, familiar to many homeless people in Las Vegas, about having problems getting ID and the catch-22 of not being able to get work without it.

KEVIN: You got to have ID to work here, that's the most definite. As far as between jobs out here, if you don't have ID, you're not gonna get no work. I'm waiting on Social Security and a birth certificate to get an ID. There's probably plenty of work out here, but you got to have all the credentials.

KURT: And you came out here specifically to find work? What type of work?

KEVIN: Construction.

KURT: Where were you coming from?

KEVIN: Chino State Prison.

I am surprised by the revelation.

"Yeah," Kevin says, staring directly at me.

I decided to carefully ask more about his prison experience. "How long were you there, if I may ask?"

"This time I was only there six months," he replied. "I just finished. They discharged my number. But I been in, did six years all together. They actually got me back in Detroit because I ran. It's all finished now, so, been living in California. I don't want to stay there anyways."

Kevin told me about his extradition to California from Detroit, where he had been working in construction. After he had served his sentence, his sister, who now lives in Las Vegas, encouraged him to move to her city because work was plentiful.

"She just told me that there's a lot of work if you want to work, day labor, labor comp, max labor, all these places [that hire temporary laborers]. If you get there early enough and you have the right ID, they put you out there on different jobs, supposedly, if you have any experience . . . give you a shot at whatever. It don't pay much, but it gets you off the street."

Kevin was right about the good number of temporary labor jobs available in the city. However, I think it was inaccurate to say that it "gets you off the street." Snow and Anderson (1993) found that those who are more recently homeless have tried to use this type of employment as a way to acquire cash quickly without paperwork. The authors note, though, that the work is often short-term, poorly paid, exploitative, and irregular. Snow and Anderson believe that this approach to earning money in order to end homelessness is often frustrating and that, in general, homeless people's "experience with the world of wage labor leads to diminishing reliance on it as a subsistence strategy" (1993, 134). Kevin's other descriptions of his experiences seemed to confirm Snow and Anderson's analysis.

KURT: Have you been working since you've been in town?

KEVIN: I worked two days since last week 'cause I just found somebody that would pick you up for labor without ID. And I called him yesterday and Monday, and I can't get a hold of him, and then I ain't got money to call today. Maybe I'll be able to call him tonight or something.

KURT: What type of work was it?

KEVIN: Actually, he's an electrical contractor, but he's branching out doing block walls, masonry. And that's what I did in Detroit, so it kind of felt good, for me.

KURT: Masonry work? That's a very well-paying job usually.

KEVIN: It is back East. It ain't here. If [you're] union . . . that's good money, but if you're just fly-by-night labor, then they give you forty dollars.

KURT: Forty dollars for an eight-hour day?

KEVIN: Pretty much, pretty much. I went from eighteen to five dollars an hour. That's pretty bad.

Snow and Anderson note that homeless people who try to use work to end their homelessness and are not successful usually resort to or perform additional subsistence strategies, such as relying on family or institutional support. I asked Kevin if he had considered staying with his sister in town. He said what homeless men usually tell me—that they don't want to impose on their parents or siblings.

"Her kids are grown-up and on their own and she helped me out, but I mean I don't want to put that burden on her, you know? I'm grown. I should be able to fend for myself, you know?"

Like other homeless people I have interviewed, Kevin discusses the shame he has felt at being homeless. The shame ironically might well perpetuate his condition, since he seems unwilling to ask family members for a place to stay. His conclusion that he should be able to fend for himself stresses autonomy, but at the expense of getting even temporary housing that he might need to become self-supporting.

KURT: You told me you didn't want to stay with your sister, but she bought you some camping supplies?"

KEVIN: Right, right. Sleeping bag, backpack, clothes, new clothes, stuff to stay warm with. It was nice of her. I got here, all I had was—I didn't even have nothing. I had a pair of pants, a shirt, and I think a flannel shirt, and that was it.

KURT: Did you get released directly from prison?

KEVIN: Yeah.

KURT: Did they give you anything, money?

KEVIN: They give you two hundred dollars, but by the time you get a bus, you eat, drink, whatever you gonna do, it don't go far.

He said he had been camping out under an overpass for three weeks and now was considering going to a shelter in the homeless corridor because the weather lately had been so bad. He had described how helpful some of the services could be to homeless people, if only they would use them. He clarified that the homeless corridor depressed him because the people he saw there didn't seem to want to change their situation, to do anything.

KEVIN: Tonight I think I'm gonna try to go to St. Vincent's, sleep in a regular bed, you know, the homeless shelter. [Saturday's weather] was miserable, everybody was complaining. I feel sorry for the people that only had blankets, let alone no clothes to bundle up in. That wind was cutting through everybody.

KURT: How do you meet your hygiene needs, shower and that type of thing?

KEVIN: Salvation Army has showers from 10:30 to 1:30. Saturdays, Sundays, [they're] 12:30 to 3:00, I believe, and you just go down there and you show them any type of paperwork or any type of ID you have. They'll give you a towel, soap, [and you can] take a hot shower, just stay clean. I don't understand why a lot of people don't do it.

KURT: There are a fair number of people who don't do it, you say?

KEVIN: Oh, yeah. I mean it's pretty obvious [referring to some of the people sitting around us at the DTC].

KURT: You mentioned, too, that you like to hang out more here at the bus station compared to the shelters. Why is that?

KEVIN: It's just a bad crowd there. It's—you don't do that. You got to get out and do something. You got to get out and do something, not just sit around all day just sitting there, waiting for someone to come to you. You got to get out and get around, you know.

Kevin seemed to be suggesting that he had trouble relating to other homeless people and that he thought their values were skewed. Despite his past, Kevin seemed to be arguing for the value of honest hard work as a means of ending homelessness. Kevin noted his activity in comparison to other homeless people's passivity:

"I ride the bus or go wherever I have to, you know, go eat wherever, go get new clothes at wherever I can. Job comes along, I go work 'til that ID comes, you know, do whatever I can do."

:: :: :: During part of our interview, Kevin kept mentioning his difficulties in getting identification and how the lack of ID was preventing him from working and thus ending his homelessness.

KEVIN: They were supposed to give me a printout, told me it would be ten to fourteen days. You give them an address and they mail it to you. If you don't have an address, they send it to the Salvation Army 'cause it—they take people's mail there. I checked every day now and it's about the eighteenth day. I don't know if it was 'cause of the holidays that makes it not working days that it's not there, but it's still not there.

KURT: You need that to get the other cards you'll need to start work?

KEVIN: You need a Social Security card and a birth certificate to get the ID. You need your ID basically to get work, so until that happens it's more or less wherever you can find, you know, by word of mouth that will take you as labor or day-labor type of deal without going to the day labor place, which don't pay worth a damn. But it's better than nothing if you can get the work.

KURT: What time do you get to the day labor in order to pick up work?

KEVIN: You got to get there early. Try to get there when the doors open at 6:00, 7:00 [A.M.], you know. A lot of these guys are getting there real early and there ain't no work after 8:00.

KURT: If you get there after 8 A.M., you can't find work?

KEVIN: Yeah, nine times out of ten. They give you tickets to go out. They usually have the work just the day before, unless somebody's calling in that morning, but [if] you get there too late, the work's already given out to everybody. You might get lucky. But you got so many people in there after that time, they come late, very rarely you'll find something for the rest of the day.

:: :: :: At the end of our first meeting, I asked Kevin about his future plans. He said he wanted to get back to a good-paying union job back in Detroit but was hoping to perhaps join the union in Las Vegas as well. Either way, he was tired of being homeless and of the problems that came with it.

KEVIN: Work in the union out here during the summer or during the winter, work back there in the summer and then go back and forth, that type of deal. That's my plan, that's my goal. Hopefully it will work.

KURT: So Las Vegas has been kind of an experiment for you to try out?

KEVIN: Yeah, pretty much. I haven't been here since I was a kid, you know. This place—it's something else, that's for sure.

KURT: It's changed a lot?

KEVIN: Let's put it this way: There's a lot of building goin' on, but if you don't have no money here, you're a nobody.

:: :: :: Three days later, in the early evening, I am waiting at the DTC for the bus to the homeless corridor. There I see Kevin again, walking with a group of passengers, carrying his backpack and sleeping bag and wearing the same black jeans and flannel shirt from days ago. I make eye contact with him as he approaches. He is scowling, looking angry. He marches up to me, stops, shoves his hand into his pocket, and then extends it.

"You want your money back?" he shouts, showing me a few crumpled bills.

"No!" I reply, confused.

We repeat this exchange a few times. I explain that I gave him some cash after our interview as a way of thanking him. I've taken to giving $5 to people after I interview them to let them know that I think their time and insights are worth something and because, frankly, I think they can use the money. He tells me instead that he doesn't need the money, that he now has $130 in food stamps and that he doesn't even need to be out here. I am not sure why he wants to give me back the money or what he's trying to tell me.

A space clears along a nearby bench and we sit. He tells me, after looking around quite a bit and lowering his tone, that he doesn't need to be out here, because he's a member of the Aryan Brotherhood. Reaching into his pocket, he pulls out folded sheets of paper with phone numbers scrawled on them, numbers he says are for fellow Aryan Brothers he has run into since coming to Las Vegas.

"I'm a bad guy, Kurt," he tells me.

"No, you're not," I say, even though at the time I wasn't sure what kind of guy he really was.

"Yes, I am," he yells. When he quietly tells me how he hates niggers, and those Mexicans who have taken over California, I suddenly wish I could leave.

During our initial interview I had felt bad for Kevin. Despite having committed crimes (which I was nervous to ask about), he had served his sentence and was now trying to find work. Even if he wasn't staying with his sister, he seemed to have kept a good relationship with her. Now a few days later, after revealing his membership in a criminal gang and saying that he was a bad guy, I was worried. He seemed eager to create tension between us, and I wanted badly to reduce it. I particularly didn't want him to be bad around me.

"People are getting to know you out here, Kurt," he says. He looks away from me, squinting. "They know what you're doing, and they don't like it." He turned close to face me. "I swear, if you ever do anything to hurt these people out here, man, I will string you up. You know what that means?" he says, raising his eyebrows. "I will beat you so badly . . ." he trails off. Kevin stands up, shakes his head, and starts making fists.

I am now upset but realize I need to address him rationally. I stand up to face him, look him squarely in the eye despite my fear, and tell him in a measured tone that I am not out here to hurt anybody. I say I'm just trying to talk to homeless people so other people can know how miserable it is to be homeless. I'm hoping that something can be done to help all these people. The last thing I would want to do is hurt anybody, I say.

"You're not with the police?" he suddenly turns and yells, moving closer, tensing his shoulders.

"No," I say in the calmest, most casually dismissive way I can muster. I am conscious that even though I'm sincere, I also need to convince him that I'm sincere, because he's agitated and threatening. I try to get more out of him. He gets to his specific concern—that if anything ever happens to those people he has told me about who do drugs under the overpass where he camps, that if the police find out about them, he will come find me and hurt me. He guarantees it, repeating my name while threatening me.

This is only the second time I have felt threatened while doing my research. The other time was also while talking to a former convict, named Spirit, in 1996. He relished intimidating me in front of other homeless men while squatting in an abandoned motel on the south Las Vegas Strip. He wanted to make it clear in front of the other squatters that I would be allowed to stay on the property because of him, and only because of him.

After talking to Kevin, I thought about how former convicts in general might feel out of place and somewhat powerless on the streets. In prison they seem to learn that strong, threatening men command respect, or at least fear, if they can back up what they say. Intimidation is an attempt to gain some control, the only source of status some former convicts have.

It's a hyper-masculinity that contrasts directly with the emasculating status of homelessness.

"I don't want nothing bad to happen to nobody out here, Kurt," he tells me. "I help these people. I look out for them." An old black man searches the ground for a cigarette butt nearby us, and Kevin offers his. At various points he makes benevolent displays to people. Oddly, he even makes these toward minority group members he presumably hates.

"Can I give you some advice?" he said to me. "Go home. Get on the bus and go back to where you came. Stop doing this before you get hurt."

I just stand, staring at him, unsure what to say or do next. I keep wondering, Why is he acting this way? Why is he so different from our interview before?

"Are you afraid out here?" he suddenly asked me.

"No," I said dismissively. "Homeless people really aren't scary. Most homeless people I have talked to are pretty nice."

He took a sideways stance, like he might be ready to throw a punch.

"You carry a gun?" he says.

"No," I laugh and shake my head.

"You carry a knife?"

I shake my head.

"You know how to fight?"

"Not really," I replied, worried about the direction of this line of questioning.

"Good!" he shouted, smiling.

He suddenly pulls a piece of paper from his pocket, a receipt for a food stamp purchase, and throws it at me. He makes a nasty face and stalks away. I am confused again. He has left his bag with all his valuables by the bench. I look in the direction I thought he went, and he isn't there.

I stand, looking at his stuff, then looking in the direction he walked off, and wonder about his behavior. Is he disgusted with me? Is he testing me? I think of leaving, but then I think better of it. Then, in my peripheral vision, I see he has come full circle around the nearby hot dog stand—he disappeared only to watch me from the side. I feel unnerved, shaken. He breaks into a smile and approaches again.

He suddenly tells me I'm all right, and hugs me. It's not a compassionate, gentle hug, but a muscular hug, an embrace around the shoulders—he thumps on my back with his fist. I try to hug back, but I am wary. He sees a black woman trying to throw away a fast food wrapper and quickly takes it from her, throwing it away himself. She laughs at the strange, seemingly helpful gesture. I think she initially misunderstood it, thinking that he wanted the wrapper for whatever leftover food might be in it.

Finally, he tells me he is drunk. I am relieved to know the root of his bizarre behavior. He had two shots earlier, after finding out that his Social Security card still had not arrived. Although I didn't smell alcohol on him and he didn't slur his speech, now I see how red his eyes are. He's not a big man, and perhaps he hasn't eaten. He's also been spitting a lot—I can see a wad of tobacco slowly disintegrating underneath his lower front teeth. During our interview the first day we met, I had wondered about the large brown stain in the gap between his lower teeth. It seemed too dark to be simply from smoking.

After his admission and all the drama of the previous twenty minutes, I wanted to get away from him. When the bus to the homeless corridor came, I told him I was going to the shelters.

"You're going there, at night?" he replied, incredulous.

"Yeah, it's fine," I said.

"I'm going with you."

I withered at his reply but also felt conflicted. I worried that his comments might be true: that people on the streets might be getting to know me and that those people didn't like what I was doing. I also feared that, with some active campaigning, Kevin could make other people not like or not trust me. He intimidated me, but I also wondered how I had failed to sufficiently convince him that I was a researcher and why he thought instead that I was a policeman or a nark.

I noticed his bus pass was very tattered, as though it had gone through a washing machine. I hoped it wouldn't work, but no such luck. He followed me on board and then, to my surprise, sat several rows behind me.

He began talking to a Hispanic woman, asking her if she was OK and if she needed anything. Through brief glances and her verbal responses, I realized he was intimidating her. His forceful, direct statements, combined with his tendency to touch the people he approached on their arms and head, was threatening. Even larger men looked him directly in the eye when he spoke, giving him a steady glance—I had learned that few people ignored Kevin. As we approached the stop, he yelled my name, making sure I would exit.

:: :: :: We walked through the Catholic Charities complex, then up Owens Avenue. He said "hey bro" and "hey man" to several people. Trying to make conversation with him, I said that he seemed to know a lot of people.

"I don't know any of these people," he replied. "I seen some. Visually I know them, but I don't know them and they don't know me." I noticed he had a stiff, swaggering walk and always held his head up.

"I want to introduce you to somebody," Kevin said as we walked the incline up Owens to the Salvation Army. "This woman sits on this bench all day. Her kids died. She's been sitting out here ever since. Her family's rich—she doesn't need to be out here." I thought about this variation of the urban legend I've heard so many times—the secretly wealthy homeless person—until I realized he was referring to a woman I had seen dozens of times on the bench. A middle-aged black woman who seemed not to care about her hygiene, she always sat by herself and talked to herself. I had tried speaking to her before but had never been able to keep a conversation going.

Kevin approached her and asked how she was doing. When she didn't immediately respond, he grabbed the top of her head in one hand and turned it, forcing her to look at him.

"Hey, are you OK?" he shouted at her.

"I'm fine, I'm fine," she said, looking right at him. Though I had watched her talk to herself on many occasions at this bus stop, her responses to Kevin were direct and sane.

"Do you need anything?" he asked, releasing her head while she withdrew.

"No, I'm good."

"A cigarette? You need a cigarette?"

"No thank you," she replied. "You have any beer?"

"No," he replied, whereupon she turned away.

As we walk away, I tell him I am amazed that he was able to talk to her, since I could hardly get a word out of her, and he just laughs. Perhaps, though, she's never had any compelling reason to be direct and lucid around me.

:: :: ::   Near the Salvation Army yard, a disabled Native American man slowly asks us for change. Kevin reaches into his pocket and gives him some. The man appears thankful.

At the Salvation Army, Kevin checks at the front desk to see if his Social Security card has arrived, but the people there haven't heard anything. He turns, takes a handful of folded toilet-paper bunches that sit in a basket on the table, and we head to the restroom and showers. The smell gets stronger, and the moist, locker-room air hits us as we approach.

The bathroom there is always disgusting, even after a cleaning. Maybe it's the dirt forever ground between the floor tiles combined with the lingering smell of exposed body parts that have been marinating in the same clothes for days or weeks. The toilets don't have doors. There's a hole between stalls where the men can see each other. The painted concrete walls are also filthy, and the fluorescent lighting completes a dismal gray effect. A cockroach crawls across the wall in front of the air dryers while I sit outside taking notes. Two elderly black men see me writing; one says to the other, "He's writing a book about the shelter." For a second I am shocked—Kevin's statement that people are becoming aware of me seems true. The second man then replies, "It's gonna be a short one," whereupon they both laugh hard. I realize I'm getting paranoid.

"Leave him alone!" Kevin yells at them from the stall. "He's with me!" They chuckle while walking out.

After Kevin finishes using the toilet, we head back toward the bus stop. Several times on the way back, my "guardian" repeats the word *depressing*, shaking his head. He clarifies that it's the setting of the Salvation Army that has depressed him. He talks about the people who sit around there all day and how he never wants to be like that.

:: :: ::   We walk several blocks from the Salvation Army to the express bus stop that will take us back to the DTC. Three police cars are attending to an accident near our stop. Kevin becomes motionless when he sees the police and wants to avoid them by going into the 7-Eleven.

In the parking lot we see the same Native American man who had earlier approached us for money. He asks for money again. Kevin angrily tells him off, reminding him that he's approached us before. The Native man puts up his hands, saying, "OK, OK," trying to avoid Kevin's wrath. Kevin has stressed several times that he wants to help homeless people and views himself as their protector, but like most people, he shows little tolerance for someone approaching him for a handout twice within a short time.

Inside the store he gets a large can of beer and I get a hot chocolate, which he initially offers to buy with his food stamp card but then forgets to pay for. A new friend of Kevin's, a drunk who wants a burrito that Kevin also offers to pay for, probably distracts him. Kevin's purchase is successful, but the clerk chides them both for heating the burrito before paying for it. Apparently this is a familiar scam in this convenience store—heat the food, then reveal that you don't have enough money on the food stamp card to buy it and hope that the clerk will simply give it to you because technically it can no longer be sold. The other clerk yells at all three of us as we try to exit the store, because the drunk is trying to leave with two 40-ounce beers in his hands. Kevin quickly disassociates us from the man as we exit. He yells at him, "Don't screw around with someone who's trying to help you."

At the bus stop, Kevin takes out his beer. He gives it a look, then says, "I shouldn't do this." He chugs it. I don't know how he wants me to respond to his statement, but I am afraid to, so I do nothing. I watch as trickles of beer stream down the sides of his face.

He soon is bending over, feeling sick. I'm wondering why he's having this sudden response from just one beer. When he starts spitting, I realize he's also probably been swallowing his chew juice. A security guard near the bus stop tells us to move on, and Kevin ignores him. I finally compel Kevin to move when I say there's another stop close by.

The bus finally arrives. On board, we sit near three young black men. They are dressed in street clothes. One holds a bouquet of flowers. They are talking about prison time they've served and the people they know in common.

"Let me smell those," Kevin says to one of the men, reaching forward to tilt the bouquet toward his nose while leaning in. My eyes widen as Kevin makes this bold move. I only wish I could have seen the man's initial expression as Kevin tilted the flowers. Kevin does it again, and now I can register the men's bemusement. Kevin then asks the man what he is planning on doing with them. "Whatever I want to do with them," the man replies. Having been put in his place, Kevin now leans back in his seat, tightly crossing his arms and ignoring the men. At times he looks at me and sneers.

Much to my relief, we finally arrive at the DTC. I have been rehearsing my exit. At the stop Kevin keeps saying to me, "Roll with me on Fremont tonight, bro."

"I can't, Kevin. I have to go home and write up notes. I've got a ton of things to write just from visiting the Salvation Army."

He repeats his plea, and I quietly but steadily decline. I begin to see him as drunk and friendless. He must feel lonely a lot, I think. He hurts and acts aggressively, causing people to avoid and fear him, so he gets lonelier.

:: :: :: Two days later, I see Kevin again on the same stretch of Owens Avenue. I tense up. This time it's daylight, though, and his demeanor is visibly different. His right arm is wrapped in bandages up to the elbow, treatment he says he got at the free clinic near the Rescue Mission. His denim jacket is covered in dirt, and he has the same pants and shirt on from days ago. He appears sadder, almost embarrassed from the other night. Perhaps he's hung over. Or perhaps his sad look is just an expression of his physical pain combined with the dark stubble on his cheeks.

He begins explaining his most recent injury and what had happened the day he was attacked. He says a "bunch of Mexicans" jumped him after he ate a meal at the Rescue Mission. He tried to tell them in Spanish to calm down, but he says one of the guys twice tried to attack him and take his backpack. He violently reenacts the beating he gave to the man who attacked him and says the man ran off into the bushes afterward. Kevin imitated the man's crying. The workers at the free clinic who bandaged Kevin told him to come back in a few days when the swelling went down and they would see about fitting him with a cast.

Recalling the other night, I wondered if he had been sober when he had been attacked. I imagined him calling his attacker "bro" or some other familiar name before the fight. I wondered if he had tried to touch him on the arms or head before their conflict.

"I hate to ask you this, bro," he began saying to me. "I need a dollar. Actually what I really need is two dollars, but I'm only going to ask you for one." I hand him two, and he gladly takes the money.

"Thank you, bro," he says, reaching forward to hug me. I hesitate, but lean forward. The hug is less muscular than before, and he doesn't fist thump my back, perhaps because of his injury.

"Take care, bro. You need anything? You OK out here?" he asks as we begin walking in different directions.

"I'm OK, I'm good," I reply, turning away.

:: :: :: A week later, I see Kevin briefly again at the DTC. He is drunk. He holds out a dollar, and asks, "You want your money back?"

"No, no. That's yours," I reply, going through the routine.

No matter how drunk he is, he never forgets the cash I gave him. It seems to bother him. Sometimes he asks for money, and other times he is stubbornly self-sufficient, I think, walking away.

As I catch another bus, I wonder if talking to him initially was a mistake.

:: :: :: Another few days pass. On December 16 at the DTC, I am sitting in a waiting area, and a scuffle breaks out. Three marshals appear and begin interrogating a man standing in the middle of an open circular space surrounded by seats.

"I didn't hit anybody," the man tells a marshal. "Those guys left."

The marshals look over everyone in the waiting area, and one announces, "If you aren't waiting for a bus, you need to leave. If you are waiting for a bus, you need to get on it." The marshals begin asking each person sitting there, "Are you waiting for a bus?" and if the person says yes, they ask, "What bus are you waiting for?" or "Do you have a pass?"

The officer sees me sitting with a homeless friend, looks me in the eye, and says, "Move on." I am familiar with this type of story from talking to Ricky and other homeless people about the way security guards and the police treat them, but I was stunned at the blanket generalization he's made about me, about everyone waiting in this area. I had arrived from a bus three minutes earlier to sit in this public space, and suddenly I was, in his eyes, a loiterer. The officers started leaving in a group.

"We'll be back," one of them says in a booming voice while walking away.

Kevin appears minutes later. His eyes are bloodshot. His hand is wrapped in white medical tape supporting his metal thumb splint, and all of that is wrapped in a gauze bandage. I ask him if I can take a photograph of his hand. He agrees.

::   ::   ::   He sits for a while. Kevin then tells me to lean closer, that he has something to tell me. I do so, and Kevin looks off into the distance.

"I've killed eleven people."

I'm unsure what to do with the unexpected admission. I begin asking questions.

"How?"

"With a gun. I'm a good shot." Four of them were by stabbing, he adds.

"Did you know them?"

"No no no," he says, making a sour face and shaking his head. "I got paid two, three thousand. Except for the child molesters."

A large, unkempt black woman in sweat pants and a T-shirt is sitting across from us in the DTC waiting area, asking passerby for money in a loud voice.

"Don't beg!" Kevin suddenly shouts at her. She looks back, furious.

"Stand up!" she yells. "Get over here!"

Kevin lurches up like a cowboy ready to draw his gun, then saunters over to her. I'm afraid there will be a fistfight. She orders him to lean toward her, and he does. She then grabs his head, shakes it, and makes fun of his bald spot. Suddenly they are both laughing like old friends, and he walks back to me.

::   ::   ::   I smile at him as he returns from his pseudo-confrontation with the African American woman and hope that he remembers he has just told me about being a murderer.

"Does it bother you?" I ask.

"Sometimes I cry at night about it," he says, surprising me with candor. "Can't do nothin' about it now, though. I just gotta keep going."

Friends often ask me if I think Kevin was telling the truth. I imagine that the four stabbings could have been group attacks on child molesters in prison, but I will never know. I tell people that I think he has killed at least once.

Kevin sees a black man, and he gets up to greet him and follow him. As Kevin leaves, another homeless man whom I had interviewed a few weeks before sits near me. He looks over at Kevin and says, "He scares me."

"Me too," I nod in agreement.

"Sometimes he just goes off down here, screaming in the middle of a group of people."

As I picture the scene he described, Kevin returns. I decide I want to leave, and I tell him that I had better go because the marshals had earlier said to move.

"You're a man, aren't you?" Kevin suddenly shouts, glaring at me. "You're a man, right?"

"Yeah," I reply, hesitant.

"They're a man, too. Just 'cause you don't got a badge don't mean you're not a man," he says. I try to figure out what he's saying. "Fuck them," he says jerking his head back. "I don't fear nobody," he adds, clarifying his meaning.

As I leave, Kevin offers his good hand, which I shake. He crushes my fingers while smiling. I wince, but act playful as I smile and leave.

I never saw Kevin again.

DISCUSSION

Individuals like Kevin who are particularly aggressive are difficult to talk to. I believe his violent presentation of self harms his chances of getting a full-time job or finding friends. His intermittent use of services for homeless people seems to suggest that he is simultaneously needy, critical, and prideful.

I think now about how his attitude toward the police and authority figures is totally different from mine. His life seems defined by fear, respect, and intimidation. His code seemed clear: Respect me, or I will mistreat you. I will kill you or hurt you badly before I let you hurt me.

I don't know where the violence in Kevin's life started. It probably began in his childhood. It could also have come later, as a teenager. His association with the Aryan Brotherhood also likely involved violence, and he certainly encountered it in prison.

Kevin's story suggests that certain policy changes might reduce homelessness. First, it is crucial to remember that all prisoners, short of those who die while incarcerated, will eventually return to your neighborhood and mine. It then seems crucial that we strongly promote rehabilitative programs in prison, including employment training and, in the case of violent prisoners like Kevin, counseling and programs that teach empathy.

In discussing forms of emotional intelligence, Daniel Goleman (1995) notes that child molesters, rapists and many people who commit family violence lack empathy. Such people are able to hurt others, he argues, because they can lie to themselves that they really aren't harming their victims, thus allowing them to carry out their actions. Goleman states that new treatments are being developed for such offenders, programs in which offenders read impact statements written by victims of such crimes, watch videotapes of victims painfully recounting their experiences of molestation or similar forms of violence, and in which offenders reenact a version of the crime but this time in the role of the victim. William Pithers, the psychologist who developed this therapeutic approach, reveals that "empathy with the victim shifts perception so that the denial of pain, even in one's fantasies, is difficult" (cited in Goleman 1995, 107). Such treatments give hope that even long-established patterns of violence can be greatly inhibited through rehabilitation and retraining.

Developing increased empathy would seem to benefit someone at any stage in life. School curricula that teach children to recognize, name, and feel their emotions when they occur might greatly reduce later hurtful behavior caused by repression of those feelings. Learning how to recognize and manage emotions, sometimes called emotional literacy (Bocchino 1999), should therefore become a universal component of school curricula.

I believe that developing empathy toward those in pain would also benefit those in Las Vegas who hate, ignore, chide, take advantage of, or deny the presence of homeless people. Kevin's story is suggestive of the demeaning, vicious nature of homelessness in Las Vegas. His need for immediate cash leaves him vulnerable to employers who pay him cut rates for his skills. He endures the cold of the outdoors rather than sleeping in what he sees as the depressing conditions in shelters in the homeless corridor. He feels helpless while waiting weeks for simple identity cards to come to him at local shelters. He fights embarrassment at having to accept assistance from his sister. He cannot even take a few dollars from me as my way of thanking him for his time and willingness to be interviewed. He wants so badly to be masculine, dominant, and in control of his life. However, his increasing depression seems to indicate a growing awareness of his limited future. He is trying to find regular work at blue-collar jobs but is frustrated. His situation raises questions about the extent to which violence and aggression are innate, learned, and/or promoted by particular environments.

It is also possible that, no matter what his past or present circumstances, Kevin is a sociopath, one among a limited number of people in any society who appear to be without a moral core. Fears of ever-present violent homeless men, though, seem rooted in stereotypes like those promoted in *Bumfights*. News media accounts implicitly promote such fears by how they report stories of homeless men who are involved in crime or violence—the label of "a homeless man" or "transient" often precedes or directly follows the name of the criminal or suspect (Borchard 2005, 7). Such media accounts suggest homeless men are a homogeneous group that poses an ongoing threat to "our" communities and safety. Demonizing this category of people so as to justify aggressively policing and segregating them then becomes easier, as when Las Vegas Mayor Oscar Goodman requested that local police specifically evaluate how much crime in downtown Las Vegas was caused by homeless people (Moller 2001).

Such a focus should perhaps raise another question: Is it beneficial, or even appropriate, to use such stereotyping and community resources to possibly justify withholding help to most homeless people?

FOUR

Living Outside the Mainstream with Chronic Alcoholism

BRUCE AND ALASKA

Bruce and Alaska were both alcoholics living in an open field in the homeless corridor of Las Vegas. Their alcoholism seems life threatening. Their stories suggest how difficult it might be to help them conceive of, and work toward, a life without addiction. I believe their stories also suggest the need for nonjudgmental social services so that such committed alcoholics do not have to choose between receiving life-sustaining services and their addiction, allowing some a better chance at recovery.

In November 2005, I was sitting at a bus stop in North Las Vegas across from Gabe's Bar. The area is on the border of the homeless corridor. A black man dressed in a suit and leather shoes sat down near me. He began talking to me about being an Ethiopian Jew, but he soon spoke to anyone nearby, shouting and slurring his speech. His spittle hit me when he spoke. He was drunk. He said that the Jews' pain has been caused by the shooting and killing of Jewish babies. He repeated this theme, with slight variations, for several minutes. He was annoying, but he was not threatening anyone. Everyone waiting at the bus stop was quietly enduring him.

Soon, a young white man and his grandmother came to the stop. The young man greeted the Ethiopian man—he remembered that they had worked together at a casino. The young man and his grandmother sat on the bench next to the Ethiopian man, who immediately began talking about the same hardships. We all looked knowingly at one another. The pair of new arrivals would soon realize that the man was drunk.

The grandmother, though, did not seem to care that he was drunk. She said she had also experienced hardship and discrimination as an immigrant and told him he was not the only one who has ever suffered. The Ethiopian man then raised his voice, shouting, "They killed babies! They burned the babies! The Nazis killed the babies! No one knows the pain of the Ethiopian Jew! No one knows the pain in our hearts!" He began sobbing. The boy and his grandmother were clearly uncomfortable, because the intensely emotional man would not stop talking.

I couldn't stand being in his presence any longer. I got up and walked to the next bus stop a block away.

Several minutes later, the bus came. On board were the young man, the grandmother, and several others from the bus stop. The Ethiopian man in the suit was not on board.

"Well, we made it!" I said to them, referring to our escape from the Ethiopian man's diatribe.

"Yes!" the young man with his grandmother said, laughing and smiling. "I just remembered him from work," he told me, indicating why he had spoken to the man in the first place. "I'm just glad he didn't have a bus pass."

A few of us smiled and shook our heads as we rode. Eventually I met up with Bruce, the out-of-control man, again, although it took me a long time to realize it was the same man I had walked away from that day.

:: :: :: In mid-February 2006, I went to an open field across from Jerry's Nugget, a local casino. I entered the field through a part of the fence that was knocked down, next to Gabe's Bar. The field was actually an abandoned mobile home court. Dozens of homeless people, mostly men and a few women, were now making it their home. Their campsites were varied and creative. Some had just a few blankets and personal items on the concrete slabs where mobile homes once stood. A few seemed to have made wind barriers out of tall piles of tumbleweeds or out of blankets tied to posts. Two men with two dogs on leashes had a store-bought tent. Several people were camped near the concrete wall on two sides of the field, using tarps and blankets along with solid posts and shopping carts to create their homes.

A black man at one campsite asked me for thirty cents. I gave it to him. He thanked me and asked if I was staying in the field. I told him I was doing a study about homelessness. He told me to follow him.

He had black hair and brown eyes and wore blue dress slacks with cuffs, black dress shoes, a black-and-white sweater, a brown leather jacket, and a red baseball cab with a white Nike swoosh logo. His sideburns revealed a few gray hairs. He had slightly puffy cheeks and bloodshot eyes, and I noticed a gap between his top incisors, the only defect in his otherwise perfect teeth.

He showed me his campsite on a concrete slab. Outside it looked like a box, eight-feet wide, six-feet long, and three-feet tall, made of the gray patchy wool blankets that charitable agencies often distribute to homeless people in this area of the city. He removed two heavy rocks holding down the bottom of a blanket, marking a space I soon learned was the door. Inside he revealed a frame constructed out of four shopping carts placed on their sides. The interior held two twin mattresses and his personal items, which were scattered wildly about. I asked him if he had gotten very wet last night, since it had rained. He said no, showing me that the thick layering of blankets was now relatively dry.

A black woman in a gold dress came by and asked the man if his girlfriend would be back tonight. He said no, that she was gone. He said he had to be on his own. The woman left, saying she would seem him later tonight.

The man introduced himself by his full name but then told me to call him Bruce, his street name. He said he needed to go to the store to get his beer. I followed him, taking notes.

He called the woman I had just met a crack whore and said that she would do anything to get more crack. Right now she was fine because she had something to drink, but that could soon change. He said there are several such women in this area and that whatever money they make won't last long. He said you have to be careful, though, because many of them have diseases.

"I know girls who come here after working at the Palomino Club [across the street]. No amount of money [they make] is enough," Bruce said. "She will give you a blow job for five dollars if she doesn't have any money left." He says even beautiful women sometimes end up here.

He described different types of homeless people, saying that people become homeless for a thousand different reasons. He said that most of the guys in the field are alcoholics and that drug addicts don't stay in the field much because they become paranoid and need a better area in which to hide.

"Out here, you can't hide," he told me.

Bruce's assessment that the majority of people sleeping in the field were alcoholics and drug addicts deserves consideration. In Las Vegas, a primary approach to helping homeless people, called the Continuum of Care (CoC), was mandated in 1995 at the federal level by the office of Housing and Urban Development (Walters 2001). The typical CoC model of programs "begins with outreach, includes treatment and transitional housing, and ends with permanent housing" (Tsemberis, Gulcur, and Nakae 2004, 651). If addicts, such as those sleeping in the field, try to access longer-term shelter in the homeless corridor, they are typically asked by agencies to participate in treatment programs before they are provided with steady housing. Committed addicts, then, usually find other ways to rest and survive while homeless.

Bruce said people find many different ways to make money while living in the field. Some people work jobs; others make ends meet with the help of nearby recycling companies.

"Some collect cans and make a quick thirty dollars for their efforts," Bruce explained.

Bruce began to talk about homelessness. He had been thinking about it a lot while sitting out here in the field, but his thoughts seemed to overlap with how he might be feeling about himself.

"The more you are homeless, you feel yourself less," said Bruce. "You feel society has abandoned you—you stop caring. If you've been a long time homeless, you just give up."

Bruce's ideas parallel some of Snow and Anderson's (1993) work on homeless careers. The researchers state "a general proposition: the longer a person is on the streets, the more difficult extrication becomes" (300). It often takes years for a person to fully identify with the role of homelessness; but Snow and Anderson believe that once that identification happens, it becomes very hard "for rehabilitative caretaker agencies to assist that person in extrication" (301). That those who have long been homeless "just give up" and "feel less," as Bruce observed, might be manifestations of their feelings of dissociation and a loss of agency, or perhaps are psychological defense mechanisms that now allow them to survive.

Bruce had been camping in the lot for nearly three months. He had taken note of and summarized the different characteristics of the people with different addictions.

BRUCE: In this area, drug addicts are paranoid. Alcoholics don't care.

KURT: You worried that your things here might get stolen?

BRUCE: No. By the time you are living out on this lot, you know everyone around you is destitute. It's safe because you have nothing to lose.

Snow and Anderson also observed similar patterns in their study. Those living outside have usually shed objects of value and experience increased vulnerability, perhaps not to crime but to other forms of loss:

Personal possessions, such as tools and clothes, are likely to be sold, pawned, or lost. It becomes progressively more difficult to maintain a car. Work skills and history become more remote. And the possibility of physical disability increases. (1993, 301)

:: :: :: As we walked, Bruce explained why we were going to Rite Aid, a nearby convenience store: "Alcoholics know where to buy alcohol cheap. Here [at Rite Aid], it's $1.09. At the 7-Eleven across from the camp it's $1.49."

Inside the store Bruce showed me a can of Steel Reserve, a malt liquor. He pointed out that it is 8.5 percent alcohol and comes in a twenty-four-ounce container. He clarified how much alcohol that is: "That's about three Miller cans."

He seemed to know that he had reached a stage of alcoholism where he needed a drink just to function: "When you have a few beers, everything feels normal. You don't feel angry or bad anymore."

Although he seemed to like hypothesizing about homelessness, he was careful about stereotyping. He often returned to the theme that there are many reasons for homelessness and that preconceptions of homeless people don't always stand up to closer scrutiny: "Any five people in the camp will all be different. Some drink, use drugs. A lot of people think homeless people are dirty. Some homeless people take better care of their hygiene than people with housing."

He seemed to feel compassion for those around him, noting that they had addictions they couldn't stop, even if some of them were in denial about their actions. He also noted, though, that many of those around him continued working.

"A lot of homeless people, they gamble and can't help it," Bruce said. "If homeless people tell you they don't drink or gamble, they're lying. For some, nothing else exists except that pipe. Crack and meth are on every corner [here]. This lot is mostly alcoholics. About thirty-five people crash here. Some of them keep working. They work during the day."

We eventually return to his campsite through a hole in the fence. He pulls out a plastic milk crate and tells me to have a seat; he sits on the ground. He showed me his identification cards for various casinos that had employed him around town. At some point Bruce had realized, though, that his commitment to alcohol made full-time work impossible.

"I used to work full time. When you drink, you can't wait to cash out that [pay]check," he said.

He then made perhaps the most edifying statement of our interview, looking at the beer in his hand: "This is the best friend I have."

:: :: :: Bruce told his life story in fragments that I later pieced together. Now thirty-five years old, he has been in the United States for thirteen years. He had been living in Chicago for a few years when a friend talked him into moving to Minnesota. There his drinking increased. He moved to Las Vegas eight years ago. He has worked many jobs in town—as a bartender's assistant, a runner, and a dealer, but he found his last job to be too difficult to perform while he was hung over. He said he preferred the swing shift because he could start drinking at midnight and continue until 6 A.M. Eventually, he says, "I started drinking twenty-four hours."

He seems aware of the impact alcohol has had on his life, but for now is unwilling to change. "Right now I can't work casino, just day labor. It has to be a temporary job, not a steady job," he said.

He describes the many problems he has had since he lost his ID:

"I lost my Sheriff's card with my old wallet. Without my Social Security card or ID, I can't get a job. I lost my license because of a DUI. I'm in and out of jail. Sometimes I'm released, and I still don't know what I've done.

"The way I drink is not normal," he adds without prompting.

Bruce seems to be able to objectively assess his drinking and the problems it is causing him, but also seems incapable of stopping. He appears to be constructing his life the best he can now, coping with his alcoholism like anyone else with a disease he's learned to live with. He doesn't discuss his alcoholism as a problem but treats it more like a fact that defines his life, even while he hides it from others.

"Most people don't know I'm an alcoholic, but I know," he says.

:: :: :: I ask him if the police bother him or anyone else much in this area.

"Here you don't stand around, you sit down," he tells me. "You don't want the police to see you. This is private property. There are big signs," he says, referring to the large "No Trespassing" signs posted around the former trailer court.

When I ask him if he has used any services in the area, he describes a few and what they offer. He also criticizes the Salvation Army.

"They have people lying on the floor," he says, drawing with a stick in the dirt. He draws rows of people lying close together. "There's no space to walk. You have people stepping on you—you see the print of shoes on the mattresses people walk on."

Because of conditions he describes, the charity that the Salvation Army and other agencies in the area offer seems to Bruce to be something they don't have to make decent, much less appealing.

"So they're saying, 'Fuck you—if you want to stay, stay. But if you want to leave here, we don't want you here.' There's too many people—it's way out of hand," Bruce explains.

Bruce's ideas about the Salvation Army seemed to parallel the principle of least eligibility from the early English Poor Law Amendment Act of 1834. He indicates that this charitable organization provided a minimal form of help to discourage overuse. He also notes that, even given its unappealing conditions, the shelter is still full—there is far more need than available bed space.

He also explains why he had difficulty getting into St. Vincent's shelter and why it isn't so appealing, either.

"St. Vincent's is a problem because it's only seasonal. The first [people they accept for shelter] are disabilities, then they [the second group accepted for shelter] have to be fifty-five. You sleep in a hallway where the light is on twenty-four hours."

Bruce knows that he cannot access St. Vincent's shelter services because he drinks. However, he also notes somewhat bitterly that others, who are less easy to detect as addicts, get to sleep there:

"They also have a Breathalyzer—I can't get in. I know people who smoke twenty-four hours of crack. They can get in. It's very easy—alcohol is an easy way to target people [for the denial of services]. They say, 'You're an alcoholic, you can't get in,'" he says, pointing his finger at me.

I ask him where he stores his personal possessions. He shows me a key to a locker that he rents at St. Vincent's where he keeps his personal items and clothes. He also has a ring of keys on a multicolored belt loop embroidered with the word GOD.

"What are your plans for the future?" I ask. He pauses.

"I know this is going to be over," he says.

As I think about his statement, I consider the different ways it could be taken. He then clarifies: He will eventually stop drinking and learn from this experience. Being homeless will have been a necessary stage in his life, something that will make him a better person.

BRUCE: I need to get my papers back, then I'll be OK. I drink less than I used to. This has taught me a lot, to be humble.

KURT: Where can you use the bathroom around here?"

BRUCE: You can go to the casino [pointing to Jerry's Nugget]. If you are respectful and don't do anything wrong, they will allow you to come in and leave. You can go to the bar [pointing to Gabe's], the shelter [pointing to St. Vincent's]. But you can always piss out here [waving his hand at the ground].

KURT: Do you feel safe out here?

BRUCE: I haven't had many fights. There are plenty of arguments between people, though, especially drunks. [He shows me the broken bottle he keeps as a weapon near his bed.]

You have to protect yourself. People will slit your throat. You can't borrow money. If a guy is smoking or drinking, they'll need that money back now. There are very nice people who are homeless, but when they get drunk, they get ugly.

He has been following world news on his radio since coming to the camp. He says it helps him put his own problems in perspective.

"I listen to BBC, NPR. There are car bombs going off in the world, tragedies. It's hard out here, but there are lots of tragedies in the world. I have to live day by day—let tomorrow take care of itself."

He also has learned a lot just by watching the activities outside his camp.

"You sit and watch out here, it's amazing. You should see it once it gets dark. The dealers out here, they sell to smoke. They do deals fast," he says, making a swooshing sound and moving his hands back and forth.

"I've seen people awake for three days," he continues. "At night, this place changes. It's like cockroaches—daylight comes, they go away—swoosh! But at night, they all come out. There [pointing near Gabe's Bar] you see Jaguars, BMWs, at around 11 P.M. or midnight. Most are users, but probably some of them are dealers. Then, five o'clock in the morning, it's all done."

Bruce points to a small concrete wall inside the field that encircles lots of bedding and two bicycles.

"Five guys, over there by that wall? One guy who sleeps there works underground construction. He makes eighteen dollars an hour. He drinks like a fish and smokes like one too. You see his bike? It sits there unlocked, all day. You couldn't leave a bike like that in the [housing] projects [across the street]—it'd get stolen. Here, no one would steal it. If they did, they'd have to not be from here. Or they'd have to leave here. Don't look back."

He summarizes the unspoken code of those around him: "In this field, it's 'Don't fuck with me and I won't fuck with you.' This is the bottom—there's nowhere else to go. So people don't steal here."

Bruce seems to consider both his surroundings and his social position as "the bottom." He also describes the disorder of his surroundings—people urinating in the open, fighting, and others selling drugs from luxury cars to those without any property. He further notes the same moral code of the streets that Snow and Anderson found: the norm of reciprocity, or "what goes around comes around" (1993, 107). Although it is arguably the most basic code of most social orders, it must be continually reinforced in places such as this field.

The code also seems to indicate the sense of social isolation found in the field. Bruce sees that his alcoholism isolates him, but at other times it seems to become his respite from being misunderstood.

"Sometimes I don't know why I drink. I have my own pain and anger to deal with. When you become an alcoholic, the loneliness is the most beautiful thing you have. There's a guy, an old man, over there [in the field]. I drink with him sometimes. But once he said, 'Let me give you some advice.

Leave me alone now,'" Bruce says, smiling. "You don't want nobody judging you—it's just you, on your own. Sometimes I hang out with friends who have a normal life: friends, family. We're the opposite. We don't understand each other at all."

Bruce had never known about this depressing part of town before he lost his housing. Although he occasionally says he realizes he needs to stop drinking, he also seems caught in an impossible situation.

"In the eight years I had been here, I had never been in North Las Vegas," Bruce said. "It got out of hand. You're seeing me sober today. I went to worship this morning. Sometimes I hate drinking. Sometimes I think I should kill myself; then I think, 'Drink today, forget about it.' I've thought about suicide more times than I can count. A couple of guys sold me a gun, but it didn't work. The trigger jammed. I ended up selling it for three times what I paid for it.

"I don't know what I'm going to do when I'm sixty-five. I've run into traffic so many times. I caused an accident on Sahara once. I felt bad, but I thought, 'I would be done. No [more] pain.'"

He then suggests that most people he knows in the field do not want to be here. He mentions the idea of predestination, which seems to help him make sense of so many of the pointless and frustrating episodes he endures daily.

"People always think homeless people have a choice. It isn't a choice. Would you choose to be out here? It's fate."

:: :: :: I again notice Bruce's keychain on his belt loop, the one with the word GOD on it, and recall his comment that he went to services today. I begin remembering something.

"What religion are you?" I ask him.

"International," he says. There is a moment of silence while I write.

"Actually, I'm Jewish," he tells me.

My sudden memory is confirmed. Bruce is the same man I sat with at the bus stop months ago, the drunken man who couldn't stop talking about the pain of being an Ethiopian Jew, who went on and on about how the Nazis killed his people's babies. I had not recognized him until that moment. Today he was soft-spoken, articulate, and engaging—everything he was not the first time I saw him and had felt a great urge to leave.

I did not reveal that we had already met, and I realized from his behavior today that he didn't remember. I knew, though, that everything he said to me about being an alcoholic was true, except one thing: People surely did know he is an alcoholic. When he was really drunk, it was obvious.

I usually give people I interview a few dollars as a way of thanking them for sharing their stories and to show them that I think their time is valuable. I did not offer Bruce that money. I realized that he would only use it to buy more alcohol. Earlier, he had bought one large beer with the help of my thirty cents, and I thought that should be enough to keep him from getting delirium tremens. He said he wanted to get up the next day, and I thought any more beer might prevent that.

Homeless people are often treated like children by social service agencies—agency workers often act as if they know better what the client needs than do the clients themselves. In an attempt to offer some dignity to homeless people, I have often given them cash, feeling that homeless people have the right to do whatever they want with their money. In Bruce's case, though, nothing he said made me think that giving him money would help him. He admitted to being out of control, and I surmised that he needed either the help of a harm reduction program or to reach bottom before he could address what was killing him.

He asked me if I had a flashlight. I said no, but that I would bring him one next time I was by the camp. When I stopped by a few days later and he wasn't there, I left it for him under the flap of his house.

::   ::   ::   In early March 2006 I returned to the camp, where I met Carol and Kiki. Both were African American women—Carol was in her mid-forties, and Kiki was in her early thirties. Carol talked to me first.

Carol was wearing a T-shirt, jacket, sweats, and a hat. She seemed to have something wrong with her tongue, because it impeded her speech. She is from Texas, her mom and dad are still living, and she has two grown children. Carol came to Las Vegas a year and a half ago with a truck driver. When they arrived in Las Vegas, he told Carol he did crack. As she watched him use, his personality changed. She told me she came out here because she was "a bad girl."

I asked her what she thought of Las Vegas. She said, "I hate it here." She has had two Greyhound bus tickets sent to her since coming. She lost one at the bus station, and the other one was stolen. She says she likes the people out in the field but doesn't trust everyone.

Kiki wore pajama bottoms and a gray tank top, and she shook and moved her head quite a bit while speaking. She tells me she is pregnant and has five kids. She moved to Las Vegas from South Carolina. Her dad has recently been diagnosed with lymphoma, and her mom passed away in 1988, when she was eleven years old.

Kiki said the people in the field who were homeless didn't have to be homeless—she said they were homeless because they had made a choice. She also said she'd be embarrassed to contact her brothers or her dad for help.

"There's a reason they call this place Sin City," she said.

I had brought food and clothing with me to give to Bruce in case I ran into him. I offered it to the women, and they took all of it. When I asked them if they happened to know Bruce, they initially puzzled over who he was. Finally, Kiki remembered him.

"You know, that drunk guy. From Ethiopia," Kiki said.

"Oh yeah! Him. He's so funny. He's cool," Carol replied, and Kiki nodded in agreement.

It later hit me that Bruce could be described in both ways. The first way, being viewed as a drunk, was causing him to lose out on social services in the area, and his Ethiopian heritage was perhaps the source of some of his pain. But the second way Carol viewed him emphasized his personality and framed him as someone likeable. His life was having an impact on others. Even if he was dying in this vacant space, the women remembered him and liked him.

I liked Bruce and felt sympathy when listening to his everyday life events and story. I wondered if any local social service providers knew Bruce and thought he was likeable. I wish Bruce knew how likeable he was. I later thought about what a waste it would be for him to die in that field.

:: :: :: A week later, I returned to the camp. A newcomer—a Caucasian man—and his male African American friend greeted me near the spot where Bruce had been lodging. The large man white man with green eyes also had a goatee and a long blond mullet underneath his baseball cap. He explained that he called himself Alaska, "because that's where I'm from, so that's what everybody calls me." He said he was forty-seven, that he had a bachelor of science degree in fish and wildlife management from Montana State University, and that he was most of his way toward earning a master's degree in education. I was happy to meet someone else in Las Vegas who originally hailed from Alaska, but I first enquired about Bruce. His African American friend told me simply, "He's in jail." When I introduced myself as a researcher, the friend said he had to go to the store. Before walking away, he said to me, "If you're really his friend, you'll go get him out of jail."

Later that night, I thought hard about that comment.

Alaska agreed to talk to me about himself and how he had come to the field.

"I came here about Tuesday," he began. "I was gonna check out the job situation, 'cause I'd been working in St. George [Utah]. And I was gonna check on my friends and if they were still here and how they were doing. I had a bunch of money, like seven or eight hundred dollars, with me.

"The first thing I did was I stopped at Jerry's Nugget and I took two hundred dollars, and got fives for it, and walked down the [railroad] tracks and gave everybody five bucks that I could find that I knew."

"The railroad tracks," I said.

"Yeah. And then I ran into this guy that I kinda knew, let him borrow my truck, and it got towed away. Now I don't know where it is and all my stuff is in my truck. And so I'm sitting here in the God-knows-what behind Gabe's Bar, with my old friends that I knew from 2003 from up on the tracks. It's just amazing that they're still here, but as soon as I walked down the street there by the Salvation Army, everybody recognized me. I guess I'm recognizable or whatever. And they told me that Allan and Monica were down here, Jamaica was down here, and here I am."

Alaska told me that he was seeing the same homeless and chronically alcoholic friends he knew from at least two years earlier. I learn that Allan was the man I just met and that Monica had said hi to me earlier through the tent. It amazed me that the same people seemed to be doing the same self-harming behaviors in the same area of the city for months if not years. It was a small community—they knew each other.

Social scientists have begun investigating what might most help members of such communities. Researchers Tsemberis, Gulcur, and Nakae (2004) have studied programs for homeless people who are chronic alcoholics and who have a psychiatric disability to learn what might help them sustain long-term housing. Their findings challenge the long-held assumption of many Continuum of Care supporters that chronically homeless alcoholics and mentally ill persons are "not housing ready" (2004, 654). The researchers argue that in New York City, a housing first program, along with an Assertive Community Treatment (ACT) program that provides formerly homeless residents with assistance from professionals such as nurses and substance abuse counselors, was much more effective at helping formerly homeless people stay housed. The idea that clients of the program receive housing first but then have *choice* about the services they use and the level of sobriety they maintain seems key to the program's success:

> Participants' ratings of perceived choice—one of the fidelity dimensions of the Housing First program—show that tenants. . . . experience significantly higher levels of control and autonomy in the program. *This experience may contribute to their success in maintaining housing and to most consumers' choice to participate in treatment* offered by the ACT team *after they were housed.* In addition, contrary to the fears of many providers and policy makers, *housing consumers without requiring sobriety as a precondition did not increase the use of alcohol or drugs among the experimental group compared with the control group.* (Tsemberis, Gulcur, and Nakae 2004, 655; emphasis mine)

Members of small drinking groups like Alaska's, then, would appear to benefit from housing first, followed by being given a choice to participate in programs to reduce alcohol consumption.

:: :: :: I asked Alaska what had caused him to leave his northern home.

ALASKA: Me and my wife got in a real nasty divorce. I got two little girls up there. I had a guide service, probably the biggest salmon service in interior Alaska. And pretty much lost everything through the divorce and what have you, and up to that point I'd been sober for twelve years. I got to drinkin', and things just kind of fell apart on me. I lost all my guide service and my boats and my house— I was driving a brand new Suburban, paid for.

KURT: Wow.

ALASKA: Yeah, tell me. So I got a little down on myself.

KURT: How did you choose Las Vegas to first come to? What was appealing about it?

ALASKA: Well, my mom lives in St. George. She wanted me to come down here so I could be close to her. She's not doing that well.

KURT: So you go back and forth between there?

ALASKA: Yeah, but I'd been in Las Vegas several times, and I knew that once I got down and out I knew that they had some kind of homeless services here, you know, maybe where I could get some shelter and help or whatever. And it's not what it's cracked up to be. The homeless services around here are terrible, really bad.

I ask him to clarify what things need improving. He says that the social service agencies need to provide better help to people who are searching for jobs and that homeless people should be able to get into a treatment program if they want to.

"And I know all that is expensive and everything like that," he adds, "but it's also expensive to have five or six thousand people living on the street, panhandling every day, you know?"

I mention how expensive police services are for the city, and he says I should consider the cost of medical services for indigent people in this area as well.

"Ambulances—ambulances are up there at the shelter every day."

As Alaska spoke, the vulnerability and exposure that is characteristic of homeless living, I thought, could well be connected to the overuse of such crisis care and police services in the area. One unintended consequence of the city's not providing enough preventative services for people to help them avoid homelessness or to house them once homeless, then, might be a very expensive overuse of publicly funded, crisis-oriented services.

:: :: :: I wanted Alaska to tell me more about his life at his previous camp. "You mentioned you were living with a group [of] thirty people, in a camp on the tracks. You said it was like a society. Tell me more about that."

ALASKA: We all had our own little jobs. Like, the big tough guys that could stay fairly sober, they were security. And you didn't let anybody strange come into your camp or walk through, and we didn't allow any drugs. There wasn't any crack smoking in our camp. We did drink a lot of beer. And uh, we had a camp cook. It was like a little town up there. Town clowns . . . [laughing]

KURT: Good friends, though?

ALASKA: Yeah, we made a lot of friends. Obviously.

I asked him if they shared resources, like food stamps for making the meals and other things, and he says yes.

"We didn't share our women, though." We both laughed.

As I had with Bruce, I asked Alaska how he met his hygiene needs living out in the field.

ALASKA: Well, the only place you can take a shower is at Salvation Army, and that's about the size of it. But you can only do it certain hours, and it's kind of a rathole. I took a shower today, but I don't have any clothes to change into. There's times where you can't even get in there to take a shower. And when it's hot out here, you need to take a shower all the time. It's pretty difficult. There's not enough services to even take a shower. You get a hundred people standing in line to take a shower, it ain't gonna happen.

KURT: Can you store food out here, or do you go to the Salvation Army or other places for food?

ALASKA: Once in a while we walk up the street to eat. I don't have a food stamp card, but usually somebody does. We get a little bit of food here and there, and we have it here. Sometimes we cook. We can't be cooking in here because the police haven't allowed us to make the fire, I don't think.

KURT: So no one in this area makes fires then?

ALASKA: I don't think so. We did on the tracks.

KURT: Did you face a lot of police harassment on the tracks?

ALASKA: Not really.

KURT: Is it the same here or different?

ALASKA: I haven't even been here long enough to know. They didn't bug us much in front of the tracks. We pretty much behaved ourselves. Like I say, we were just kind of a self-sufficient community up there. Some of the guys were in charge of getting the beer, and others were in charge of keeping the fire goin', and they helped out one way or the other.

Alaska's discussion of a self-sufficient community reminded me that, in this part of the city, the everyday norms were completely different than in the tourist area of Las Vegas. People living here were outside the mainstream economy of Las Vegas, but this economically marginal area seemed designated for them. Here people could be drunk and even disorderly, could live self-sufficiently in camps, and could go for long periods of time without being disturbed by the police or told to leave.

In what Hopper and Baumohl (2004) discuss as abeyance theory, those outside the traditional economy are encouraged to both go to an area and engage in a series of activities to sustain themselves, practices that function as a form of social control for what might otherwise become a problem population. Alaska's subculture is perhaps a partial abeyance mechanism, a form of containment that allows homeless campers to live, perhaps for years, despite regular violations of the law by its members. However, if those populations became too big or visible in Las Vegas, even within the homeless corridor, the police engaged in "sweeps" to disperse those campers and perhaps send a message to others that their activities are ultimately not condoned.

Yet using simple social control tactics instead of broader, nonjudgmental forms of assistance might be self-defeating. Although life-sustaining forms of assistance (like free meals) are essential for homeless people, the provision of that most basic sustenance to homeless alcoholics could inadvertently be perpetuating their homelessness. Those homeless alcoholics who live in a marginal part of the city and who see little chance of improving their lives are arguably stuck in a cycle of drinking to escape their problems, which in turn are caused or exacerbated by their drinking. By keeping them from housing first, charities and social services agencies might be giving those individuals just enough help to promote their feelings of despair and their slow but steady deterioration rather than promoting a reason for a homeless alcoholic to want to be healthier and to address his or her personal problems.

:: :: :: Alaska and I talk for a while longer, and I tell him that his tent construction, and the whole rough living of the camp, reminded me of when I lived in Alaska. We share a laugh over the comparison, but he jokes that even camping in Alaska was safer.

ALASKA: Like I said, I'd rather deal with a bear than somebody who's whacked out on crack.

KURT: Well, if you were in my place, studying homelessness, what would you look at, how would you approach it? Any ideas or thoughts?

ALASKA: I think the state or whatever, the powers that be, are trying to get everybody in a shelter. But there isn't enough shelter space, and there's people like me that won't stay in a shelter. And then you've got [people] who can't stay in the shelter because they're doin' drugs or drinkin' or hookin', or doin' whatever they're doin' to get by. And so, they're trying to clean up the city, but nobody, none of the tourists come out this way. Geez, we're out here, a long ways from the Strip. I don't know where they expect everybody to go. There's probably— have you walked down the tracks?

KURT: You know it's funny, I've walked down the tracks maybe once or twice. But most of the time I'm on Owens Avenue, and I will talk to people outside of the Salvation Army or St. Vincent's. But I sort of felt like I was a real visible outsider on the tracks.

ALASKA: You definitely would be. [We both laugh.]

I tell him that, for my own safety, I'm not sure I should do interviews on the tracks. I also say that I've tried to talk to some people living underneath the bridge nearby but that they weren't interested in talking to me, and that I understood why.

"If you were gonna walk down the tracks, you'd wanna have someone with you that they knew down there," Alaska tells me. "There's probably a hundred people living a couple hundred yards down the tracks from the Salvation Army, living in tents. They're supposed to be out of there by the tenth—that's tomorrow. I don't know where they expect them to go."

Alaska's ideas caused me to think of other reasons why the police might conduct only intermittent sweeps of homeless campsites. It might be fairly intimidating for single officers or even small groups to confront a hundred people living in an area generally removed from public view. Also, in a city with a good deal of serious crime, it would seem logical that addressing less-threatening violations of law, such as homeless camping, would be a lower priority for the police.

In response to his last comment, I tell Alaska that I agree that there do not seem to be other places for those people to go. Because of a shortage of shelter space, those individuals might just be told they need to move on.

KURT: Well, what do you see as the future, what are your plans for the next couple days, week?

ALASKA: If I can find a way back, I'm gonna go back to St. George. Gotta come up with the twenty bucks to get the bus ticket. I got a place up there to stay and everything, and clothes, and . . .

KURT: You literally just have to get back there.

ALASKA: But coming up with twenty dollars here is not easy either.

I try to think of other questions.

KURT: Since you were here in 2003, would you say homelessness here has gotten better, gotten worse?

ALASKA: Worse. A lot worse.

KURT: Yeah? And how so?

ALASKA: Just because ah, you run out of places to go. We used to camp out, after we got in trouble on the tracks, we camped out in that field right next to the Salvation Army. They moved everybody out of there, so everybody moved back down on the tracks again. And then, uh, people started moving out here. Down on the tracks is kind of a dangerous area—lot of [he coughs], dang it—

KURT: It's OK. [I wait for him to clear his throat.]

ALASKA: Lot of drug activity and what have you. It's kind of a dangerous place. So they're supposed to be moving out shortly. But you're gonna let loose a hundred crack heads and drug dealers out on the street, and they got no place to go. So they're either gonna rob, steal, or something to find a place to go.

KURT: You mentioned before that you were sober for twelve years and then you fell off the wagon. What types of resources are there for people with alcohol problems? I've heard Westcare [a nearby inpatient alcohol treatment facility] has some things.

ALASKA: I've been in Westcare. They let you sleep there for three days and then they put you back out on the street. There's no treatment going on. I mean, you can't get treated for alcoholism in three days.

That's all it is—just a detox place, basically. I went there voluntarily, I walked over there, because I thought maybe I could get into treatment somehow, you know? Not a chance. Not even a chance.

I tell him that I think he's right, that they need programs that homeless people would *want* to access in Las Vegas for things to change. Recent research (Tsemberis and Eisenberg 2000; Tsemberis, Gulcur and Nakae,

2004) recommends that agencies serving homeless people view those individuals as *consumers* of their services, a term emphasizing that homeless people have a choice as to what services they might use. Homeless people can use services that reflect their goals and values, services that also allow those consumers to see models of healthy lifestyle changes and to think about and make steps toward healthier living.

At the end of the interview, I gave Alaska five dollars, explaining that I usually do this at the end of an interview. It was the same amount he said he had been giving to his friends on the railroad tracks only days earlier. He gave me a look of utter disbelief, staring at the bill and then back at me before taking it.

"Thanks, man," he said in a high-pitched tone. "Wow, this is great," he said sincerely. I felt like I had just made his day.

:: :: :: Near the end of March 2006, I went at dusk to visit the same camp in the abandoned trailer park, only to find it gone. While waiting across the street for the bus back to the terminal, I recognized Alaska as he stumbled by me. He was wearing the same baseball cap, but now wore a dirty white sweatshirt that was too small—it had a teddy bear drawing on the front—and blue jeans. He sat down beside me and reached out to shake my hand. After realizing how smashed he was, I don't think he really recognized me, particularly in the dark of night. It seemed he simply wanted to befriend someone.

He slurred as he told me he had just finished beating up a man who had tried to rob him. The man had pulled out a pistol, which Alaska had thrown out onto the street. He repeated this fact several times while he pantomimed throwing the gun toward the street.

Before my bus arrived, Alaska began talking about fighting and mimicked fighting moves with me. I decided then not to hang out with him but to let him sober up alone.

Before the bus arrived, I said I had noticed that the open lot where his camp had been was now cleared. I asked him where he was sleeping these days.

"Wherever I fall down, that's where I sleep," he said before I boarded the bus.

DISCUSSION

Bruce's and Alaska's stories are about serious, life-threatening alcoholism. They seem to represent individuals who need help to overcome an addiction yet who also appear to refuse programs that insist on complete abstinence as the route for becoming sober. They are largely unable to access shelter services in Las Vegas because most shelters have rules prohibiting alcohol use. Their connections to former friends and their families of origin seem to have been strained or to have ended because of their alcoholism.

Time in jail will allow people to briefly sober up but will not solve their problems. Nearby treatment options in the homeless corridor, like Westcare, provide detoxification facilities. The number of beds available at any given time is far fewer than the number of people needing such treatment locally. Outpatient treatment for alcoholism is also very limited in Las Vegas and is available mainly to those with insurance.

In the United States, individuals are thought to have the freedom to succeed and the freedom to fail. Las Vegas offers both the freedom for tourists and residents to enjoy alcohol as they wish and the freedom to overindulge. Strangely, the city advertises itself as a destination for hedonists but also punishes those individuals who cannot control themselves. It wants to profit from liberal alcohol laws promoting limited self-control but does not have a systematic, supportive response to addicts like Bruce and Alaska that it will inevitably attract or create.

Communities like those Alaska mentioned—separate subcultures of addicts where people have different roles, their own codes of behavior, and ways of life—exist across the United States. The police in Las Vegas intermittently disperse such homeless camps, but many addicts will simply find new ways to continue their marginal existence. Criminalizing the behavior of homeless people does not provide the social support for treating individual addicts. It simply harasses individuals who, for now, want to drink.

Listening to Bruce's and Alaska's stories suggests that alternatives should be considered to programs that require abstinence as a precondition for charitable or social service assistance beyond subsistence. People often think that the abstinence-only approach forces the alcoholic or addict to quit drinking or using. While that might be true, the effects might not be long-lasting. Malcolm Gladwell (2006; 2009) writes about a man named Murray Barr who, after years of homelessness and alcoholism, participated in such a program in Reno, Nevada. The program, which was the equivalent of house arrest, allowed him to maintain sobriety. Yet after his graduation from the program, he received little continued support, and he returned to drinking within a week.

Requiring abstinence as a precondition for assistance also fails to consider the disproportionate expense of social services provided to a few alcoholics because of excessive emergency room visits, arrests, and court costs. One of the police officers who regularly came into contact with Murray and other chronic alcoholics in Reno investigated the total expenses that were incurred by such individuals and shouldered by the public. All of Murray's expenses, including medical bills and substance abuse treatment over his ten years without housing, totaled more than a million dollars. Gladwell argues that "it probably would have been cheaper to give him a full-time nurse and his own apartment" (2006, 98).

Harm reduction programs and housing first programs are increasingly being implemented and evaluated in Canada (Wellesley Institute 2009) and some areas of the United States (Ending Community Homelessness Coalition 2009).

Allowing chronically homeless alcoholics to access immediate housing and social services emphasizing harm reduction could well be key to reducing public costs. Such an approach also provides an alternative to abstinence-only programs that clearly are not appealing or of long-term use to some alcoholic and chronically homeless people.

The Disconnect of Mental Illness

PAUL, MELISSA, AND CORY

When I met Paul, we had a series of difficult-to-interpret interactions. I believe that he had serious mental illness. He seemed to have problems with communication, maintaining personal hygiene, and maintaining personal relationships. He also seemed to use drugs and to sleep outside.

I first saw him in early November 2005 sitting alone, staring out into traffic. He sat cross-legged on gray wool blankets on a trailer pad made of concrete. The trailer court itself seemed largely abandoned, with only five trailers still on the massive lot next to the Piute Indian Smokeshop and within walking distance of the homeless corridor. The court had been condemned, though some of the few trailers left on it seemed occupied—two had lights on, and one had a working television.

Paul had scraggly dishwater blond hair, clumped in the back, and was wearing a blue-striped T-shirt with a logo, turned inside out. His black-and-white zip-up tennis shoes sat five feet from us, and I stood next to his socks. There was a large cache of water bottles behind him, but he seemed to have no other personal items. Halfway through our talk, I realized that his jeans were unzipped and, because a large patch of hair was showing, that he wasn't wearing underwear.

I tell Paul I'm doing a research project on homelessness, and he says, "I'll talk to you, but I'm higher than fuck on cocaine and crack right now," with a staccato emphasis on the last several words followed by a laugh. "I got high at noon today, the twelfth." I am confused, and try to tell him that I think today is the tenth, to which he replies, "Well, I got high on the twelfth." Perhaps he means noon.

The staccato rhythm of his speech draws me in, as do his eyes. He has riveting eyes that match the intensity of what he had to say, eyes like light turquoise pools of water I associate with pictures of Caribbean inlets. It is a distracting feature that captures my attention, though I occasionally venture a glance at the bright pink sunburn peels coming off his forehead and his entire nose. I also notice his nearly nonexistent pupils.

"I wanted to smoke this crack cocaine," he says, tapping the clear lid of a small black condiment holder sitting in front of him. "But this is what they gave me, this crack. I can't smoke it," he says, shaking his head and laughing lightly.

"What is it?" I say, trying to look down into the condiment holder.

He grabs it, shakes it, and holds it up for me to see. "Granola," he says in a serious, disheartened tone. I realize it is a terribly small container of granola, and I become confused. Was he talking about the granola when he was talking about the crack, or simply holding the granola, motioning to it, while talking about something else?

After a few minutes of talking, and his telling me about how he got to this particular spot and a couple of far-fetched statements, I realize his speech is so rapid and unique that I want to capture it on tape. When I ask him if I could use a tape recorder, he said, "You don't need no tape recorder. You just need to sit down here and listen," motioning to the slab.

He begins to talk while staring at me, a large crease forming between his eyebrows when he emphasizes a particular point.

"I had a six-hundred-thousand-dollar dog, and when I came back, the dog was gone. They took him. I had the keys, but he wasn't anywhere around. It'll happen to you someday, you'll find out," he says, nodding for emphasis.

"You'll take your keys, and they won't work. I loved that dog. Twenty years ago, it was worth two million dollars. Two centuries ago, it was priceless. There'll never be a dog like that again. And it was all Nibco. They knew everything about that apartment, and they took it from underneath me. That's why I ended up staying at the fucking Moulin Rouge,[1] then those fucking assholes kicked me out."

At certain points in the conversation about Nibco, nearly every other word from Paul would be *fuck, fucking, fucker,* or *motherfucker.* Then, abruptly, the profanity would stop.

He made reference to having stolen wire and included details about building materials so often that I thought he must have worked in construction. When I asked him who or what Nibco was, he pointed at the fence and said, "A fencing company." He mentioned it so regularly that I thought it might be the key to understanding a lot of his life and current condition.

"You see Nibco, Nibco is in charge of the casinos. They have them linked together, underground. They construct the spaces that connect the casinos together underneath, the whole city. You see, they're foundations on top of foundations." He started drawing boxes in midair, side by side. "This is how they're able to function. Nibco," he said, nodding.

"Nibco," I repeated, nodding.

"What was your dog's name?" I ask.

"Valencio Solo," he says.

"Valencio . . . ," I trail off, struck by the first name but trying to remember the other.

"Solo," he repeats, taping his fingers on the clear lid of the black condiment container. I look at the lid and suddenly realize that the raised brand name on it is Solo.

Although I am not a psychiatrist, I can recognize that Paul's seemingly disorganized speech and behavior, his hallucinations, and his delusions are all symptoms of serious mental illness. It suddenly hits me that Paul might be doing a free association between the immediate things around him and real events in his life, stringing together a narrative with the things he can remember, pieces of his life today (like the dog nearby, barking intermittently) and other stuff. He is constructing, combining things in his mind with objects around him. It reminded me of the visual metaphors Nathaniel Lachenmeyer (2000) used to describe the speech and thinking of one schizophrenic homeless man:

> You sense there is a meaning in these objects, that this strange world is important to the people who constructed it, but you cannot connect it all. In the mind of every person suffering from schizophrenia there exists an entire city of thought which is inaccessible to anyone other than its architect. (22)

Paul's thoughts also seem to me like dreams, fantastic stories about a $600,000 dog and magical keys that at times blend with the dog and seem to become the dog, combined with fences and the nearby barking he endures. In a sense, even his stories are "making do," piecing together nearby abandoned junk and fragments from his mind that seem stuck in feedback loops, stories and stuff patchworked together in what seems, at moments, an inspired, impassioned attempt at communication. When I nod or simply repeat parts of his statements, it seems to momentarily calm him or causes something to come back to him that becomes linked to something else remembered, fabricated, or nearby. As the themes are repeated I begin to think of Freud's dream work. On the bus ride home I puzzle over what the different objects that he was discussing might represent and what he is really saying.

Paul also seems to embody the characteristics of homeless men frequently represented in *Bumfights*: living in public space, disheveled, and "crazy." As such, he might parallel the dominant popular stereotype of homeless people: a group of people who are visible, primarily mentally ill, and out of control—people who are lost to the world, worthless, and unsalvageable, and who seem to be prime candidates for someone else to take control of their lives. They are seen as people who don't fit anywhere, who have either abandoned their families or have been abandoned by them, who are a public nuisance, and who will likely deteriorate mentally and physically until they die.

:: :: :: Serious mental illness is found disproportionately among chronically homeless people. I cannot diagnose Paul. However, I want to consider one specific and severe mental disorder, schizophrenia, in order to understand the assumptions that have been made about the presumed limits of possible recovery from the disorder. As recovery from such a severe mental illness is increasingly thought possible, I believe it illustrates more generally how homeless people with a range of mental illnesses might be helped.

Schizophrenics might seem doomed to experience a progressively debilitating condition. Such a bleak view is largely rooted in the assumptions of Emile Krapelin, the researcher who first identified the schizophrenia. He understood it to be an unremitting organic disorder of the brain leading to steady deterioration of mental function and premature death. Krapelin's initial research set the stage for a century of thought that recovery from the disease seemed hopeless, and it was used as a justification for doctors, legal representatives, and institutions to assume control of the patient's life (Davidson 2003, 35–36).

The deinstitutionalization movement in the United States in the 1950s and 1960s meant that mentally ill patients were, by the 1970s, understood as citizens with equal rights and were then often released from mental hospitals. Newly developed psychotropic drugs were promoted as a way to control the symptoms of disorders like schizophrenia, allowing individuals new options for treatment. Community mental health systems were supposed to take the place of the many mental hospitals closed in the 1960s; but largely because those community mental health systems were inadequate and underfunded, "more than 60 percent of people with mental illnesses receive inadequate care and the mentally ill make up approximately one-third of the nation's homeless" (Lachenmeyer 2000, 123–24).

Ironically, a lack of insight into schizophrenia is relatively common among sufferers. According to Lachenmeyer,

> As many as 40 percent of people who suffer from schizophrenia are, as a function of their disorder, unable to examine their behavior and thought processes independent of their delusional system and constellation of symptoms; they simply do not believe they are suffering from a mental illness. (2000, 96)

Some might see this lack of self-awareness as an additional reason to control a person experiencing schizophrenia. However, recent research questions Krapelin's assumptions about the disorder. While schizophrenia involves genetic and biological factors, an individual's exposure to stress and social vulnerability are also key variables related to the disorder's onset and course. Longitudinal studies now indicate that people with schizophrenia might experience a range of possible outcomes, including full recovery. People with schizophrenia currently have a 50 percent chance of at least partial recovery (Davidson 2003, 12).

Larry Davidson's (2003) qualitative research on people experiencing schizophrenia suggests that a partial or full recovery from it depends to a large extent on the individual with schizophrenia developing an "outside" view of the disorder (174). As the person with schizophrenia gets to view him or herself through the eyes of caring others who see value in the person despite his or her disability, the person with schizophrenia gains key social support and self-esteem. The Krapelin-based understanding of schizophrenia promotes the control and dis-abling of a patient, leading the person with schizophrenia to become completely dependent on powerful others. Current research indicates that an individual's recovery involves his or her sense of self-determination and value, senses that are reinforced by others' acceptance of that person and by that person's sense of belonging to a community. When these are bolstered, the person with schizophrenia becomes more grounded in reality, his or her sense of agency increases, and the skills he or she needs for recovering from the disorder are enhanced (Davidson 2003, 182).

Studies like Davidson's suggest hope for individuals like Paul through housing first programs and community mental health centers and outreach that all provide strong, ongoing, esteem-building social support and that help the individual develop his or her own agency in the recovery process. While medication is still thought to be important in controlling the symptoms of most serious mental illnesses, the social support of caring others is now also recognized as vital. Dismissive actions rooted in the stereotyping of mentally ill homeless people, then, are the opposite of what many might need for recovery from their illness. In around half of all cases of people with schizophrenia, treating those individuals as if they are valuable and capable of recovering from their illness appears to be a precondition for their recovery (Davidson 2003).

It is important to note that the approach outlined above will not work for all people with schizophrenia. The condition can lead to further social isolation, either self-imposed or rooted in the rejection by others (Lachenmeyer 2000). As a friend of mine put it, "The problem with mentally ill people is that they act mentally ill." At times, it is very hard for the person with a serious mentally illness to have social relationships, ironically the very relationships that might help connect that person to reality and address the illness. By "acting" mentally ill, those individuals are at great risk for several factors leading to homelessness, including having few friends and primary social relationships.

Therefore, perhaps another policy implication of Davidson's study is that people with serious mental illnesses should be encouraged to contact their extended families and be provided with the means to do so. Family members of a person with severe mental illness, even those long estranged, are probably the best candidates for making a long-term commitment to support that person. Of course, not all individuals with mental illness will come from healthy families or have family members willing to help them, and not all seriously mentally ill people can recover. Some might even reject those caring people who are committed to helping them. Such is the case in Steve Lopez's account of Nathaniel Ayres, a schizophrenic homeless man whom Lopez unsuccessfully tried to reunite with his sister (Lopez 2008). It is perhaps most important to remember that all homeless individuals have the right to self-determination and dignity, even if "we" at times think we know better what "they" truly need (Lopez 2008).

:: :: :: So for forty minutes as Paul rants, laughs, pauses to put together his next statements, stretches out, sits up, stares intensely at me, and looks away, I at times think about serious mental illness, homelessness, and what Paul needs. When I gesture toward his collection of water bottles and ask him whether the water pipe behind him works, he says, "Oh yeah," then gets up and takes a drink directly from the faucet. He comes back and says, "That's right. I want to thank you for your assembly of that."

There is no easy solution to helping homeless people who have serious mental illnesses; but promoting housing first, along with caring, compassion, empowerment, and a sense of community might go a long way toward helping someone like Paul. For Paul, a sense of community seems unavailable. As we talk I begin to notice the group of seven people on the concrete pad behind him, conversing and sharing cigarettes. I wonder to myself if Paul is ever invited. He might invite himself, but the fact that he's getting food from the garbage would indicate that he does not. They look our way several times, but none gestures for us to come over or even acknowledges us. I think Paul is alone. Even everyday exchanges with nearby strangers might lead those others to avoid him.

He begins ranting hatefully about blacks and Hispanics, and then suddenly turns more subdued. I begin to think Paul is agitated, and mindful that he is larger than I am, I decide to gradually make my exit. I begin with subtle signals over ten minutes followed by clearer statements, pulling my backpack closer to me, throwing it over my shoulder, and saying, "Well, thank you for talking to me" as I stand up.

"And you have to know how many times Nibco has done this. Fucking Nibco. They're always taking the dogs. That's why they got the apartment. Nibco."

"Yeah, Nibco," I reply, nodding. "Thanks again for talking to me." I wave goodbye. "Take it easy, man," I say.

"Yeah, you too, brother," he says, looking back into the traffic. He begins talking to himself as I walk away.

:: :: :: The next day Paul is sitting on the same concrete pad. He perks up when he sees me, giving me a hoarse but resounding "What's up?" He's wearing different clothes, a red short-sleeved T-shirt with a logo from a Chicago-style restaurant, gray shorts, and the tennis shoes. The jeans from yesterday lie behind him. His hair is still matted in the back, and his shirt is spotted, but he doesn't look bad. I ask him what he's eaten today.

"I got this stuff at Albertson's," he says, pointing to a large box next to him. "That's part of what got me homeless," he says, and I wonder if he's making a reference to theft. The box next to him has the remains of spoiled fruit and looks like it has been taken from a Dumpster. He pulls out a package containing one squashed tomato, holding it up.

"To-mae-to, to-mah-to," he says, alternating the pronunciation. I ask him which Albertson's grocery store he means, as I haven't seen one anywhere nearby.

"Albertson's, Vons, they're all over. There's one that way, that way," he says, pointing in different directions. "They've got all kinds of fruit. Grapes." I noticed the remains of grape stems at the bottom of the box.

I ask him if he ever hangs out with the group of people we saw yesterday who are still behind us on a nearby pad.

"Yeah, I gave them a bunch of chicken but they didn't want it, so . . ." he trails off. He seems more lucid, but he begins punctuating the ends of his sentences with a whinnying "Riiiight."

About thirty feet from us, a purple Subaru without license plates is parked, facing the road. It strikes me that it might be his—it might be where he keeps personal items. When I ask him if that's his car, he says, "No, that's somebody else's car. They're trying to sell it. That's your car."

I look surprised at this unexpected turn, and he goes back to discussing it as being someone else's.

"They're selling it for forty thousand dollars. Forty thousand, that's what those cars go for, Mercedes, Porsches. Forty thousand, with the T-T, O-O. You can get a lot of tomatoes with that," he says staring at me and starting to nod.

"Yeah," I say, smiling.

So far today he hadn't mentioned his dog or Nibco. I had hoped those topics were temporary obsessions, brought on by something unknown to me, or maybe from being agitated by my presence, or my mention of a tape recorder, or from the barking dog, or the temporary effects of drugs. Things were looking more promising for our sustained interaction today—he seemed to recognize me, his speech wasn't laced with profanity, and he was talking about what seemed to be real things. Then his disorganized speech pattern returned, interspersed with letters and spelling.

"The T-T, O-O, that's what it is, riiight. Yeah, Mountain Dew," he says, looking down at the soda bottle in his hand. "It could be the C, O, U, N, T, but there's a P-P, R, U, T. C Y R I S U T. That's how it becomes thrifty. The I F T becomes a B U, like Subaru. L X Q, U-U. That's spelled X X U A B R U. Y? Thrifty has the two T's, the T-T, Y-Y. That's why those cars cost so much money. X X U B A R U T-T Y-Y. Riiiight!" he says, smiling and laughing.

I nod along, occasionally repeating portions of the spellings to try to figure them out, and so I can recall them later.

"That's thrift, because the I-I is under the U-U, followed by the T and the Y, Z, X, R. Thrift," he said, looking at me directly and simply, like he had unveiled a significant, useful insight. "Followed by the S, the Q-Q, M, P, R, Z, L-L. They're underneath."

Paul creates an avalanche of similar patterns and combinations for ten more minutes, causing me to mentally lose track of which letters were under each other, which occurred in pairs, and which were related to Subarus or Porsches, and how the topic always seemed to come back to thrift, unless it came back to forty thousand. In other constructions, though, forty thousand became four thousand, or thirty-eight thousand, followed by "that's still a lot of money." He engaged me and lost me at the same time.

I also began to wonder when Paul's mental illness set in. He still had a full set of white teeth, a smile rare on the streets. I wondered if his self-care routines, like brushing his teeth, were so engrained from childhood that they might stay with him for a long period. When we're children, we learn things that become routine in us, routines defining us. Teeth like Paul's healthy ones usually are the result of care. I remembered recently watching a homeless man carefully clean his toothbrush and put it away in its plastic case after brushing by an outdoor spigot at the Salvation Army.

Eventually I become mentally worn out from trying to follow Paul's thoughts, and I get up to leave. He has been quieter today, laughing a bit more at times. Maybe seeing me has helped him, if only briefly. Maybe it has been good for him to talk to someone willing to listen, though I will never really know his mind's inner workings.

"Take care," I say as I go. He repeats the same phrase. I stop to watch him briefly from a distance as he gets up and paces near his campsite.

::   ::   ::   Paul's speech associations linking reality and fantasy are common among certain types of mentally ill persons. Lars Eighner says mental health practitioners use the phrase "word salad" to usefully describe the speech patterns of some mentally ill people (1994, 170). Of course, speech patterns vary by person. Unlike Paul, Melissa and Cory never engaged in word salad. They slept outside and far away from the homeless corridor of Las Vegas and its services. They subsisted by asking for donations. Their most fascinating characteristic for me, though, was a shared paranoia.

::   ::   ::   I first met Melissa and Cory in late February 2006 at the corner of Maryland Parkway and Flamingo Road. They were "flying the sign," or trying to solicit donations indirectly by holding a sign that read "Anything Helps" while walking slowly past drivers who were waiting for the light to change. Melissa had long dark hair and was slightly overweight, while Cory had brown curly hair, a beard, and was fit. They were both Caucasian, and it struck me that they were both the same height and had the same color blue eyes. Each spoke with a southern accent.

What I thought would be a simple discussion of their experiences while indirectly panhandling quickly turned into a complex explanation of how they had become homeless. I was interested, as I had never been able to interview a homeless couple before. While Cory was holding up his sign to passersby, Melissa spoke quickly and urgently about how she had become ill while staying at a motel on Boulder Highway (the name of which I have changed).

"I was working [there] in 2000, and I'd noticed that people were getting lethargic, couldn't get out of bed," she said. "One day the manager asked me and a friend of mine, 'Could you get a ladder out of the attic?' So first [a friend] got up there, popped his head and he fell back down, and I said 'OK, I'll get up there.'"

She said that once she was in the attic, she saw strange things: "I seen something green, and I said to myself, 'What?' It looked like neon lights, 'cause the attic's dark, but I could see a film of white. You know like when you're in a snow blizzard, it's all white, or [like] snow on a TV? 'Cause my efficiency [room] was below the attic, at night I would hear [she makes a strange noise], and I thought, 'What is that thing I'm hearing?'

"Then I thought to myself, 'When I wake up in the morning, is there going to be a white film in my room?' Because there was only a piece of plyboard between the attic and my roof in my room. I thought, 'OK, they're making drugs, they're doing something like that.' [Then I thought,] 'No, I been around drugs, and I know what drugs smell like. This ain't drugs.'"

Melissa then said she began noticing her growing illness.

"I started getting fevers, I started getting hot, and I thought, 'Something's not right here.' Then the lady in [room] number sixteen with the three-year-old come to me. He had the fever for six, seven, eight days. So I got the baby's fever down with alcohol rub . . . but I seen his eyes going cross-eyed, so I knew something was desperately wrong."

Melissa saw a mysterious, glowing substance in the attic, and she then became ill. Her story sounded somewhat fantastic. She then revealed that mold was discovered on the property, adding credibility to her account. Mold doesn't glow, but health concerns related to its occurrence in buildings made national news in the United States in the early 2000s. Las Vegas had flash floods in 2003, and high water had damaged several local buildings. Without cleanup, mold could cause illness (Babula 2003).

"So the mold was already in the walls, but my concern was what was in the attic that he was keeping," Melissa continued. "I know that it was plutonium, [which is] something you [use to] make germ warfare. Sammy [the manager] had given away so many clues. When Sammy would go to the store, I would [be in charge of renting] the rooms out. K.G. and the Ferrel brothers are also part owners.

"I was verbally hired, and then they tried to say in court later that I wasn't hired. [They changed the] receipts with my name on them [so they no longer said] 'Rent Received by Melissa.'

"Up in the attic, Sammy would keep four air conditioners on at all times. I mean, I'd go in there and it would be fifty degrees. It's summertime—I'm thinking, 'Why is it so cold in here? He's trying to keep the chemicals that could leak out from getting into him.' I figured that out."

I began thinking that Melissa seemed delusional. She then mentioned local health and safety department officials she had contacted about her concerns. She said some of them had investigated and responded to her complaints. It was hard for me to tell what in her account was true and what was imagined.

Melissa's story continued. She claimed that one of the owners began yelling at her in front of a local health inspector. Melissa said that the inspector told the owner that the district attorney would soon be involved.

"At that point, the owner looked at me. I thought, 'Oh, boy, this guy's got money,' so I'm scared. That night I noticed Sammy was listening to my phone calls. I would be in the middle of a phone call, and click, it would hang up. The person I would talk to would call back and I'd say, 'I didn't hang up, I thought you hung up.'

"I said, 'What is he up to?' Well, I started to pry. Well, remember I told you that plyboard, it was in between? I tried to look up it one night. I seen green lights. I thought it was a monster. I believe in Jesus Christ very much. I thought, 'Oh, God, the Devil's up there,' but then, I heard [she makes noises]. I just sat and listened."

Melissa began to think that the illnesses around her were caused by exposure to radiation, a radiation she was convinced was in the walls. She also said she was infected with stachybotrys. When I looked up the term, I discovered that it is the name of a toxic fungus associated with diarrhea, fatigue, dermatitis, and depression.

Melissa told me she next witnessed a man from the local health department take a bribe from the motel owners to ignore the health code violations.

"Two days later all them motels were open, and nobody came in and investigated. The yellow tape was gone and there was no cleaning up of it. Then in the next two days, I get an eviction notice from county. So I go to the judge. [A fellow tenant and I show him] an album full of pictures of mold. The judge didn't even want to look at them. Wouldn't even look. So we had twenty-four hours to get out. Now I'm homeless," Melissa concluded.

Melissa said she stayed with a former husband and began filing claims.

"I filed for workers' comp. They denied me. Then I said 'OK, I'm going to go file for disability.' I've got to because I'm getting sick. I called FEMA. Big mistake. [The motel owners] had gotten a check from FEMA in 1998, but didn't use a dime of it to clean up the motel. I found out from other tenants the water was this high [putting her hand about two feet from the ground] in the rooms in '98. He didn't even change the carpet."

Some of what Melissa said, like the spreading of mold in her old hotel, seemed quite possibly true. The theme of a conspiracy against her by the motel owner and managers, though, seemed more the result of her beliefs and interpretations. Listening to Melissa's story, it seemed that her thoughts were geared toward rational things like survival and problem solving, but that her paranoia might impede those skills.

"I'm six months pregnant now by my ex-husband. I know K.G.'s chasing me, so I'm scared. I'm in another motel with two of my friends. So I call back FEMA, and this guy Mr. Silver in Oakland, so I talked to him," Melissa said.

"He calls me back the next night and says, 'We want you to meet us about mid-afternoon at Boulder Station and we're going to take you to a private room.' So I ask, 'Can I tell my friend where I'm going?' 'Oh, don't you tell anybody where you're going.' I said, 'I'm sorry, Mr. Silver, I cannot do this. I won't help you.' They could have took me out to kill me."

Melissa then explained to me that K.G. and his brother, who were part owners of the motel, were from India and that they had a lot of money and local influence.

"I mean they're rich. They own five hotels alone here in town. I'm not saying that Mr. Silver took a payoff, but somebody told him to shut his mouth or shut my mouth, so I backed off."

Melissa said she then gave birth to her daughter. During that time she re-met her current partner, Cory, whom she had known since childhood.

"I've known this man since I was three years old. He is the first kiss of my life," said Melissa.

"Cory?" I asked.

"Yeah. I kissed him at three years old—scared the dickens out of him. We were at a wedding. I was the flower girl, he was the ring bearer, and he was dancing. I kissed him. He cried. He just kept pulling my hair. I've loved him since then, I can honestly say that. But I've been separated from him for eighteen, nineteen years. I left."

As I begin thinking about her on-again, off-again relationship with Cory, Melissa changed the topic back to the other people she had known who became sick after living in K.G.'s motels. Then in what seemed like a blend of racism, paranoia, and an effort to find out about her seemingly real illness, she said she now thought K.G. was conspiring with local doctors to interfere with her medical care.

"I know the blood work was botched at [a local clinic]. The doctor was from India. [So I said to myself], 'Oh, K.G.'s relative. Boy, I'm just getting railroaded right to him.' [Then] they send me to this internal medicine doctor. There's nobody in the hospital but him and his nurse. He [just] has me walk a diagonal line, [then had me walk] back, and says I can go.

"I looked at him. I said, 'You didn't swab my mouth for saliva, you didn't take any blood, you didn't even weigh me, and I can go?' He said, 'You can go now.' I just walked out thinking, 'K.G. bought [him off].' Then I looked back at the picture on the wall—he's Indian, from India. 'Oh, here we go again,' I said. Every doctor I was getting directed to was of his ethnic race.

"I know they're going to stick together. I mean it's like us as Americans, we're black Americans, we have black pride, we have white pride, Mexican, right? We stick together, and they stick together."

:: :: :: Melissa explained to me that she was on welfare when she gave birth to her daughter, Charlotte. Although the state had paid her medical expenses, she had to submit to drug tests. Her daughter was then taken away from her briefly after she tested positive for marijuana. She said she had smoked half a joint to relieve some of the stress of living on the street.

"You know, hey, it's my fault," she explained. "You had to know my situation. I was on the street pregnant, running from K.G., staying awake, walking, staying awake.

"I'd get into motels when I could and I panhandled when I could, and I'd get what I'd eat, and I'd ask people for food, and some nights people bought me food, so I have Charlotte. I'm the only one there. Cory still doesn't know that I'm even pregnant."

I thought about her homelessness and paranoia combined with her pregnancy. Her homelessness, unstable relationships, and paranoia seemed all of a piece. Impending motherhood only seemed to add to her troubles.

"I get on the Housing Authority list. I had already completed the paperwork. I was staying with this Hawaiian family. I said, 'I'm not staying at your house anymore, but can I still get my mail here? This is important. I'm having the baby. I need to have [the Housing Authority contact me about] a place to go when I come out.' They said, 'Sure, no problem.'

"So I called Housing Authority the day after I had Charlotte. [They said] 'Well, you didn't get our letter? We sent it to you. You're first on the list to have an interview.' And right there, I just dropped the phone. I started crying. So I called the Hawaiian family. The mother tells me her oldest daughter maliciously sent back the letter to the Housing Authority. Now I'm back [down] to number eight hundred and thirty on the list."

Melissa tells me that she had supported that Hawaiian family for years, sharing food stamps and paying rent, because she had been in a relationship with the parent's son, whose name was Phil. Phil was an alcoholic, and he eventually died from cirrhosis of the liver. Melissa had thought Phil was the father of their child until Phil explained that he was impotent. Melissa then remembered a one-night stand she had with another man during her relationship with Phil. Still, she had listed Phil as Charlotte's father on the birth certificate.

It was difficult to keep track of the characters in her stories as well as the focus of each story. I found that my ability to follow her different threads was impaired by my trying to simultaneously figure out what was true and what was fiction. I was glad I had the tape recorder on.

Listening to Melissa suggests that she has a strong fear of others, especially people of different races and cultures. Her disorganized thinking parallels her disorganized patterns of living. Her difficulties in maintaining a stable life also seem to reinforce her paranoia—her paranoia combined with her problems breeds her open mistrust and dislike of others, quite possibly causing them to dislike and mistrust her.

People experiencing mental illness are considered outsiders even among homeless people (Snow and Anderson 1993). They can be antisocial, unpredictable, and irritating and can easily exhibit behavior disqualifying them from local shelters. There is also a range of mental illness, from mild, to moderate, to severe. Paul's illness seems to be more severe than Melissa's if only because Paul seemed more incoherent and alone. A range of community mental health services and forms of mental health outreach, then, should be offered to homeless people in Las Vegas and nationally.

Once the deinstitutionalization of mental health facilities occurred across the United States in the 1950s and 1960s, community mental health programs were supposed to provide care to those with mental illness. Many communities such as Las Vegas, though, have weak or nonexistent community mental health programs. In 2005, then-Governor of Nevada Kenny Guinn made a commitment to greater funding of such facilities. Other researchers have noted that even his proposed funding increases would likely not match the need for mental health services in Nevada (Landreth, Brandenburg, and Gottschalk 2005).

:: :: :: Cory eventually stopped panhandling and came over to visit us. He told Melissa he thought it was unsafe to continue to fly the sign. Even though they are not breaking the law by directly soliciting people for money, they have both been cited in the past for disrupting the flow of traffic. The police are intermittently monitoring the area.

"I just saw ten cops in ten minutes," Cory said. "They're everywhere."

"You got to understand us homeless, we fly our signs out here, like I do," Melissa says. "I need food. I won't lie. When I have people hand me food, I'm delighted. I go give it to my friends. They'll drink their beers or whatever, so I make sure I try to give them greasy food." Having been a bartender, Melissa says, she knows that this helps her friends sober up. She also says she worked for twelve years in Las Vegas as a Keno runner, for a while as a maid, and doing other jobs in six different casinos.

"It's not like I'm not a worker," she states, perhaps to refute the popular idea that homeless people do not want to or have not worked.

I asked her what had happened to her daughter. After further problems with K.G., she said, she and her daughter began sleeping outside.

"I ended up sleeping behind the dentist's office that night with my daughter. I had a sleeping bag around her and a blanket around her and she had her stroller. She was fed, she was clean. I knew that morning I was going to go get a thousand dollars from my ex.

"Then, the police come. A man outside of the bar might have had something to do with [calling the police]. I wake up in the morning and say 'Come on, honey, let's go eat. She's happy, smiling, [saying], 'I love you, Mommy.' I put her in the stroller. My baby's clean—I brush her hair, even brush her little teeth. Then the police come. They said, 'Melissa, you got two warrants.' I started crying. I said, 'I know. You're right.'

"They said they had to take Charlotte. I said, 'Oh, God, take me to jail, but please, don't take my baby. Please.' I explained to them what happened, and they said, 'I'll tell you what. You put Charlotte in the car and we won't take you to jail.' When I put my daughter in the car, she started screaming, 'No, Mommy, no.'"

Melissa's story helps illustrate the bind homeless parents are in while trying to care for their children. Once a family becomes homeless, it becomes hard for those families to find shelters that will house all members, particularly as a unit. Homeless families then seem to have an incentive to be less reliant on social service agencies to help end their immediate homelessness. However, if Las Vegas police discover a homeless family living outside or in a car, those parents will likely lose custody of their children, at least until the parents regain housing.

:: :: :: Soon Melissa was staying in an abandoned building with friends, including the father of her child.

"I'm staying in this gutted-out place. Now Johnny's over there stealing my money out of my backpack. I run back to the backpack, there's seven hundred dollars. Four hundred dollars was missing. So I grabbed my backpack, ran into the room next to his where him and Dan were, and I said, 'Quit stealing my money.' I'm thinking, I'm praying, 'Do I tell him he's Charlotte's dad? Do I tell him? What do I do? Mohammed might kill him. I can't chance that.' I looked at him. I said, 'Help me.'"

Although I can't quite follow her narrative, Cory soon interjects. He seems to follow Melissa's train of thought.

"The terrorist," Cory says in reference to Mohammed.

"He's a terrorist," Melissa said, "and all of a sudden he started talking about his uncle. Oh, my gosh, I put it together."

"K.G." Cory said.

"I put it together," Melissa said. "Him and K.G.—K.G. had sent him after me."

I begin to wonder how Cory comprehends her while I feel so confused. Melissa and Cory's interaction suggests they might share the same view of key events. Seeing the same racist, paranoid patterns, their interpretations of events were mutually reinforcing. They had become each other's material, social, and emotional support, even while on the street. Even though they each seemed paranoid, they also seemed to listen to each other, to care about each other.

Melissa begins discussing a local doctor who tried to help her with her illness.

"He was one of the only men who would give me the truth. This was in year 2001. He said, 'There is no cure for what you have, if you have what I think you have. They haven't begun to work on a cure.' And I'm thinking, 'How bad is it?' And he said, 'It's pretty bad.'"

"A man came to me yesterday," Cory added, "and brought some medicine for it. The government is trying to cover it up. The government sends this guy to give us medicine from Hawaii."

"That's a really good man," Melissa says, "so I know I can trust him."

"He's a good man," Cory says. "He's scared to death."

"Of K.G.'s people," Melissa interjects.

:: :: :: Cory eventually began to explain why they have not gotten Charlotte back.

"We went through all the classes and all that stuff to try to get her back, but the State will not help us, any kind of finances or anything to try to get up off the street to get a place or anything. They just keep giving us this red tape."

Melissa continued.

"The social worker says 'You have a case plan to follow, but I couldn't find you.' I said, 'You couldn't find me because I was in jail. I was in jail for a four-year-old traffic ticket that I get a month for, thirty days."

"She's in the system," Cory said. He also seemed frustrated about the social worker not contacting Melissa. "She missed her court date. All she had to do was look in the computer—she's in the computer."

:: :: :: "How do you make ends meet besides flying the sign?" I ask.

"We go to churches," Cory replies. "We go to our reverend, down here on Maryland Parkway. There's a park in the back. They have soccer games and stuff out there for everybody. They have no church, but we hold church outside, and they bring food and clothing for everyone out here."

I asked Melissa and Cory if they have been in touch with their families. Cory does not want to talk about it on tape. Despite being far from Louisiana, Melissa says she has a large family network locally and saw her brother just yesterday.

I asked them if homeless people in Las Vegas form a community.

"Yes," Melissa said. "Everybody works together and helps each other to try to come up with stuff. You know what? Oscar Goodman, he made this statement that all homeless people should be put to sleep like lying dogs. He did say that."

"He tried to retract it," Cory added, "but he said it and he meant it. He's been trying to build a place outside of town to take the homeless and put them outside the town and lock them up like prisoners because they're homeless, like a concentration camp."

Some of what Cory said was true. In 2001, Mayor Goodman did propose sheltering homeless people in Las Vegas in an abandoned prison approximately thirty miles away in Jean, Nevada. At least one local newspaper used the phrase "concentration camp" in an article about the proposal (Silver 2001). The mayor had become known for his strong and at times outlandish statements against homeless people in the past, including that he "would like to kick them as far away from Las Vegas as possible" (Casey 2001).

Melissa and Cory then both explain how local marshals recently ticketed Gail Sacco, a local homeless advocate. She was cited for distributing food in Huntridge Circle Park to a group of more than twenty-five people. (See chapter 10.) Any group of more than twenty-five people in the park required a special permit to gather. Melissa and Cory saw the incident as another example of how homeless people in Las Vegas are harassed and how homelessness is criminalized. In an additional example, Melissa said a police officer once told her that homeless people are targeted for jaywalking tickets.

:: :: :: Soon Cory's friends come over to us. They are done flying the sign for now. I ask them if they have had any experience with the shelters in the homeless corridor and why they are here instead of the homeless corridor. Cory answered first:

"At St. Vincent's or any of the shelters here in town, there's cockroaches. If you're homeless, you have to pay ten dollars a night to stay in a place that stinks. The government's paying for that facility for the people to stay at night."

"Hey," Cory calls to two nearby men. "Any of you guys ever stayed at any of the homeless places here in town?"

"I have," one man says. "I got my stuff stolen."

"Never," another man adds.

"They have all stayed one time," Cory says. "What was it like?"

"Cockroaches, fleas and athlete's foot," the first man says. "They had bed mites over there."

Thinking that I was looking for a place to stay, the second man spoke directly to me.

"Don't be a mission rat," he said. "Stay with us. We'll make sure you're all right. You'll eat better. Trust me."

Cory doesn't tell the man that I am a researcher. "Us homeless people out here take care of each other," he says instead. "We band together. And we fight against the corruption."

"Don't be a mission rat," the second man says. "No, no, no, no, no."

Melissa chimes in.

"If he does, he's going to clean a lot of toilets with a toothbrush."

Melissa and Cory's friends reveal that some homeless people recruit other homeless people to stay with them. Such recruiting helps homeless people form a collective with shared resources, one in opposition to the degrading condition of being a "rat" in local shelters ostensibly designed to assist homeless people.

Studies of other homeless persons have had similar findings to the views expressed in my group discussion. In a 2008 study of more than 500 transcribed interviews with homeless people, Hoffman and Coffey found most respondents described social services in "sharply negative terms, with experiences of objectification and infantilization being commonplace" (2008, 207). Many of the respondents said that in order to maintain their dignity and self-respect, they no longer used the social service system. Such findings suggest that many different homeless people wish for and would make more use of social services if they were more consumer driven and facilitated a positive self-image.

:: :: :: I clarify to everyone present that I am researching homelessness, which is why I am holding a tape recorder. No one seems to mind. I explain that I am interested in how they manage to live outside the homeless corridor.

"Well, I go through Dumpsters and I do runs and I collect clothes and food and everything and give it to everyone else," Cory replies.

"How did you do the other night when it was raining?" I asked. "Did you have a tarp or anything?"

"We find a place where we camp at, under a bridge," Cory replied. "We just get on the ground and find a place to hang our stuff and get out of the rain."

"Go in at dark time and leave at dark time," the second man says. "That's the rule." Three people in the group nod.

"Wherever we go, the police roll up on us," Melissa says. "They give us a warning and tell us we got to get out. We don't go near businesses. We'll go in a field and—"

"And don't leave no traces," the second man adds. A third man joins the conversation: "Always take all your trash. Take all the bull with you, that way no one knows you're there, always."

I mentioned that others I have interviewed on the same corner said they try to keep the area clean for the same reason—to avoid problems from the police or nearby businesses. The group's description reveals that group survival means following norms and looking out for collective interests. Camping together means safety, but it also means they must avoid attracting the police.

Eventually Cory tells me more of his thoughts about Las Vegas Mayor Oscar Goodman.

"He's covering up all these things that he knows about K.G., with all the chemical spills and the terrorist chemical warfare and all this thing going through the wash," Cory says, referring to streams of water that run through Las Vegas. "He's paying people to come out here and clean up his mess that these terrorists are doing. The terrorists are paying him off so he might as well be in their back pocket. And these guys are getting hurt and dying with high fevers and stuff right down here at Sunrise Hospital. You can go in there and check out all of them."

As it was growing dark, the group decided to break for camp. I thanked them for their time.

DISCUSSION

While I am not a trained psychiatrist, I believe Paul, Melissa, and Cory suffer from mental illness. National studies estimate that roughly 30 percent of homeless people might experience mental illness (Shlay and Rossi 1992). Many researchers believe that the deinstitutionalization of mental hospitals in the 1950s and 1960s in the United States contributed to a significant rise in homelessness nationally. It is easy to see how an individual's mental instability can lead to his or her material instability. Mental illness, though, also undermines a person's sense of comfort and safety in the world, contributing to homelessness in another way.

The concept of "home" can refer to a physical residence or to a sense of emotional connection to a place and the people who live there, or to both. While homelessness is often thought of as being without a physical residence, it is less often thought of as being without a sense of connection to a place or people. Mentally ill homeless people would likely benefit from housing first programs combined with caring social interaction and treatment options, perhaps also allowing them the initial social support and esteem-building they might require to recover from mental illness (Davidson 2003).

Paul, Melissa, and Cory also illustrate a common problem in diagnosing mental disorders—the issue of co-morbidity, or a person having more than one disorder or disease. Each individual seemed to be using alcohol and/or other substances, for example, as well as having mental problems.

There is a general perception that continuum of care approaches are the best model to help mentally ill and homeless substance abusers gain housing, despite recent evidence challenging that assumption (Padgett, Gulcur, and Tsemberis 2006).

CoC models usually require that an individual starts treatment first before being offered a stable place to sleep, and thus "gaining access to services requires relinquishing control and choice" (Padgett, Gulcur, and Tsemberis 2006, 75). Instead, it might be better to provide housing first and consumer-driven service models, even to individuals with co-morbidity. One study of homeless mentally ill persons placed in programs following the CoC steps to permanent housing revealed "a consistent (and probably underreported) use of illicit substances by individuals enrolled in treatment first programs despite abstinence requirements" (ibid., 81). By contrast, "consumer-driven programs that practice housing first and harm reduction are not linked to increased substance abuse [by residents] despite the absence of restrictions" (ibid.). Providing housing first, then, might be as effective in reducing substance use among homeless mentally ill persons as would making such individuals attend treatment and meeting "abstinence requirements" before being granted stable housing. Housing first programs would have the added benefit of reducing the number of mentally ill and substance abusing homeless people living outside, individuals who would otherwise be at much greater risk of developing illnesses and disabilities that would likely be treated using public funds.

It is also worth considering why homeless people of all types avoid the centralized services found in the homeless corridor. Melissa, Cory, and the group of homeless panhandlers I met explained that the corridor was unappealing. The charities there were filthy, and they charged money for homeless people to stay there. Some of the men I spoke to drank intermittently while we talked, further explaining why they might not like social services that restrict such behavior. Through local church assistance, Dumpster diving, panhandling, and camping under bridges or in open fields, this small group of homeless friends both enabled each other and worked collectively to survive. They seemed to resent policies that criminalized their living practices. They camped in hidden areas and restricted their panhandling to avoid problems with nearby businesses and the police.

Cities in the United States increasingly use "quality of life" ordinances and citations in a seeming attempt to force homeless people to use services they dislike (National Coalition for the Homeless 2004). The response might create a vicious cycle—some homeless people might then work harder to subsist away from such services, supporting themselves and each other in groups. I believe Las Vegas might better assist homeless people through a range of different programs, including programs that recognize homeless people as people first. Many people in the course of their life engage in self-harm or self-defeating behavior. Most people have difficulty making significant and immediate life changes. Providing supportive housing first might grant self-harming and mentally ill individuals some stability and self-esteem that would then allow them to consider change. Also, strong funding and support for a range of community mental health services, in Las Vegas and nationwide, is crucial.

Dealing with the Iron Cage of Bureaucracy

GARY

Gary is a long-time drug addict. He is also a veteran, a group that is esti-mated to comprise one-third of homeless people in the United States. I met him in late October 2005. He was Caucasian, and he spoke with a Pennsyl-vanian accent, which I couldn't place at first because he also had no teeth. He had sandy blond hair, a moustache, and thick glasses. He stood about five-feet-seven-inches tall.

Timmy, a small, gaunt heroin addict with a substantial beard, had introduced Gary to me. I had first seen Timmy near my bus stop. He was panhandling from traffic in front of the Hard Rock Hotel and Casino with a small cardboard sign that said "Anything Helps." Timmy would ride the bus from the Hard Rock Hotel back downtown where he spent his eve-nings. One night we were both riding downtown, and I struck up a conver-sation. He told me about his heroin addiction and how he had lost most of his toes from gangrene, which explained why he walked with a cane.

I asked Timmy if I could interview him for my research and said I would buy him dinner. I suggested a place where they served steak. He twice told me that all he wanted was a hot dog, so I said OK.

He initially agreed to be interviewed, but after we got off the bus and I explained that I hoped to tape our conversation, he changed his mind. I explained that I could also just take notes as were walking toward the DTC. Timmy stopped to take cigarette butts out of an ashtray near Fremont Street when he suddenly said he had an appointment. As we were walk-ing, though, we saw his friend Gary, and Timmy said, "He'll probably talk to you."

When I explained my project to Gary, he immediately agreed to talk to me, even before he saw my Informed Consent Statement. He gave a clear, concise interview and explained a lot about his life and how he became homeless. Though I saw him twice after our initial conversation, that first interview revealed most of his present situation and life story.

GARY: I moved here in 1980. Before I left Pennsylvania, I had my records sealed. I had a possession of marijuana charge, and when I come back from Vietnam in 1972, I had three joints. I think it was under about four grams of marijuana.

KURT: What branch did you serve in?

GARY: I was in the Air Force in Vietnam. I was in a construction unit. They call them Red Horse units. So anyways, all [the charge amounted to] in Pennsylvania was a sixty-two-dollar fine and thirty days probation until I paid the fine off.

When I come out here, I never said anything [about the conviction]. I worked in the gaming industry. I dealt poker from 1981 or so. I went to dealer's school, and I started working in casinos. I had my gaming card renewed from 1981 up until '98, maybe '99; '98, I think it was, when they pulled my gaming card for that.

So I get it renewed all those years, four, five times. I go to get it renewed again in '98 and they want to know why my records are sealed in Pennsylvania. And I told the lady, I said, 'If I wanted you to know, I wouldn't have had them sealed.'

I should have never got smart with the lady. [He grimaces.] I should have told her right up. That was a mistake. I was havin' a bad day and I got smart with her. [So] they give me my card, and about three months later they come into the Horseshoe [Casino] where I was working, pulled me off a table, took my gaming card, and that was it. No more work.

I was surprised that this would happen after Gary's years of working at the casino. I thought about how a criminal record like Gary's might not have been traceable through a national computerized database until recently, possibly explaining why local gaming officials only asked him about it years later. More important, it didn't seem to make sense that someone who had worked in the gaming industry for seventeen years would suddenly lose his right to work over a misdemeanor charge from twenty-six years earlier.

Gary agreed with me. "And I was dealing poker almost seventeen, eighteen years, something like that," he said.

"And this was for an infraction that was old?" I asked again.

"1972, correct," Gary replied. "So that's how I lost out. No gaming card [means] you can't work in this town."

Gary was right about the necessity of having a gaming card to work in casinos in Las Vegas. He caused me to also think more generally about the role that bureaucracies, identity cards, and paper trails play in our contemporary bureaucratic society. Homeless people so often seemed to have run-ins with bureaucracies that require such information or credentials. If Gary was telling me what really caused him to lose his gaming card, it seemed like an infraction that reasonable human beings could resolve, allowing Gary to keep his job. I thought about how bureaucracies can be very efficient at times but, because of inflexible rules, inhumane at others.

:: :: :: Gary and I decided that we were going to dinner at Binion's, the casino where Gary used to work. On the way, Gary spoke more about himself.

"I had money. I made good money. I made about between forty, fifty grand a year all those years, and I had a nice chunk of change put aside for my retirement and that, and next thing I know, a year or so later I'm homeless. I can't get a job. I will be fifty-five in a couple weeks, and I don't have no other trade. I'm also a drug addict."

His candor surprised me, but I also wanted clarification. "Which one, if I may ask?"

"I was on—when I come back from Vietnam, they put me on methadone."

"Oh, OK," I said, knowing this was the government-approved substitute for heroin, used in treating the addiction.

"I've been on and off methadone all those years, but I always worked," he said. Looking back on the interview, Gary seemed to have stressed that, although he had an addiction, it hadn't stopped him from being a productive citizen. He was proud of his work record and seemed to have a right to be.

I was trying to follow his thoughts, and for a moment I got confused over where we were in relation to Binion's. I mentioned the steak dinner deal they had, and Gary, despite not having teeth or dentures, seemed interested. Gary pointed the way to his old employer.

"So you were on methadone right after the war?" I said, returning to the previous topic.

"Yeah. When I got strung out over there in Vietnam, when I come back, the VA [U.S. Department of Veterans Affairs] put me on methadone, but I always worked and I never got in no trouble. I had one possession of marijuana charge and then in 1988, I had a driving under the influence charge. I was at my nephew's wedding. I had three stinking beers, and I tested 1.0 on the nose after blowing in the machine three times. I can't get a driver's license and I can't deal, so I'm stuck."

I wondered why he had forgotten his DUI charge, but I didn't pursue it. Maybe it slipped his mind, since it had happened seventeen years earlier. I often found it hard to recall all the specifics of a story myself when I was downtown, with all the distractions of neon lights, noise, and people.

Gary's drug problems and military experience seemed another important reason for his homelessness. The stress of direct involvement in war can sometimes lead a soldier to turn to drugs. The National Coalition for Homeless Veterans (2010) notes that a "large number of displaced and at-risk veterans live with lingering effects of post-traumatic stress disorder (PTSD) and substance abuse, which are compounded by a lack of family and social support networks." Each of these problems, I learned, was part of Gary's story.

:: :: :: "And so, if I may ask, where do you stay at night?"

"In the streets next to the highway. Once in a while we run into a little money and we rent a room, get a room for a couple nights, get cleaned up. At least five nights a week we're on the streets and two nights a week we're in a room probably."

"What hotel is your preference, if I may ask?"

"Oh, we go to the ones that are twenty-five dollars a night."

"Oh, OK. Down, like down Fremont Street?" I said, referring to a block of seedy, cheap hotels.

"Down Fremont Street, right."

Like other homeless people I met who had drug or alcohol problems, Gary did not seem interested in the services for homeless people in the homeless corridor. He slept outside most nights but could occasionally pool money with friends for a cheap hotel. He was telling how he got by, even though he was homeless and addicted.

"Just for background, have you ever been married, do you have any kids?"

"I was never married, but I lived with three different women like six, seven and eight years. You know, seems like seven years is the magic number; it's over. But I was never really married, no, and I don't think I have any children, no."

"Would people at Binion's know you if you were in there today?"

"Well, I've been out of there since '98."

"Yeah, that's seven years now," I said.

"A lot of the people that used to work there are gone, because Jack Binion still owned it when I was there and then his sister took over. His sister ruined the place."

I wanted to hear more about his current circumstances.

"So how do you make ends meet in terms of getting food to eat, and—"

"I mean this is where it's a little sticky," he began. "You know, I go out and steal movies and stuff like that. I don't know if that's—but you know what I'm saying, I'm a little—"

He had been quite candid, but now hesitated. I assured him that I would be changing the names of all interviewees in any published material, in case that was his concern.

"I go out, do a little boosting," he continued, using the slang for shoplifting. "I never got arrested. The judge asked me about four, five years ago, he said my name and then he said, 'I don't understand something. You got one charge. You're forty-nine years old, fifty years old. Then all of a sudden, boom,'" Gary said, referring to his suddenly facing several criminal charges.

"I said, 'Your Honor, they pulled my gaming card. I can't work,' I said. 'I was making a good living and all of a sudden, I'm stuck.' I said, 'I don't—I don't know how to survive.' I said, 'I refuse to beg money off of people. I won't do it.'"

"Yeah," I said, opening the door to Binion's.

"I'd rather go out and steal stuff and sell it before I—you know, it's embarrassing," Gary said.

Gary's story seemed to emphasize his relatively stable life before he lost his gaming card. He had been in trouble for minor drug possession and a DUI after returning from Vietnam. He also became addicted to heroin in Vietnam. He had used a methadone program upon his return to the United

States, though, and had held a good job for eighteen years. It seemed that since losing his job his life had spiraled downward into illegal drug activity, petty crime, and homelessness.

:: :: :: A long, winding line formed up the stairwell from Binion's basement restaurant where I had hoped we would eat. I turned off the tape recorder, and Gary and I tried to decide if we should wait or go to another restaurant. We decided that the line was too long and that we could go to the Gold Spike, where I knew we could get a good meal for a similar price but more quickly. Gary was fine with the idea, and so we left. I turned the tape recorder on again.

"You just mentioned combining resources with friends sometimes to get a hotel room," I prompted him.

"Yeah, we try to get a room at least two nights a week so we can shower, you know, don't look too bad," he said. "I mean, some of these people on the streets look really bad. I know I'm not at my best, but I try to look halfway decent."

Several homeless people I have spoken to frequently tried to distinguish themselves from other, more apparently marginal homeless people. Most people are taught as children and teenagers to care about their appearance, so much so that it becomes central to their self-definition. Kevin (from chapter 3) had also mentioned how some of the homeless people around him seemed to have lost interest in staying clean and trying to work. It was as if individuals like Kevin and Gary, so aware of the stereotypes about homelessness that could now be applied to them, wanted to clarify that they were not as far gone as "*those people* over there." Also Gary, like Ron and Ricky (from chapter 1), put a premium on looking "decent," on perhaps not appearing visibly homeless.

"Where do you store your stuff otherwise?" I asked.

"Most of my stuff is gone. What I have stored, I have stored in friends of mine's places. I mean one girl I know, she's a very old friend of mine. She's got most of my clothes, my winter stuff, put away. I'm goin' to have to go out there and get it pretty soon, and then I'll give her my storage, and I keep maybe a pair of blue jeans, a couple pair of shorts, about half a dozen different shirts, and that's it, underwear and socks and everything else, she got it. My suits and that—I worked the floor in these places. I had suits. I had a whole bunch of stuff."

"You had good clothes," I said.

"Yes," Gary replied.

"Well, speaking of storing things and whatnot, sometimes people will talk about how safe or unsafe they feel, maybe sleeping in bushes and being kind of in public. How's that been for you? Have you felt safe?"

"It's dangerous. Luckily, I stay around with a couple friends of mine. There's safety in numbers, but we have never been bothered," Gary said, referring to some friends of his I had met. "But I also sleep with a piece of reinforcement bar, a half-inch [thick], you know, what they put in concrete? About fifteen inches long. If someone comes up to me at night, they better be prepared 'cause I'm gonna hurt 'em."

"So, you've got a big metal club?"

"Yeah. You have to have—you know, I ain't gonna get caught out there, you know, with nothin.' If I'm goin' down, someone's gettin' hurt. I'm gonna hit somebody. Someone's gonna pay."

I thought about how Gary, who just a minute ago had been discussing the suits he used to wear to work, was now telling me about the club he kept near him while sleeping outside in order to protect himself. His becoming homeless had completely changed his everyday activities and concerns.

"But it is dangerous on the streets," he continued. "You got to know how to handle yourself, you got to know how to talk to people, situations like that. I mean there's—some of these drunks, they're bad, they're homeless, and I mean I can understand where the mayor gets so pissed off. I mean these people are downright obnoxious. They just go up and try to intimidate people. I don't do that, and none of my friends do it. But there are, you know, there's some bad dudes out there that are homeless."

Again, Gary was drawing distinctions between himself and other homeless people. Gary understood Mayor Goodman's anger at homeless people, even though Gary felt he was different. Gary seemed to appreciate a community leader wanting to socially control such dangerous people, even if he happened to make overgeneralizations about homeless people. Gary seemed to think that there was a bad element within the collective body of homeless people but that he was not a part of it.

:: :: :: "You mentioned just a minute ago having a good friend who you store your stuff with," I said, returning to his earlier statement. "Did you try living with any of your friends before you were on the street?"

"I lived on and off with friends, but that gets old. They can only do so much for you. They can help you out a few months—one, two months here. But I was goin' back and forth among people I knew and I was working. You know, you're good to people, people are good to you, and luckily, thank God, I was raised right. My mother told me, you always be nice to people. What goes around, comes around. She didn't use those words, but to those effect."

"Sure," I said. "I imagine it would burn out a friendship if you're staying with people for too long, like you say."

"I mean I lived with this girl. She got my clothes in the summer for six weeks. She got three kids. I try not to be a burden on her, but still."

"Yeah. That must have been hard for everybody."

"It's so goddamn hard, you know," he said, sighing.

:: :: :: We opened the doors to the Gold Spike and felt the immediate change of the semi-cooled air, cigarette smoke, and dim light. We ordered our food and chose a booth in the dingy restaurant.

"OK. Before, I went off on a tangent there. I lost my gaming card in '98," Gary said.

"Thank you," I said to the waitress serving me.

"Can I have a knife and fork, please?" Gary asked her. "I lost my gaming card in '98. I had enough money put away, I guess, for about eighteen months or so of livin', rent and everything. I figured by then I could have somethin' else, but it just didn't work out. I don't have a driver's license. I thought I could drive a cab or somethin' like that, but I've been on the streets probably since midway through 2000, and—"

"That's five years," I said.

"Yeah, it's close to five years."

"Wow," I said.

I wanted to return to an earlier story he had told me.

"I know you said it makes you sick, and I don't want to talk about things that are really upsetting, but earlier you mentioned an interesting story about how the city sometimes affects people in a negative way. You mentioned Timmy, your friend, and how he had come into some money but then unfortunately lost it at a casino, I think it was."

"Gambled it away. Yeah," Gary began, discussing the man who had introduced us. "His mother passed away, and the estate was worth like probably $200,000, but him and his sister split it up. They got about $80,000 each after the government got their cut. And he didn't have that money three months. I mean that's ridiculous. I mean, that's absolutely disgusting."

"He spent all of it in the casinos?" I asked.

"Oh, no, took the drugs, partying, but most of it in the casinos, right." Gary continued.

"I mean, it's bad enough gambling—and gambling's fine—but you got to have a clear head. You cannot get high, drinking or otherwise. Why you think casinos pass out this liquor when they gamble?

"I worked eighteen years in the gaming industry; I know," Gary said, beginning to explain the tactics casinos use to get an edge on gamblers. "Someone starts winnin', they start openin' up, they start gettin' a little heavy on the drinks. Usually, it's a shot, they give you a shot and a half. Not a lot, just a little bit more. Now, it might be a little different. I've been out of it about seven years now, but that's the way it was then. You don't make good decisions when your mind's messed up."

Gary started eating with his plastic knife and fork.

Gary was describing another potential cause of homelessness in Las Vegas. The city's major industry, gambling, is designed to separate individuals from their money. The industry profits from unstable individuals, individuals who lack self-control, or individuals who might feel stress from a bad life situation. The gaming industry is not built on the idea of shared responsibility and mutual aid for members of a community. It is built on individuals losing money. As forty-eight states now allow some form of legalized gambling, the idea that gambling is fun and entertaining is fairly common for many people in the United States. Perhaps the redefinition of gambling as entertainment, along with the everyday emphasis in the United States on individualism and self-reliance, has helped the gaming industry. But some people will lose everything by gambling: their friends, family connections, job, health care, and housing.

Gary had been in the gaming industry for years. I asked him how people in that business view homeless people.

"They don't like 'em 'cause they don't want them in their casinos. It's bad for business. I mean that's why—"

"Did they ever kick you out?" I asked, hoping he could give me specific examples of policy or things he witnessed "I'm not allowed in a few casinos, but that's why I try to look halfway decent," he replied. "I mean I realize I don't look the best, but I don't look like some of these people either, sittin' on a corner drinking a beer, you know, and trying to bum spare change."

"So it's partially about how a person's perceived?"

"Right."

Gary was reinforcing what Ricky had suggested to me—that homeless people felt a need to blend in, or appear as tourists or individuals with housing, to take part in key tourist activities in Las Vegas.

:: :: :: I asked Gary background information about his life.

KURT: You said you moved here in 1980?

GARY: Yeah.

KURT: If I may ask, where did you grow up?

GARY: I was born and raised in Pittsburgh, Pennsylvania. I graduated from high school in 1968 and I went in the Air Force. I went to University of Pittsburgh for a few years. I wanted to teach math and history and coach soccer and volleyball.

I played soccer and volleyball in high school, and I had a partial scholarship offer from the University of St. Louis to play soccer. Back then they didn't give full scholarships for soccer. And the University of St. Louis was a soccer power. And so I went in the service, that's it. I really didn't want to go to college. I wanted to get in the action. There was a war going on, and I was stupid.

KURT: I think a lot of young people had that reaction with 9-11. [referring to a rise in military enlistment after the attacks on the World Trade Center and the Pentagon on September 11, 2001]

GARY: Yeah, but, see, Vietnam was completely different. Half the people thought it was wrong, and I was in the other half that thought you were supposed to do the right thing and fight for your country, which I got educated on. I became a hippie real quick.

My father worked for the steel mill. He raised five kids working in the steel mill. He never made more than ten dollars an hour, but we never wanted for anything. I had good parents, God rest their souls. My mom was a housemother. It was funny. Her Social Security number was the same as my father's only it had a dash and an s for spouse. She never had a Social Security number of her own.

KURT: I've never heard of that.

GARY: Neither did I until when I was doing some paperwork after my father passed away and I seen that.

I noted that Gary was reading a book by W. E. B. Griffith, *Brotherhood of War.*

"I like to read," he said.

Gary again mentioned the three different women he had lived with in his life and told me more about his last relationship of eight years.

GARY: The last one passed away, God rest her soul. She was the best one I ever had. She died April 2000, and I went on the streets probably October, November of 2000. We were together when they pulled my gaming card, and still together until she passed away.

KURT: Did she work in town?

GARY: She's an ex-working girl. She was an ex-hooker. She was a year younger than me. She was about forty-eight years old when she passed away, but she made probably five million dollars when she was in her twenties.

KURT: Wow.

GARY: As a high-class call girl on the Strip.

KURT: But couldn't save much of it, or—

GARY: No. It's a crazy town, boy. Money travels one hand to the other to the other to the other. Not so much now as it was twenty years ago.

Gary's life story intrigued me. He had attended college and volunteered to serve in the military. He had drug problems and seemed to have associations with dubious people. He had had a series of relatively long-term relationships. He had held a steady job for years. He was smart, but he had made some questionable decisions.

:: :: ::   I asked Gary if he made money in any other ways besides theft. He told me he was a carrier of hepatitis C, and so he couldn't sell plasma as some homeless people do.

GARY: Some people die—are dying from it, and I just never been sick and I got it.

KURT: So you're a carrier but you don't feel any symptoms?

GARY: Yeah. I know people that had hep-C that died. My older brother passed away from it. And I have never been sick from it.

KURT: How do you get medical care?

GARY: I go to the VA. They spent God knows how many million dollars to build it. They have it seven years and the building got condemned because it was fallin' apart. They spent close to a hundred million dollars on it. Now they got different clinics throughout the city until they get a new VA.

KURT: So at least you're able to get some free health care there?

GARY: Yeah.

Between bites of food, I asked Gary what he thought generally about the future of homelessness in the city.

GARY: I don't see it getting better. People movin' here—I think it's around five thousand people a month are movin' into the city, and they have been for the last fifteen years. Now, there's—granted, there might be two thousand leaving every month, too. I don't know exact figures.

Because of the weather, the homeless come here. It don't get cold, I mean, maybe two months a year, and when I'm saying cold, back east cold is in the teens. Out here, cold is in the forties. It's different.

I asked Gary more about his employment history and job training.

GARY: I worked in a steel mill in Pennsylvania. They closed down in 1977, I guess it was. I was unemployed for a few years. I went to computer school. I used my GI Bill, went to computer school. Everything I learned in the two-year computer course was obsolete by the time I got out.

My father passed away in 1988, my mother in '92. My father was seventy-eight when he passed away, my mother was eighty-two—she died on her eighty-second birthday.

KURT: That's a long life. Any brothers and sisters?

GARY: I had two sisters, one that lives in Chicago and one that lives in Pittsburgh.

My two brothers are deceased. My younger brother died in a construction accident—oh, about twenty, twenty-five years ago maybe.

KURT: Do you stay in any contact with your sisters?

GARY: Oh, yeah. I talk with my sister once a month at least.

KURT: Do they know you're homeless?

GARY: They suspect, but I don't tell them. They know I ain't workin.' I tell them I'm applying for disability, which I am, but I—I don't want to—especially my older sister. If she found—if she actually seen how I lived, she'd die. I'm serious.

KURT: She'd be upset?

GARY: She'd be really upset.

Gary's discussion is an example of the shame that most people I interview feel about their homelessness. Cleaning up occasionally, as Gary notes, can help homeless people avoid the everyday stigma they feel about their lack of housing. Ironically, though, hiding their homelessness from their families means that homeless people cannot request substantial help from their families to address their homelessness. It would seem that reducing the shame associated with homelessness would help homeless people by allowing them to ask for help from those most likely to care about them.

:: :: :: After our meal, Gary and I leave the Gold Spike and begin walking back toward the DTC. The neon lights of nearby casinos stand out brightly in the dusk.

KURT: So what are your plans for the future? You just mentioned applying for disability.

GARY: Yeah, if I get everything I'm entitled to, I'll get about twelve hundred dollars a month—I can live nice. My buddy just got his. He wasn't in the service and he's getting almost seven hundred. He got—he got his first check a couple weeks ago. He paid off all his bills, and probably starting next month he's gonna get a cheap place to stay, and I'm hopin' to stay there this winter. But I consider myself a lot better off than a lot of these homeless.

KURT: Any other health issues? You mentioned hepatitis. How do you take care of dental needs or anything else?

GARY: As you can see, I don't have no teeth. My dentures are in storage. I don't wear them half the time. I do have what they call the PTSD. My back is throwed out. I have about half a dozen different things all added up to where I can't work, and I'm finally filin' for disability, and if I get it, everything works out, I'll be all right. Just being on methadone was an automatic qualifier back then. I'm not on methadone no more 'cause I can't pay for it. I went on methadone [after Vietnam] in 1972 or '73. I can't remember exactly, and I was on methadone until 1999.

KURT: Is it possible for you to live at the VA?

GARY: No. They have a place here called the Meadows. It's like being back in the military. You got to get drug-tested and this and that, and I'm a drug addict. I'm tellin' you straight up, I'm a drug addict. There's no way I could pass the drug test, so—I don't get involved with it.

Gary seemed to be describing the steps employed in the continuum of care approach to helping substance abusing homeless persons. As a first step, homeless people have to agree to treatment and sobriety before they receive stable housing. Such conditions now seemed curious, since Gary had managed to maintain a job and residential stability for years while having been on a government program that supplied him with methadone.

:: :: :: "I know it's a personal question, but do you use [heroin] intravenously?"

"Yes."

"And how's it possible to keep clean needles on the street?"

"Because I'm the only one that uses them," he replied. "I hide them. No one else touches it. I don't let nobody else use mine. You can go into any pharmacy, most any, and get a ten-pack for anywhere from three to four dollars. And that will last you a month, two months, whatever, depending on how much you use it. You just don't give them to other people to use. Keep them yourself or give them a new one and tell them to keep it and don't give a damn what happens. That's a big no-no."

I asked him if he had ever served time in jail.

"I've been there a few times. I did six months, three months. For petty larceny, I've told the judge my story and the judge usually gives me time served."

I asked Gary if he thought I should do anything different in studying local homelessness.

"No, no, you're doing the right thing," he replied. "You're going out there and talking to the people who are living it. You can't learn that stuff out of books. You got to go see it, talk to those people face to face. You got to see how they live. You might want to go to one of these campsites where you get to know a few of these people, spend a couple days with them. But other than that, you're doing exactly what you're supposed to."

Gary was saying something similar to what Alaska had, that the best way to understand homelessness was through talking to homeless people, hanging out with them, and perhaps staying with them.

"I got—I got to go out and make some money," Gary suddenly said upon seeing some friends near the DTC.

"Oh, you've got to run?"

"Yeah," Gary replied, already stepping into the street.

"OK. Thank you," I said, surprised that our time together was now over.

DISCUSSION

Gary seemed to be open with me about his heroin addiction, a drug he said he started using during his military service in Vietnam. Later, through methadone maintenance, Gary seemed to have been a productive citizen most of his adult life. He seemed to have been fairly stable before he lost his gaming card in 1998 or 1999.

Max Weber once wrote about the "iron cage" of bureaucracy, indicating how bureaucratic structure is inescapable in our increasingly rational, modern society (Mitzman 1985). These structures deal efficiently with volumes of cases but might not work when it comes to the exceptional case. Gary should have been able to continue working as a dealer if his petty offense was far in the past. Gary was able to have his record sealed for the minor drug charge for many years. This apparently passed scrutiny when he first applied for a gaming card to work in Nevada. When the old offense was uncovered and his job was lost, Gary also seemed unable to continue his legal methadone maintenance program.

Substance abuse is a common problem among homeless people. A larger issue, however, is how we typically address addictions and the addicts themselves in the United States. Since the 1980s, punishment through incarceration has received far more funding than treatment and prevention programs. Drug convictions were at the heart of rapidly increasing incarceration rates in the United States in the 1990s. By 1995, nonviolent drug offenders made up nearly one-third of all convicts in federal and state prisons (Nadelmann 1995). While incarceration takes drug users off the streets, prison often does not provide addicts with substance abuse counseling. Punishment is meted out in place of treatment, and those addicts eventually return to the same environments they once lived in with few skills for avoiding future drug use.

"Getting tough on drugs" criminalizes what some other Western industrialized countries view as an illness and, in addition, leads to an expensive policy of incarceration with little gained. Countries such as Switzerland and the Netherlands have taken a different, harm reduction–based approach to addressing heroin. In Switzerland, certain heroin addicts are supplied with the drug under controlled conditions by the government, and so are able to lead productive lives. The Swiss Federal Office of Public Health indicates the project has reduced homelessness and illicit heroin use in that country. Dr. Daniel Meili, the director of the program in Zubill, Switzerland, says, "Our patients have achieved more stable lifestyles, their health has improved, and some even have jobs. And many of these people have hepatitis, or are HIV positive. If they didn't get heroin here, they'd be out on the street" (BBC News 2002). England has since tested a similar approach to helping hardened addicts. In 2007 a pilot program in London supplied a small number of heroin users with the drug under controlled conditions for two years and reported a substantial reduction in drug use by test subjects (BBC News 2007).

It might be difficult to imagine U.S. citizens advocating a policy that legally provides heroin to addicts under controlled conditions. However, as things currently stand, Gary will likely continue with petty theft and homelessness to meet his habit. And if "get tough" incarceration policies continue to be popular in the United States, then Gary, a formerly productive citizen, could well end up in prison or dead.

SEVEN

Homeless, Not Criminal

JACK

Jack, a middle-aged African American man who once had drug problems, seems to have accepted his homelessness. Having served in Vietnam, Jack greatly appreciates the freedoms that come with being a U.S. citizen. He argues that not everyone can find a place in "normal" society and that homeless people still love America but resent the criminalization of behaviors associated with homelessness.

I met Jack at the annual Stand Down for the Homeless event on November 9, 2005. He is a thin, fifty-one-year-old African American man with black hair and a goatee with traces of gray. We were introduced by a local police officer who knew many people at the event and who told me that Jack would be good to talk to. Jack and I spoke for an hour while eating hot dogs provided for free at the Stand Down, which could be described as a homeless fair.

Similar Stand Down events are held each year across the nation for homeless people to learn more about assistance available in their community. The Las Vegas Stand Down often attracts around two thousand homeless and near homeless people who can then access services and information in one location, all day. Social workers distribute pamphlets on shelters, substance abuse treatment, child-care programs, veteran's assistance programs, and counseling. Local businesses donate services (such as free haircuts) and items (such as clothing, toiletries, and food). Health care providers give basic checkups and tests, and judges from city and county courts provide a "day of amnesty" for those homeless people attending the Stand Down, allowing them to resolve offenses (such as tickets for an open container of alcohol or for loitering) with the penalty reduced or eliminated entirely. This year's event, the thirteenth annual in Las Vegas, was held at the Cashman Center in the homeless corridor.

When I met Jack at the booth for Straight Off the Streets, a local activist homeless organization, he said he was a Marine who had served during Vietnam. I asked Jack how he came to Las Vegas. Throughout our interview he stared directly into my eyes when speaking.

"I lost my job in Denver, Colorado, where it's very cold," he said. "I lost my home. I was evicted, on the street. I knew that I was going to be homeless in the wintertime, so the only thing I knew about where I was, my location, was to go somewhere where it was warm, where I could survive a winter. So I came down here to the Catholic Charities' homeless program seven years ago."

He had worked over the years as a laborer and a truck driver. He had a child, but was divorced, and his parents were deceased. "Are you in contact with your family ever, do they know that you're homeless?" I asked.

"No, my family doesn't know I'm homeless," he said.

We made small talk about the size of the event. I asked him about his experiences while being homeless in Las Vegas. He said he had tried using several local shelters at first, but now slept in a child's tent near an auto repair shop in the homeless corridor.

"I stay there every night," Jack said, "not in a program, because the program [I want to use] is poor, and I was in it once before. You can't go back in until the end of the year.

"So now I'm on the street, in a tent. I use a facility called the Poverello House, which you can go once a week and do your laundry. I keep my laundry clean and I even wash up in one of the bathrooms, such as the Catholic Charities restroom, because [their] showers are closed for the winter program. I just had a birdbath in a bathroom, so when I can't take a shower, I do that."

His tent allowed him the freedom to come and go as he pleased, which more restrictive shelters and programs did not. He explained he preferred less restrictive social services in the homeless corridor, such as the Poverello House to do laundry and Catholic Charities' day shelter in the summer to escape the extreme heat. In my own visits to the Catholic Charities' dayroom, I had seen dozens of men watching a widescreen television in the air-conditioned space while seated on metal folding chairs. Men could select from more than twenty DVDs to watch. The problem was that everyone had to watch the same thing, and sometimes quarrels would break out over someone's choice. During one of my visits, after a movie began, a man shouted, "Man, this is the third time [we've seen this film] this week."

While Jack likes sleeping in his tent, he says he tries to keep it hidden from sight to avoid homeless "sweeps" by the local police. As stated in previous chapters, such sweeps force those in encampments, both in and outside of the homeless corridor, to disperse. Sweeps became a policy promoted by Las Vegas Mayor Oscar Goodman for addressing homelessness in Las Vegas in order to discourage homeless people from trying to live outside of shelters. The sweeps have been criticized, however: Despite making homeless camping illegal, the city does not provide adequate shelter for all those who need it (Borchard 2005).

Some homeless people I had met locally camped in groups. In Jack's case, he wanted solitude and a place to store his things.

"I sleep just two blocks away," he said, "right over here on the other side behind the federal building. And I'm one of the only people to pitch a tent back there. I don't like sleeping around a crowd of people. I feel secure within myself. I'm not a drug addict or drug user, even though I was at one time. So I sleep away from everything. I have a tent just big enough for me to lay all the way out. Got my laundry in there, change of socks, underwear, clothes."

Jack had few material things. Still, his story indicated he held some of the most valuable currency on the street—knowledge about what services were available where and when. He had carefully gauged which services had curfew rules and strict criteria for admittance. He seemed to have sought out charities that would help him in the way he wanted rather than those trying to change him:

"The Poverello House is [where] you can stay for one day a week," he told me. "You get a lunch, shower, have washing machines, you can go wash your laundry for free and get a breakfast and a dinner. And then you can watch TV and stay there the whole day. Every week you [can] go there to wash your laundry.

"Catholic Charities, every day between the hours of 10:30 and 11:30, has a free lunch program, and then 5:00 to 6:00 the Mission has a dinner, and it's served every day seven days a week, so we always eat. Eating is not the problem."

Many homeless people I have spoken to had used that last phrase when describing homelessness in Las Vegas. I believe they mean that food is widely distributed in the homeless corridor, but that this form of subsistence is not enough to end their homelessness.

KURT: What things are the problem?

JACK: Well, keeping yourself out of trouble is one of the biggest problems. Keeping yourself out of trouble, because they have several places, such as the Lutheran church, where you can go and get clothes once a month, get a change of clothes. And then College Park Baptist Church once every ninety days, you can go get food, services and clothes, and then there's a thrift store over on Bruce and Lake Mead where the lady will [let you use] a laundry room or [give you] a change of clothes, and then also the Mission once a week on Wednesdays, Tuesdays and Wednesdays you can go change your clothes.

KURT: You know a lot about the services here. How did you find out all that information?

JACK: They're all advertised. They don't put out fliers, but they verbally advertise. It's usually word-of-mouth too, on the street . . . I like to keep clean. Of course, we're not on public assistance. We're not allowed. Just because we're homeless doesn't make you available to public services like welfare or SSI.

I was interested in Jack's use of the plural in describing his situation.

KURT: So you don't receive any of those types of checks?

JACK: No, no. The one problem I have is I don't have money, unless I work in the day labor, or like, for example, yesterday I volunteered to help set this show [the Stand Down for the Homeless] up. The thirty volunteers [were told], "Keep yourself clean." Of course, you might not have money, but money is not necessarily the biggest problem. Every man, woman, and child in here eats every day. Then the Catholic Charities serves lunch for maybe three to four hundred people, and then the Rescue Mission serves dinner every day seven days a week, so we always get to eat.

Jack again said food was plentiful for homeless people in Las Vegas. He also knew that accessing it involved familiarity with a system and an area, one where homeless people walked several blocks from one service to another. But not having cash made him and others like him dependent on this system, segregating those individuals from other parts of the city. The everyday expenditure of energy it took for an individual to survive within this system caused me to again compare it with quicksand—those who fought to get out could well sink faster than those who stayed still, and some might never. Jack, however, valued his autonomy, freedom, and privacy. He had these while camping, but temporarily, until the police or others discovered his site.

:: :: :: "Sometimes I'll talk with homeless people and they'll mention that they feel harassed by the police," I said. "Camping out, have you had any experience with that?"

"Yeah, yeah. It's against the law to camp out in Las Vegas, I believe. I wouldn't say harassed, but I've been asked to move my tent and go away from the area. I've never been arrested for it, but I was asked to move several times."

Jack seemed to no longer think about getting ahead. He was nomadic, walking miles a day, shuffling his possessions from one site to another, scheduling when he could eat or do his laundry using recent information. After seven years, he seemed to have accepted his homelessness. His everyday activities seemed to take up most of his time. I wondered how much longer he could sustain this and thought about how one injury or illness might bring his tentatively constructed lifestyle crashing down.

"Have you had any physical problems that you needed assistance with?" I asked.

"Me personally, I haven't had any physical problems, but health care is not free."

We ate for a while without talking. I eventually asked a general question.

"Do you feel homelessness in Las Vegas is going to get better, or is it going to get worse?

"One thing," Jack said between bites. "Las Vegas, Nevada, is very tempting to a person who wants a major change in his life. A lot of people come here with the idea that 'I can go to the casinos and win a large sum of money.' It's a gambling state, so a lot of people come here and you can easily fall into the idea that 'I'm going to win a lot of money gambling.' "

"Have you ever gambled yourself?"

"Yes, sir."

"Do you like it?"

"Yeah, I do like it. It's very attractive. A lot of times I gambled my money right away, because the idea of being able to win a large sum of money for a little bit of money is really inviting."

"What type of games do you play?"

"Mostly [video] poker machines."

Like most homeless people I have interviewed, Jack's story involved gambling while in Las Vegas. He noted its primary appeal: It might bring a life-changing windfall. While some local resorts and casinos advertise smaller jackpots and are aimed at locals, many others promote the possibility of winning large amounts of cash. The odds of winning such an amount, though, are long. Research now shows that state lotteries, a popular form of gambling in the United States, are often highly appealing to and create a form of regressive tax for their poorest citizens, those who, ironically, can least afford to play (Clotfelter and Cook 1991; Nibert 1999). However, gambling gives those individuals at least the hope of a different life and a temporary thrill.

:: :: :: Jack also tried to make money by going down to the day labor hall.

KURT: What type of work have you been able to get with that?

JACK: Usually when you go down it's either cleaning up a building or labor, construction labor, or moving jobs or unloading trucks. It's usually minor labor work.

KURT: How much have they paid you, on average?

JACK: Minimum wage, which is $5.35, $5.25.

KURT: Five dollars and twenty-five cents. Do they provide transportation?

JACK: Sometimes they do. It depends on if they're sending more than two men on at the same place you're going. Then they'll provide transportation. But if it's just you by yourself, you're asked to be able to get to the job by yourself.

Other men I had spoken to about going to the day labor hall in Las Vegas said that at times they had been charged for transportation, safety equipment they had used on the job, and fees for cashing their checks. Similar practices exist in for-profit labor halls across the United States (Parker 1994).

KURT: When you go there, are you able to regularly get work or is it occasional?

JACK: It depends. Usually they send people out every day. Not necessarily you, but labor halls always got jobs.

KURT: Has any of the work that you've done for them ended up giving you longer periods of work besides just day by day labor?

JACK: Sometimes they have a long-term employment ticket and they send you on. Sometimes, yes. I've gotten a job here through a labor company, a full-time permanent job, but it was just six months. I'd say it was a full-time temporary thing for a six-month period of time.

   :: :: ::

KURT: If you could give advice to someone who was coming to Las Vegas and was new and homeless, what advice would you give them?

JACK: I would say stay in your own state and try and utilize the services there because I think that Las Vegas is overwhelmed with homeless people, and they're overwhelmed with [the need for] services. So if you're down on your luck, go to your state's social services department or your state's EEOC office or unemployment office.

I've been here for seven years, and there's thousands upon thousands of homeless people here. They're overwhelming the services, networks, and it's not a state where you can 'insta-fy' wealth, like people believe. I think people will always believe that Las Vegas is glitter and gold, and it is, but as far as the glitter and gold, it's from the wealthy [on] vacation. It's a resort town. So I think Las Vegas is not necessarily one of the places that you can go and turn your whole life around, if you hit the bottom.

Jack knew whereof he spoke. He had been in the city seven years, and I'm sure he had met many people in the homeless corridor who had hoped to "insta-fy" wealth, as he put it. The city is attractive to individuals looking for a dramatic change. That logic of instant change for the better, as opposed to saving, enduring discomfort, and making a steady transformation, has a strong appeal. Sometimes Las Vegas seemed to me like one large experiment for testing individual self-control. Although millions of tourists visit the city every year and have fun without serious consequences, the city also seems designed to prey on vulnerable individuals who lack emotional stability, a social support network, and financial security.

KURT: So you think it's harder to get out of homelessness in Las Vegas than other places?

JACK: If I could do it all over again, which I can't and I understand this, it's not a wish or a wishful thinking, I would have stayed in my state and asked my state for services, rather than coming into another state and asking for services. Because as you can see during this Stand Down, it's thousands of people at one event saying we're all homeless, and the availability of services . . . the need is overwhelming.

KURT: It is overwhelming here.

I looked out at the vast crowd.

KURT: What plans do you have for the future? You mentioned being here for seven years. Any plans?

JACK: My plans are always . . . I'm fifty-one years old. I'm a high school graduate with one year of college. I'm healthy. I don't apply to government services like welfare or SSI, because I believe in a fair chance, right? I'm black, as you know, and I believe that you do the best you can with what you have. I can't go back, my parents are dead. I can't go back and ask my brother or sister to try to support me, you know what I'm saying?

I love Las Vegas, and the one thing I really want to do is get involved in the rehabilitation work that they're going to do in Louisiana from the hurricanes. I worked in Florida during Hurricane Andrew for a company called Oil Tech, which is an Alabama-Texas construction company. Hopefully when they're prepared for people to come down there and work as laborers and clean-up people, I'd like to get involved with something like that.

It seemed that in pointing out his race, Jack was referring to racism and an unequal opportunity structure in the United States. He also pointed out that others had it worse off than he did. He seemed to be arguing that welfare and Social Security should be for those absolutely unable to help themselves. He didn't yet see himself in that category.

JACK: I want to be self-supporting as long as I can, always knowing the fact that the employment rate is very low and you can't just go somewhere and say you're homeless and all of a sudden get a job.

KURT: I've heard that there's a company that's hiring people to go down and help to clean up [from Hurricane] Katrina. Have you heard about that here?

JACK: I've heard about that, but they list the company on Merlin Avenue and it's a temporary service. I also work here for a company . . . a general contracting company. So I'm already experienced in construction labor, also in drywall finishing, and if I could get involved in something like that, I'd definitely like to go down to one of the several states that were hit by the hurricane, because I do have experience.

:: :: :: At the end of our interview, I asked Jack if he agreed with the popular explanation that drug and alcohol abuse were responsible for homelessness. His answer instead considered that although homeless people might use drugs and alcohol, they are often nonviolent, introverted, and even educated people outside the mainstream American economy.

"I would say that drugs and alcohol abuse has always been synonymous with homelessness," Jack said, "but I don't think [having] mental [problems] is an excuse. I think if you talk to men who are homeless in America, you'll find out that they're very, very educated men who have lost their jobs, lost their ways. They're usually introverted into their own life, but I do not want to say that a man on the street who is educated and who is white, and black, and the majority I would say are men who just lost their way, gave up on society, and they are brilliant. As you say, if you go into the Whipple Reed Cultural Center Library, you will meet a very large group of intellectual men who study and read and are very gifted. But they have a problem communicating . . . they are not violent. And when they do drugs, on an average they do not bother anybody. A group of people who create an unrest, unlawfulness in the United States, are usually young people. . . . The average person in the homeless shelter I would say is forty-five years old."

Jack seemed to be speaking of opportunity structures and individual choices. It interested me that he said many of the homeless men he regularly saw in the library were "brilliant." It was as if they were literally misfits, men who couldn't conform to a traditional life of work and family and therefore were "home-less," itinerant or vagrant wanderers. Jack, like Gary in chapter 6, was a veteran of Vietnam, a deeply unpopular war. War veterans, particularly Vietnam War veterans, are overrepresented among homeless persons. Research in 2007 revealed Nevada had the fifth highest rate of homelessness among veterans in the United States (Curtis 2007a). Jack's rough estimate of homeless people being near his age group perhaps spoke to an entire generation of men who went through that war and "gave up on society," as he put it. Jack then also began talking about the role of race and dominant values in explaining homelessness.

"I think a lot of people have the perception that homeless men—homeless men offend the [dominant] white values, [the values of those who are] rich and doing good. When you see a person who you might consider a bum, which we don't mind the title of bum, because we are happy being a bum in the United States saying that we live better than anybody in the free world. So even without money, even in a homeless condition, we are still great Americans and we don't want to give up the thought that we are citizens. We are just a society of homeless men who still love our America, noting the fact that probably 70 percent of homeless men over the age of forty-five are veterans."

Jack captured the paradox of homelessness in the United States as a condition between freedom and poverty. He also noted how military veterans are overrepresented as a group among homeless people in the United States. His final point suggests that military service, frequently promoted as a way for racially and economically disenfranchised young men to gain a career and social betterment, can also result in individual alienation and PTSD, particularly after someone endures the stress of war. Military service might provide skills training and a work record allowing for greater individual opportunity. However, whole generations of American soldiers, including those from more recent conflicts, might well develop personal problems as a result of their military experience, causing difficulties for them in getting and keeping employment.

Toward the end of our interview, Jack reiterated that homeless men in general were intelligent and that their homelessness should not lead to blanket stereotypes about their behaviors. They were Americans, many of whom had served their country and, because of race and restrictive opportunity structures in the United States, could not find a traditional career and housing. Jack felt, however, that all Americans deserve the freedom to live as they choose.

"I'd like to say that first I'm a black man and I never consider [that] to be equal to a white man, but to say that I'm gifted, that I was raised here under the white authority of the law, which I consider to be white all the time.

"And I would say a person who interviews a homeless man should note that a lot of men on the street, and especially Las Vegas which I live in, are very educated. Most of them are veterans and they want a fair shot to say yes, we're homeless, and no, we're not a bum. We don't fight, we don't cuss, we don't try to steal your money. Most of us are not drug addicts—even though we use drugs, we are not addicted because our situation does not allow us to be addicted—we don't have the money. But we like to get high, we like to drink, we like to group with one another and talk. The majority of people on the street are not a problem to the society of America. They don't want to be."

"What would be the one thing you would recommend changing in Las Vegas in order to help homeless people?" I asked.

"That's a hard question because then you're asking for somebody's money. We have a shelter. We don't want to be arrested all the time for little or nothing. We want to change the fact that if a man breaks the law by a misdemeanor, say [being] drunk [publicly] or jaywalking, you know, we don't want to be arrested and convicted for jaywalking. Just because we are poor we don't want to go to prison as if to say I'm breaking the law. We don't want to be arrested off the streets for minor offenses.

"I would write [about homelessness here] as a good thing . . . how nice it is for a man to be an American and how good we do as Americans, even homeless, even homeless. Go into the Catholic Charities, which is beautiful, inside and outside. You can go into—not the low end of Salvation Army, but the new office building that they just built. And in the Mission, go inside. They have a library inside. They have upstairs televisions, they have dental care, they have health care, social services, they also have a senior citizens' services, nurseries.

"You go inside there, you'll see that we're not just laying out on the street creating an eyesore. We don't want to offend the public. We want to say we're here, we don't want to offend you, but we're a part of your society. We understand who we are. We want to see you because you remind us of us a long time ago or what we always cared to see about ourselves.

"We don't want—we don't want to ever offend Americans. We want to say we're proud to be an American, even in this situation. We haven't given up on our ideal, that we are the greatest country in the world."

DISCUSSION

Jack presents himself as a Vietnam veteran who served his country, as a black man in a culture dominated by whites, and as someone who simply wants to live without harassment. He seems to have found social services that offer him assistance and allow him to maintain his autonomy. He makes a good case that many of the homeless men he sees, including himself, are not pathologically criminal but are outside of the economy.

Jack seems to be arguing ultimately for the freedom to be homeless. While noting the role of race and structural inequality in American society, he also suggests that the freedoms offered in the United States are what separate it from other countries with structural inequality. As a veteran he fought for the United States, and he believes homeless veterans are not "bums" but deserve to live their lives in the way they choose. People with housing are often able to drink alcohol and engage in minor drug use without scrutiny; Jack notes that homeless people living out private lives in public are jailed for such trivial offenses. He seems to be saying that such activities by homeless people should not be criminalized.

Jack's thoughts parallel those of Peter Marin (1987), who argued that many homeless people "are not only hapless victims but voluntary exiles. . . . people who have turned not against life itself but against *us*, our life, American life" (1987, 41, emphasis in original). Although Jack is a patriotic American, he seems to have accepted (and perhaps even helped create) his economic outsider status within the United States. He argues that homeless people are rarely harming or even bothering anyone but that they have "lost their way," and he doesn't seem to think they will either have a chance to or want to find their way back.

Jack's conceptualization of homeless people as outsiders also resembles the ideas of Mizruchi (1987). Hopper and Baumohl (1994) summarize Mizruchi's idea of the "abeyance process" as "the practice of shunting off unneeded but potentially troublesome people into various forms of substitute livelihood, thereby neutralizing the threat they might otherwise pose" (1994, 524). Hopper and Baumohl say that homeless shelters serve this function to some degree today. Jack seems to recognize he might not ever gain steady work again and that he is getting older, but he is still trying to survive and enjoy his freedom as best he can.

Despite his poverty, Jack repeats his belief that this is the greatest country in the world. He says clearly that homeless people do not starve in Las Vegas and that shelters and various charities provide many services for people in the homeless corridor. Homeless people have either been cut out of the American dream or have opted out, but either way should be left to do what they want to do because they are not hurting anybody.

At times Jack makes unsustainable claims, such as saying that most homeless men "are brilliant." Though Jack believes that most homeless people are not addicts, studies indicate that addiction is key problem for many homeless people. Despite such statements, Jack makes an interesting case that "we don't ever want to offend Americans." His phrase seems to convey that those with housing see homeless people in the United States as less than citizens, less than Americans. He suggests that in the United States, having housing is directly tied to the concept of having civil rights. He seems to be reminding us that he once fought for and risked his life for those rights.

Jack doesn't seem angry or necessarily depressed about his homelessness. He seems to just be requesting the freedom to be. Despite vagrancy laws being struck down as unconstitutional decades ago, cities like Las Vegas now criminalize many aspects of homeless living, attempting to eliminate the problem behaviors without helping the people who have them. Even homeless people outside of the economy must find ways to live and pursue happiness. Even those who live in public space, or who come from a minority group, are still, as Jack put it, "a part of your society."

EIGHT

Recently Dislocated

CHUCK

I also met Chuck on the afternoon of November 9, 2005, at the annual Stand Down for the Homeless in Las Vegas. He had a serious criminal record and an unstable upbringing. Listening to his story suggested how he had become homeless. However, he was rare among the homeless people I met because he seemed a likely candidate for rapidly regaining permanent housing.

Chuck was smoking outside the building after the event had ended. We had talked to each other three times in the homeless corridor before I had this chance to formally interview him. He was twenty-five years old, balding, with short, dark hair and a goatee. He had a round, slightly chubby face and damaged glasses, and he complained a bit about being overweight. He told me that he had come from Colorado with two hundred dollars and that he had worked as a printer.

"Yes, ran a press for eleven dollars an hour. Good job, but it was just really expensive in Boulder, where I lived, so you can't really survive—I paid eight hundred dollars a month rent for my apartment. That's what I made in two weeks, then all the other bills on top of it. And then they cut our benefits at work, and now insurance costs a hundred forty-five dollars, so it was time to go. Since it was just me, I could pack up and move."

"You said it's just you?" I asked.

"Just me, yeah, live by myself," Chuck replied. "I was on parole for a while. It's easier [for me] not to live with somebody than to have them violate your parole because your roommate's got a beer in the fridge."

Since Chuck brought up his imprisonment, I asked him if he was comfortable telling me more about it.

"I went to college and learned how to be a really good criminal," he began. "I got in trouble for stealing, embezzled money. But I didn't get in trouble for the money, I got in trouble for the fake IDs and documents that I used to steal it. I went and got educated and did the wrong thing with it. So I went to prison for a while and then was paroled. I do my parole. Lesson learned on that one."

"Was it a nasty environment? Was it in Colorado?"

"Colorado's not too bad. It's really not as bad as they say it is. I know how to handle myself well enough to get along all right with everybody. It's not like they show on TV. Not there. Everybody's split up, and there's not that many people in the facility. It's not as rough as they say. As long as you don't do anything stupid or don't be disrespectful to a lot of people, you'll be all right."

I asked him about the process of being released from prison.

"You go to the halfway house before you get out, before your sentence is done, if they accept you. When you go there, you gotta get a job and you got case management. If you screw up at all, you go back, but when you get out on parole you go to your parole officer. You have two weeks to find a job and a place to live or you go back.

"Colorado's got mandatory parole, which means I did all of my sentence, then I had three years mandatory parole on top of it. If I messed up [my parole], I went back for the remainder. But [as far as support services for the recently paroled are concerned] they don't tell you where to go, what to do. You get out. When you discharge your sentence, you get a hundred bucks, which when I finished my parole and I got released, they gave me a hundred-dollar check, and they give you a bus pass wherever you're goin.'

"Then you're on your own, and then you just got out of prison with no ID, no nothing, no birth certificate, and you got to find your own way. Most people end up back for that reason alone."

I asked more about his college education.

"I went for two years, part-time the first year, and I was a full-time student the next year. I was going to work as a paramedic, but I changed my mind and then went back for business management, and then didn't have enough money to go to school and work, the eighteen thousand dollars a year [tuition], and so I started doing stuff to make money on the side. That's how I got caught, and that's how I got in trouble."

Chuck's experiences seemed different from many of the homeless people I have met. He had been in trouble for embezzlement and forgery, which are white-collar crimes. He had attended an expensive university for two years. His current homelessness seemed directly related to having left prison and trying to move to a new city. I wanted to know more about his upbringing.

KURT: Do you stay in touch with youtr parents? Do they know you're homeless here?

CHUCK: I got adopted when I was a kid and the people that we got adopted by were horrible people, so—I haven't had any association with them in ten years, which is good. They're not very good—they were the ones that slipped through Social Services hands when they were doing the screening.

KURT: So then basically you're on your own?

CHUCK: Yeah, pretty much. My older sister lives in Germany, so she's got four kids, a husband that's a German citizen in the American military, and they do OK, but . . . She's never coming back here, so . . .

KURT: When was the last time you talked with her?

CHUCK: Oh, wow—about six months ago. It's about time to give her another call. Christmas is coming up [smiling].

KURT: OK—I got the idea [smiling back].

Studies indicate that homeless people frequently have weak or nonexistent family ties (Shlay and Rossi 1992; Snow and Anderson 1993). By saying that he was adopted and that those parents "were horrible people," Chuck indicated that he did not have a key form of social support that many people take for granted both in good times and in times of crisis. His sister lived on another continent and had started her own family, and Chuck only spoke to her twice a year. He might have felt disconnected from his family for years.

:: :: :: I remembered that Chuck mentioned he had traveled to Las Vegas by Greyhound bus, like many of the people I have interviewed. I asked him how much money he came here with.

"Two hundred dollars and a bag—that was it. When I used to live here before, that was enough. It wasn't really enough this time."

Talking with Chuck also reminded me of the larger social problem of prisoner reintegration upon release and a lack of social support for prisoners just out of prison. The problem of limited social support for former convicts has become more evident to criminal justice scholars in recent years, as the number of prisoners in the United States has quadrupled since 1975.

The United States incarcerates its citizens at a higher rate than any other nation (Parenti 2000; Raphael and Stoll 2009). The rise in incarceration is a direct result of calls by politicians to "get tough on crime" (particularly drug crime in the 1980s and 1990s). Although a "war on crime" ensued, plans were not made for what to do after the "war"—for how those prisoners, once released, would reintegrate into society to become law-abiding citizens. A lack of support for former prisoners seems to also lie behind an alarming recidivism rate in the United States: 66 percent of federal and state prisoners return to prison within three years of their initial release (Donzinger 1996).

The punishment-based approach (captured in the popular phrase "lock 'em up and throw away the key") was politically popular but has proven financially unsustainable (Dyer 2000). The expense, hopelessness, and frequent racism of such a system of punishment have critics dubbing it the "prison-industrial complex" (Davis 2000). Loic Wacquant (2001) argues that prisons now function as an extension of ghettos—a place for disposable people (those marginal to the traditional economy) to be contained. Though Chuck was Caucasian, I saw a disproportionate number of African America men in the homeless corridor in Las Vegas. Several people I spoke to during this study and my previous study (2005) mentioned having spent time in prison, and the homeless corridor itself bordered on North Las Vegas, a historically African American district. Wacquant's idea connecting prisons and ghettos helps explain the hopelessness and social marginality of those I saw regularly in the homeless corridor in Las Vegas, the geographical placement of the homeless corridor, and some homeless people there having come directly from prison.

:: :: :: When I asked Chuck about his previous visits to Las Vegas, he said this was his third trip. He had seen change over time.

CHUCK: I was here when I was on parole in 2002 and 2003, which is only two
    years ago, but property values have tripled since then and the cost of living's

gone up a little bit. It's still not too bad here, it's just changed a little bit. There's still plenty of work, just not as much as there was before, so—and then I also lived down here for six months before I got in trouble. I came down here on vacation and got offered a really good job for six months and worked on it and then went home.

KURT: What types of things have happened to you as a homeless person?

CHUCK: I got here and stayed at a weekly rental for a week. I was tryin' to find a boardinghouse. They don't have those anymore in Colorado, but they used to. When I first got out on parole, you'd go to a boardinghouse and there'd be a room with a bed and a hot pot and a microwave and it was fifty, sixty dollars a week. You could only stay for a month or two. But it was enough to go find a job and then save up some money and then go move into an apartment.

I was looking for that out here, and I think they've got one, but there's so many people here that are tryin' to get into it that. There's a waiting list, and even the cheap weekly places, I got lucky in the one I went to. The guy happened to leave an hour before I got there.

Chuck then noted that the Stand Down event we were attending had attracted thousands of people. Each person who had stood in the line outside this huge building that day was asked to take a survey with a volunteer before accessing services. Later reports indicated that some of the people who came to the Stand Down were not poor but had gone simply for the legal amnesty. An amnesty was being offered, but tickets were quashed only for misdemeanor infractions at a judge's discretion. Even those with housing who came for legal services were probably not middle class. Listening to Chuck, I thought about how legal problems seemed closely tied to some people's poverty and/or homelessness.

I also thought about how obvious the problem of homelessness and poverty in Las Vegas was on the day of the Stand Down. The visibility of such poverty on this single day of the year seemed to clearly indicate a social problem that the city faced *all year.* This event, however, was held in the homeless corridor, removed from sight of the average Las Vegas citizen or tourist. The social marginality of these people paralleling the geographic and economic marginality of this neighborhood reminded me of Wacquant's statement about our penal system, which he called "an instrument for the management of dispossessed and dishonored groups" (2001, 95).

Although some local news media covered the event, it would not be a lead story. Some homeless people benefited enormously from the event, connecting with social service agencies that could help them end their poverty and regain stability. For many attendees, however, the Stand Down represented a one-shot outreach or perhaps a form of social work tokenism, sequestered from the local community and managing the social problem of homelessness. Many people I saw were thrilled to have a new blanket, a haircut, a free meal, and some toiletries. Large changes for attendees seemed far less probable.

:: :: :: I asked Chuck how he had found work once in Las Vegas.

CHUCK: I had been here about a week and I applied at a bunch of different places, printing shops. They're union, so I was told I had to wait until the union opened their books, which is in another couple of months. Then I'll have to wait. My name gets on the list—seniority's first to actually go work at a place.

I went to work for a day labor place for a couple of days. When the guy I was working with found out that I wanted full-time employment, he offered me a job. He knew I showed up and actually worked—I was the only guy in the day labor place that went all three days. Everybody else left or didn't show up or went home sick.

KURT: You were reliable.

CHUCK: Right. So he gave me a job. It's not quite as many hours as he said it was gonna be, and I'm not gettin' paid a whole lot of money, but I should, when I get paid on Wednesday, be able to move somewhere, I hope.

I asked him how long he had been staying at the Salvation Army.

CHUCK: Two weeks and five days. They gave me a five-day extension 'til I got paid. I've been rentin' a bed for the last week. I'll rent a bed 'til next Wednesday, and hopefully I'll have enough money to move then.

KURT: Was it longer than you anticipated?

CHUCK: Yeah. I was thinking I wasn't gonna have to go in there. Like I say, the first time I came out here, I got offered a job. I was walking down the street and [somebody said], "Hey, can you drive a forklift?" "Yeah." "Well, this place pays twenty-one dollars an hour." That was when I was eighteen years old.

I thought that I would come here [again], and when I spent that first week out applying at places, I thought I'd go to work in a day or two. That's the way it had been before. Since I do know how to work, usually I can get a job pretty quick. Just took a couple of weeks longer than I thought it would.

Then there's the whole thing of not havin' anywhere to stay, so you got to find a place to stay, and I had to lock up my bag at a Greyhound station and wait 'til I got paid to get it out, which cost a lot of money.

KURT: That's where you stored your stuff?

CHUCK: Right. That's where all my clothes were. Now I've got that, so I've got enough changes of clothes. I didn't come down here with much, so half my stuff's locked up in my friend's storage [in Colorado]. It's not much at all, but he'll hold on to it until I get stable enough . . . which hopefully will be before Christmas.

Other homeless people had mentioned to me the problem Chuck described—regularly needing personal items, but also needing a reliable place to store those things when that individual did not have ongoing shelter. It seemed to me another example of the instability of homelessness that itself leads to difficulties in ending homelessness.

:: :: :: I decided to ask Chuck how he would study homelessness if he were in my position.

"I wouldn't have a clue where to start," he began. "The problem with homelessness is, other than shelters, there's nowhere for people to convene. A lot of these people just move around town—it's kind of hard. Being on parole, I did volunteer work here when I was here before at the Salvation Army. I see some of the same people I saw here [years] before when I was doing that, which is kind of horrible.

"This town—there's a lot of stuff to spend all your money on, that's for sure. These guys, at the first of the month, everybody got their checks. Now [eight days later] the shelters are starting to fill back up 'cause everybody spent their money."

I thought Chuck was referring to some of the people we saw in the Salvation Army yard where we had talked before. The yard was where I had watched homeless people fight over a box of donated clothes that someone had simply left outside the building. It was also where people slept for free during the day. Chuck seemed to be saying some of those people might receive a pension or disability check at the beginning of the month but spend it all within a week. I mentioned to him that, a week earlier, many people seemed to have left.

Chuck continued discussing why people in the city became homeless.

"Guys are hiring people, [but] you got to make eight or nine dollars an hour, pretty much, to live and support yourself. A lot of them aren't paying that anymore."

He spoke more about his current job.

"The guys I work for, they pay me eight bucks an hour because they decided that's the minimum somebody can make and actually show up for work."

"And do you get health benefits or anything?" I asked.

"No, none of that stuff. It's all right."

Chuck was more concerned about transportation.

"They're good guys, so they know what situation I'm in, and they try to give me enough warning to get down [to the worksite]. Since they took out the express buses, it takes two-and-a-half hours to get to work now instead of an hour and ten minutes, so . . ."

"So you work on the south Las Vegas Strip?"

"Right. Our shop's behind the Orleans [Resort], and I usually meet them at the shop 'cause that's easier for all of us."

"That is a long bus ride from here."

"It is. And that Strip bus takes an hour and a half. The Maryland Parkway bus takes an hour. Plus, I got to take Tropicana [Avenue] over 'cause you can't walk over the interstate. You have to take the bus to get across. I could walk faster than the buses, but there's no sidewalk goin' over the highway."

I had seen people walking on the overpass that Chuck was discussing, but I realized that crossing it by foot was illegal. Chuck had to be careful about even minor infractions of the law now. Any illegal act could cause him further legal trouble.

"Have you thought about other options besides staying in the shelter, like camping out or something?" I asked. "If you're spending over four hours a day riding a bus, you must be awfully tired."

"I can sleep on the bus, too. And I do. Most of the time, I can get enough sleep. St. Vincent's is better than Salvation Army, but St. Vincent's won't let you check in after midnight and sometimes I work late, sometimes it's 2 or 3 A.M. So the Salvation Army, I got to be back at eight o'clock in the morning. That's kind of rough.

"As far as camping out, I have to take a shower every day. I mean I work, and we do work in the casinos and in people's houses and stuff like that. I got to be clean."

Chuck was noting a dilemma common to those in the homeless corridor trying to stay employed while homeless. Until he could live on his own, he needed the services in the homeless corridor to rest, clean up, and eat. He needed shelter first and employment second. Riding the bus for hours each day was not reliable transportation and did not make it easy to work, but he felt it was his best option.

"If you're not at the Salvation Army [by] a certain time, you're screwed. The other night I had to spend the night on the bus, sleeping on the bus goin' back and forth, because they don't sell the beds past 9:00 at night and I got there at 9:10, and so I was like, 'Well, I can't find a bed, the other place was full,' so I spent the night on the bus."

Chuck explained that he had a month-long bus pass not just for transportation purposes, but to provide him a place to sleep no matter what:

"That's the first thing I bought when I came down here. And then when I got paid, I bought another one just to make sure I had it. If all else fails, I can ride the bus all night."

Though Chuck seemed very motivated to end his homelessness through hard work, he also seemed frustrated at his lack of money, which left him completely dependent on public resources (like buses) and private charities. Chuck seemed to be trying to move from the most basic level of Maslow's hierarchy of needs (meeting physiological needs like sleep) to the next level (meeting safety needs like secure employment) (Maslow 1943). Securing the bus pass appeared to be his plan of last resort for sleep on any given night.

:: :: :: I asked him what type of work he did now.

"Stone floors, anything to do with stone floors. Like maintenance or cleaning—you know when you go into a casino and everything's real flat? They don't come that way, they come in rough, and they lay all the floor— we would come in and sand it down and then seal it and epoxy it. Then after a year, we would go in there and strip off all the sealer and reseal it.

"[We also work in] people's houses," he said. "There's a lot of really nice neighborhoods out here, and these people have sandstone floors. Just yesterday we spent three days doing this lady's marble floor. Marble's hard stone. If it gets a scratch in it or a stain, or if you spill acid on it, it eats the stone. So we go in there and use acid stripper and grind the floor. It's a good job. It's not very consistent, you know—we don't work a scheduled shift." Chuck then returned to explaining why he had to rely on charitable services that are so far from his job.

"If I was to go sleep in a park [near where I worked], they would wake me up and take me to jail. They won't do that down here [in the homeless corridor] to these guys because there's a lot of people [camping out]. They're not just gonna be able to take just one. They had the paddy wagon down by Salvation Army the other morning, all the guys that sleep across from it, and they wanted to pick them all up, but they only had three paddy wagons and there was a hundred and something people out there, so they just left. They decided that wasn't a good idea.

"I think because of these high-rises they're tryin' to put up, they're tryin' to clean up parts of this city, and everybody's got to go somewhere."

Chuck seemed to be suggesting that the homeless corridor involved a form of economic segregation. He believed he couldn't sleep outside in better parts of the city because laws against loitering in those areas would be enforced. He had to stay on the right side of the law. Other groups of homeless people he saw camping illegally in the homeless corridor had safety in numbers, to some extent: The police would have difficulty arresting and processing them all. Chuck suggested that, so long as they stayed in the corridor, the behavior of homeless people was tolerated.

I asked Chuck how much he got paid an hour.

CHUCK: I get eight bucks an hour. My first paycheck I got fifty hours, which was three hundred and forty dollars after they took the taxes. That's not really a lot, but it was enough for me to go from the [free] sthelter to renting a bed. When I get paid again it should be a little bit more. I only got thirty-two hours last week. Hopefully I'll get forty this week.

KURT: So you're counting the hours?

CHUCK: Yes. Anything will help. It's real hard because the work's so scattered—I don't know if I'm working at night or [during] the day. Last night I worked, yesterday, and the day before. Monday night, we worked at a place. Tuesday night, we were supposed to go work at a place. They canceled.

Last Saturday we went to the place we were supposed to go to and nobody was there. We didn't have a key and we didn't have a code to get in, so we can't just break down their door. So that scraps that whole day's worth of work. They try to not have that happen very often, but it does. We were supposed to work today and it didn't work out.

KURT: Is that why you're here at the Stand Down?

CHUCK: Yes. Well, I needed a haircut, too. Anything I can do to save. I mean, fifteen bucks for a haircut—it saves me a little bit. That means that I can smoke this week. I don't do anything else—don't drink or do drugs anymore, so you got to have something.

For a variety of reasons, many homeless people I have interviewed have been smokers. It provided sociability and an outlet for stress, but it also was a regular expense. Lawsuits against tobacco companies and taxes on cigarettes have caused this habit to become expensive all over the United States—a pack of cigarettes can cost five dollars or more out of a vending machine in Las Vegas. Smoking regularly was difficult for many homeless people I spent time with but, ironically, so was quitting. I have watched homeless people conduct hundreds of transactions with each other in an attempt to get cigarettes. Chuck seemed to be one of the "lucky" ones who could, at least now, afford cigarettes from a store.

:: :: :: Chuck also had solid skills as a printer, a job that should pay well. I asked him to tell me why he had left his last job. His story was like those of so many people who try to make a living at manufacturing jobs in the United States today.

"I ran the printing press. There was a lead on a press. Our press was supposed to have four people on it; it only had three. Usually runnin' a press, it's fifteen, eighteen, twenty dollars an hour. If you're good like the guy that worked as my second, he made like twenty-five bucks an hour. They hired me when I was in the halfway house and on parole, so they could hire me at whatever they wanted to. I got hired at eleven bucks an hour and was told I'd get a four-dollar raise as soon as I left the halfway house.

"When I left the halfway house after a couple of months, I didn't get the raise. I was told we were on a raise freeze. Then waited 'til when Christmas came and the New Year. He came and said they were going to be on a raise freeze for one more year, and it had been like six years they had been on this raise freeze. Then in June our benefits were renewing. It was gonna cost 'em an extra—I don't know, eighty or ninety grand to keep the same insurance they had the year before, so they were just gonna get rid of benefits all together. They also hadn't put any money into their profit-sharing program in a few years. They said they weren't making enough."

The cuts Chuck described in his employer's insurance package are similar to those occurring across the United States: "the take-up rate of employer-provided insurance is decreasing" (O'Hara 2004, 64). Additionally, the cost of health care has risen each year between 1999 and 2004. Chuck thought that an employee shouldering such costs was one of several ways his former employer continued to profit at the expense of the employees.

"Somebody I worked with then went and wrote for a copy of their expenditures and profits," said Chuck. "They made something like $1.2 million in profit for that year. [And yet] they told us they didn't make any money, so I left. When we got that copy [of the report], they put it up on the poster board at work. Everybody threw a fit. The president came down tryin' to say, 'We took a loss for five years,' and we were tellin' him, 'Well, you told us that you didn't make a profit, you had taken a loss for this year and that's why everything was the way it was, and that wasn't true.' There had been rumors about him tryin' to sell the place. We figured he was tryin' to take the company, make as much money as he could as quick as he could, and then sell it and run with his millions."

:: :: :: Chuck explained more about his training as a printer, a job he had had for six years. I asked him if he could find printing work in Las Vegas.

CHUCK: I hope so. It's union down here, so the pay is so much better. They'll start at like seventeen an hour, and what they'll do is hire me as a second and make sure that I can run a press, and then I'll either wait for a lead spot to open or they'll already have one waiting.

KURT: Is it competitive here?

CHUCK: Pretty much. In this town, they print a lot of stuff. Most of these hotels and casinos go through local shops. You see all the fliers in the trash, the stripper books [pamphlets for erotic services that are handed out on the Strip], all that gets printed here. It's cheaper to print it out of a place here than to have it shipped in from Washington. So they've got something like twenty-six shops that I know of. I've applied at like ten. I'm waiting for the union to open its books and [then I'll] pay my three hundred and ten dollars in union dues. Hopefully I'll have enough money to do it.

KURT: So you'll have to join the union first?

CHUCK: Yes. When I went and applied at a bunch of places, a guy runnin' a press pulled me aside and said that it's all union. "Go join the union and the union will fill out all your apps." But he told me the union puts you on a list by seniority—the guys who have been in the union the longest go to the top of the list and get hired first. I'm sure there's a couple of shops that are nonunion, but from what I understand, it's real hard, because if you're not union, you can't buy paper because the paper plant's union, so . . .

KURT: It's all union based?

CHUCK: Right. This is a union city.

The unionization of labor in Las Vegas was a double-edged sword. On the one hand, it made the city, as Hal Rothman phrased it, "the Last Detroit," or a place where working-class people could still make a living wage, even in service sector employment (2003, 63). On the other hand, unions have sometimes made it difficult for newcomers in the city to get a decent-paying job. If the city truly is the last Detroit in the United States, it could not possibly employ the multitude of workers it attracts. Chuck could wait months or perhaps years before securing a job in his trade.

:: :: :: Toward the end of our interview I asked Chuck if he thought homelessness in Las Vegas would get better or worse.

"It's gonna get a lot worse. In ten years they're gonna have to really, really do somethin.' Property values have tripled over the last few years. The rent's starting to catch up.

"These people that own these inexpensive places on the Strip or on Tropicana or on Fremont—they ran out of room to build casinos, so now they're startin' to build them out, and there are these high-rise buildings they're trying to tear down. Just before the Stratosphere as you're heading toward the Stratosphere, places like that. There used to be an apartment complex there. Not anymore.

"If you haven't bought a house now, you're pretty much done. You're gonna have three, four, five people livin' in a one-bedroom apartment. It's already goin' on. There's a lot of under-the-table work here, and those guys are only makin' five bucks an hour. They're not really legal to work, but they gotta have jobs and pay their bills, so they're gonna have to do something."

Chuck noted that as property values increased, people would need to double up or make do with insufficient housing in order to live in Las Vegas. Although the city needed tens of thousands of laborers for all of its service sector jobs, the increasing expense of life in the city meant those workers would have a harder time staying.

Chuck described a similar gentrification pattern he saw in Denver.

"In downtown Denver, they tore out all of downtown and re-did it, and they were supposed to be building all these lofts and apartment complexes for the people that worked in that area. Instead, they sold it to private contractors who now sell them for a million bucks a piece. Now everybody that lived in those places before has to go somewhere else. It's a long commute—traffic's worse than it was before. It was supposed to solve all those problems. That's [also] what's happenin' down here.

"I understand they're tryin' to clean stuff up, but some people only make eight hundred, nine hundred a month. And they got to live. So [homelessness is] gonna get a lot worse."

Chuck then mentioned several interconnected problems associated with local homelessness.

"People move down here and they blow all their money, or they don't realize it's so expensive, or—I mean there's a lot of bad habits you can have. If you have any bad habits and you come to this town, there's a lot of ways you can end up bashed out. It's so hard to go from being homeless to not [being homeless] anymore.

"It's hard to get jobs. If you can't shower every day, you're not gonna work somewhere, anywhere. Even washing cars—if you stink, you're not gonna work. Fillin' out apps, I use the address I used to live out here before as an address, because if I put the Salvation Army's address, there's places that won't hire you. I don't understand why, but I get some of it, too—half the people [in the shelters] aren't dependable."

Chuck noted the stigma of being homeless and of being associated with agencies helping homeless people such as the Salvation Army. He thought that stigma put the people using such agencies at a disadvantage in trying to find work, while also saying that many of those using the shelters "aren't dependable." He then told me he bought a cell phone to avoid the stigma of association with a homeless shelter:

"That's another big thing is that you can have [employers] leave messages at the Salvation Army, but when they call, they say, 'Salvation Army Homeless Shelter,' and people don't like that, so . . . I bought a prepaid cell phone. Twenty-five dollars, it comes with fifty minutes. That's more than I'm ever gonna use, so now when I apply places, I can take phone calls."

He also mentioned his difficulties trying to find apartments willing to take local housing vouchers for homeless people, the same vouchers that Ron and Ricky (from chapter 1) combined to rent a 300-square-foot apartment.

"That's the other problem here. The housing authorities will give you rent vouchers and things, but the voucher's for three hundred and seventy-eight dollars. I'm sure there's places that let you live there for three hundred and seventy-eight dollars, but I don't know where any of them are. I have been trying to find places like that and I don't have a clue."

I ended the interview by asking Chuck about his future plans. He first wanted to find a weekly apartment. He described difficulties he was having trying to get a Nevada state driver's license, wishing the bureaucratic hoops he had to jump through for it were easier. He also worried about his unpredictable work hours and income.

"I've called some places around here, and when I get paid next Wednesday, hopefully, I'll be able to move. My boss wants me to get a license and they're gonna give me the van. The only problem is the DMV does not accept my certified copy of my birth certificate, the one that I have. I don't know why. I don't know what's wrong with it and neither does the State of Colorado, so I'm tryin' to get my license here. I gave it up years ago—I was on parole and I couldn't drive, so they made me give up my license."

Like Chuck, many people in this study described problems with getting documents they need (like Social Security cards or valid birth certificates) to obtain licenses, government benefits, or employment. Homeless people naturally have difficulty keeping such documents safe. It is also hard for homeless people to know what documents to carry on their person, because they don't know when those documents will be needed. A potential policy implication of this study, therefore, is that homeless people might benefit from special assistance in securing and perhaps keeping these documents that are required for life in a modern, highly bureaucratic society. As digitized records are increasingly used, perhaps digital repositories for what were once paper records could be developed specifically for vulnerable populations such as homeless people. If not having such records can prolong homelessness, increasing an individual's access to such records can reduce it.

Chuck continued discussing his future plans.

"I have to take a written test, and they'll give it back here—so I'm gonna try and get that all taken care of. I don't know what I'm gonna do about my birth certificate. We'll deal with that later. Then I'm tryin' to move out by the Tropicana. I don't think I can afford any of those places. There's a couple of weekly places that are here on Fremont Street. I've called a few of them. I think there's one of them that I can afford to pay for two weeks, and then when I get paid again, pay another two weeks.

"My boss pretty much knows that [my limited pay and hours] is just not gonna cut it, so when another job comes, I'm gonna go. Now, if they get busy and I'm workin' sixty hours a week, that's different. Hopefully, maybe one of the press places can call me back."

DISCUSSION

Chuck shared several characteristics with what Snow and Anderson would categorize as a "recently dislocated" person (1993, 46–47): He was using both agencies and charitable organizations as a way to meet his immediate needs for shelter, and he was actively seeking full-time employment. Snow and Anderson also identify this type of homeless person as somewhat younger, having been homeless for a shorter period of time, and behaving in a manner consistent with getting off the street.

Chuck seemed committed to ending his homelessness. His discussion and priorities seem consistent with his determination that his homelessness was temporary. In this regard, he seemed to reflect national studies indicating that the use of shelter services for most homeless people is temporary (Gladwell 2006; Shinn and Tsemberis 1999). He described quite well, however, the catch-22s that recently dislocated people often face. The right supportive housing program would allow him to meet his most basic needs for several weeks or months while he gained employment and saved enough to live independently. Without such a program, he scrambled to avoid a total dependency on public resources and charities, a dependency that might seriously inhibit his chances of ending his homelessness.

If recently dislocated homeless people like Chuck who are committed to ending their homelessness have such problems using charitable services while trying to work, it is no wonder that such individuals often feel frustrated with their situation and might perhaps fall into longer-term homelessness. Chuck is very resourceful and determined, but as he works without insurance, one stroke of bad luck like an accident could quickly set him back. Although there are programs in the homeless corridor for individuals who work, a range of such programs and supportive housing located throughout the city (especially in more economically viable areas) might better serve homeless people who are eager to work and would place them closer to employment. Chuck noted that gentrification throughout the city would likely lead to more homelessness and that those homeless people displaced by such neighborhood improvements would face frustrating, stressful conditions.

Chuck's narrative suggested how his homelessness was related to his incarceration, subsequent release, and decision to move to Las Vegas. Providing a better and more sustained form of social support that would help former convicts reintegrate back into civil life after they have served their sentences is one potential policy implication of Chuck's story. Before a former prisoner can have a stable, productive life after prison, that person first needs housing and social support. Because Chuck did not have family to return to, he was at some risk of recidivism, or returning to crime, without some other form of strong social support.

Chuck did not have a stable family background and said he did not want a roommate or friends who might get him into trouble and jeopardize his parole. His story suggests another possible policy change concerning prisoners reentering civil society, one that might help reduce their rates of homelessness. Soon-to-be-released prisoners could be systematically evaluated specifically for their social networks before leaving prison. Those with more fragmented and/or unhealthy networks could be offered more direct social support programs upon release to help ensure that they will not return to prison. As the average taxpayer cost of imprisonment per inmate per year in the United States was more than $24,000 in 2001 (National Institute of Corrections 2010), providing better social support programs for former convicts to help them avoid reincarceration might also be cheaper than their return to prison.

Angela Davis argues that a lack of support for the large number of former prisoners trying to reintegrate back into society will create pressing social problems in the future. A prisoner's problems that were not addressed in prison or upon release will continue once a prisoner is "outside" and will only perpetuate high recidivism rates (Davis 2000). If those people only receive punishment for their crimes rather than rehabilitation and transitional assistance once their sentence is served, they are being released without either the skills or the help they need to be productive, healthy citizens. Researchers Langan and Levin (2002) reported that in 1994, two-thirds of those individuals released from state prison were later rearrested for serious offenses. That statistic shows that we need to listen to the difficulties Chuck is facing upon release, including his homelessness, to develop social programs that will help him avoid further prison time. The alternative of not helping such individuals promises to perpetuate recidivism, failing everyone.

Avoiding Centralized
Programs and Shelters

KAREN AND DAVE

Like Melissa, Cory, and their friends (see chapter 5), Karen and Dave seemed to work hard to stay independent of and miles away from the social services provided in the homeless corridor of Las Vegas. They had developed alternative means of survival, including sleeping outside and using a sign to solicit cash. Their story indicates the other ways some homeless people subsist, and perhaps even thrive, while avoiding centralized programs and shelters for homeless persons.

On February 13, 2006, I visited the corner of Flamingo Road and Maryland Parkway, because I had long seen homeless people there holding signs asking for help. On that day I met Karen, who would carry her sign and walk slowly past drivers who were stopped and waiting for the light to change.

Karen had a good suntan and wore baggy blue sweatpants, work boots, and an oversized purple sweater with a zipper on the collar, and she carried a plaid work jacket across her arm. Her clothes were visibly dirty. She has brown eyes and curly brown hair with blonde streaks, and I noticed her top two front teeth were jutting out. She was forty-five years old, and she walked with a limp.

When I asked her about panhandling on that corner, she corrected me. "I don't panhandle," she said. "I don't ask people for money."

She let me read her sign into the tape recorder. The first line said "Homeless and Hungry," followed by a second line that said "Willing to Work." The final line said "Please Help God Bless."

"[On my sign] I say I'm hungry and willing to work, and I have worked.

I have been told by a police officer that you can't ask for cash. He said I could walk on the sidewalk. I could get a ticket if I'm in traffic for obstructing traffic," Karen explained.

Ordinances that criminalize panhandling are now common in metropolitan areas across the United States. Homeless people have therefore developed strategies to get money from passersby without breaking the law. For example, Lachenmeyer (2000) describes his homeless father's technique of indirect solicitation for getting cash. His father found out that it was against a city ordinance in Burlington, Vermont, to ask people openly for money, so instead he would simply ask people, "Can you help me out?" (2000, 203). Unfortunately for Karen, walking with her sign between cars stopped at the light put her in jeopardy of violating traffic laws. She seemed at times to be willing to risk breaking the law, though, since doing so allowed her to pass directly by a driver's side window, making it easier for drivers to roll down their windows and give. It also forced the immobile drivers to see her limp, and offered her a chance to look those drivers in the eye, perhaps causing some to feel guilt or sympathy.

A supportive response to her sign, though, was not guaranteed. I asked her if she had experienced negative reactions from people.

"I've had people spit in my face, throw pennies at me. I've had a guy that followed me with a sign that said 'Help Yourself.' They hired another guy to videotape and photograph it. The guy dressed up in a costume, a homeless-type of costume, and followed me around for a day. College kids—too much of daddy's money and nothing better to do," she said dismissively.

We talked about how bizarre that experience was. I wondered if the "college kids" following her were perhaps hoping to make a *Bumfights*-style video recording.

I asked her if she had any positive experiences and about the general reaction others had to her sign.

"Most of the people that give are minorities who can't afford it," she told me. "The Mercedes and Hummers might give you a dollar or nothing at all. The other day I spent four hours [and was given] ten dollars, [and then I made] ninety bucks in an hour, all last week. I really got [sun]burned bad at the end of last summer. I need to get sunscreen," she added.

Karen seemed to be suggesting that this form of panhandling-like activity had, for her, many elements of a job. She had observed patterns in who tended to give money, and she used that information to increase her chances of success. Like other solicitors, she had to deal with angry responses and rejection and had great days and disheartening ones. She was also vulnerable to the elements and, like many workers today, had good reason to invest in equipment (like sunscreen) to do her job before earning any money.

She told me about herself.

"I moved here to buy a house. Been here three years. I came from L.A. via New York. I lost all my family—brother, mother, and grandparents—in fifteen months' time. I inherited money, but I put it in a storage unit and it got stolen."

I wondered why she had put her money in a storage unit instead of a bank, but thought it did not matter now. She then described living in an inexpensive and crime-ridden apartment complex near the University of Nevada Las Vegas campus. The complex she mentioned rented studio apartments by the week or month. She then said she became homeless after a series of health problems.

"I broke my back in 2001–2002, the year my relatives died. Knocked my teeth out—I hit the divider on D.I. [Desert Inn Road] going fifty-five. I lived [on East Harmon Road near the Las Vegas Strip]. Now I sleep on the side of a furniture store behind some shrubs. I sleep with two men protecting me—actually I protect them," she said, smiling. "I met them out here. One's from England."

Karen's story suggested that she had lost important figures in her family and probably her major support network. When she had subsequent accidents she might have had problems holding down regular employment.

"I got robbed several times [in Las Vegas]—[I lost] cash, clothes, a computer, books, my brother's ashes . . ."

Karen then paused and cried. I turned off the tape recorder, but she motioned to start it again. About thirty seconds later, she continued.

" . . . artwork, stuff from my inheritance. There were five main break-ins when I was living in the studio. I had plenty of money when I came here, but I didn't know that neighborhood was so bad. It was pristine during the day, but at night the vultures came out."

I was familiar with the area where she once lived. It had a reputation for drug dealing and prostitution. I wondered why she had chosen to live there if she could afford to live somewhere else. Some things weren't adding up. Of course, not everyone I spoke to was candid about his or her personal problems, particularly during our first meeting.

"They should have a 'beware of people' sign when you enter this city. I've been to Oakland, L.A., New York, and I've *never* seen such bad, unsavory people. There's a few kind people, [but] they're few and far between. But when you hold a sign, you see the good."

I asked her how she had chosen to display her sign at Flamingo Road and Maryland Parkway. She, like other people in this study, told me her practice was called "flying the sign" and indicated that the corner was a popular place to solicit cash. Like Jessi (see chapter 2), men had also offered to pay her for sex:

"I came over here because I was working with another guy, but then it became a turf war. There are people who come out here and fly the sign who aren't homeless. They don't deserve to be out here [with a sign asking for help]. Some people want you for sex, some people want to work you to death. I once got arrested for solicitation. This guy kept asking me for sex, and I said I don't do that. He said, 'You sure I can't talk you into it?' So I said, 'For a hundred bucks you can come on my back.' I was being facetious. And this officer comes out of nowhere and arrests me. I shouldn't have done that."

"Do you have any other family and do you stay in touch with them?" I asked.

"My oldest son is a physics major at Columbia University," Karen said. "He's switching to law. My youngest son is talking about majoring in business. I keep in contact with them but I haven't recently. They don't know about my situation. My husband does. He's dying of hepatitis c, waiting for a liver transplant.

"I'm diabetic and I have a bad heart. I was very sick, and I went to the hospital. A doctor from a private hospital told me I had to go across the street [because] I didn't have health insurance. When I came to, I was in a nut hospital. I never got treated for what I came in for. It was illegal to put me in there [the mental health facility] without my permission."

Karen's crying spell, her arrest for solicitation, and her involuntary confinement in a mental health facility caused me to wonder about her mental stability. Despite saying she had successful sons, she had certainly seen her share of hardships.

"Have you tried using the services in the homeless corridor?" I asked.

"I'm waiting for my ID card to be replaced," she replied. "I would use the services, but I can't without ID."

She then told me she should get back to flying the sign and asked me if I could give her any help. After I gave her five dollars, she told me to come back sometime and meet her friends.

:: :: :: The next day (Valentine's Day) on the same corner, Karen introduced me to Dave. I soon realized he was one of the two men she said slept by her outside the furniture store, the man Karen had said was from England. Dave was a thin, fifty-five-year-old white male originally from London. His skin was brown from the sun, and he had receding dishwater blond hair and a beard. We talked under the shade of the nearby Long John Silver's restaurant sign in the parking lot. He was waiting for Karen to finish panhandling at 4 P.M., when he would take over in what he called "the shift change."

Dave explained how they camped by a building near shrubs and an open field in this area. He mentioned the positive aspects of his present location. It was far from the homeless corridor, which he found threatening and depressing. He could fly the sign regularly on the corner with his friends. He also explained there were useful facilities within walking distance, such as the public library, a grocery store, a homeless outreach program, and a community center.

He said that he and Karen panhandled together. Each would alternate as a lookout, watching for the police. He, like Karen, said the police would ticket them for disrupting the flow of traffic.

"If I see any [police] coming down the street, I blow my whistle," he said.

Dave was showing me through example how homeless people working together in small groups were able to subsist outside of the homeless corridor. By having one person act as a lookout, others flying the sign could reduce their chance of arrest or a fine. Also, as Melissa and Cory (from chapter 5) suggested, sleeping outside but in a group offered protection to each individual by reducing his or her vulnerability.

Dave said he first came to Las Vegas in 1999.

"I've got a friend here I've known for thirty years. I came to visit and ended up staying. We lived in a place for four years, and one month he didn't come up with his rent. I didn't have enough money, I lost my job, and at the same time the guy moved to California, so I became homeless around 2004."

I asked him what kind of work he once did.

"I did bricklaying. I helped construct patios for people's houses. I've done landscaping, computer work. We did detailing—we detailed cars, mobile detailing. It's—I just hate going to work. You know, I worked for years and years like in factories, welding, and it's the grind. It's dull. I'd like to do computer work, but you have to have some kind of a degree, and I'm fifty-five."

Dave was sleeping outside and seemed destitute but also seemed candid about having made lifestyle choices embracing the freedom of homelessness. Unlike Karen, he did not frame his reasons for homelessness in a way that might cause pity. He clearly did not like certain jobs he had worked; but although he had fallen into poverty, he also had arguably found a way to do other things he enjoyed.

"I love the computer," he continued. "The reason I chose this location is the library's right over here, and you can get on the Internet two hours a day. They're open from nine to nine four days a week, and from ten till six other days. And you got the one-hour computer. You can study or you can watch music videos. I put my earplugs in and listen to the news from London."

"Oh, really? On the computers? That's great," I said.

"Yeah, on Real Player. Every night at midnight on PBS radio on FM, they [also have] broadcasts from the BBC."

Dave said that a long time ago he had been a roadie for different bands, such as Hawkwind. He said he likes going down to Circus Circus casino, on Las Vegas Boulevard, to see the circus acts and to play the midway games, and he visits there with his niece who lives in the city. He continued speaking about computers and was knowledgeable about various web pages. He drank a beer while we spoke.

During his interview Dave didn't complain about homelessness, except to say he hated having his stuff stolen.

"Before I knew it here, I was out in the desert by the railroad tracks, and people [were] just stealing things constantly. You come home and there's no blankets. Someone stole my shoes one night. Luckily, I had an extra pair, but I didn't have any of my clothes. So now I've accumulated a bunch of clothes. They're dirty," he said, looking at his bag.

To avoid having his things stolen, Dave carried several items with him in a black rolling bag and said he had other things hidden in the desert. He had also purchased a small white device called a Mini Alert Motion Detector. He would turn it on and leave it on top of his bag when he was sleeping or when his bag was out of his sight momentarily. He had me walk toward the bag, which set off the device's shrill alarm. I thought again of how homeless people used some technologies, like that mini motion detector, in inventive ways compatible with their mobile lifestyles.

:: :: :: Dave had found ways to survive away from the charities in the homeless corridor, and he mentioned different techniques he had for meeting different needs.

KURT: How do you manage to get clothes?

DAVE: People give me them, [I] find them. Like these pants were just sitting there, over at the bus stop. They were clean yesterday. They're the perfect size, and these were brand new. I found two pairs of shoes up near the post office.

KURT: How do you eat and how do you store food, or do you store it at all?

DAVE: I eat a lot of food by people giving it to me out of the cars standing here. And sometimes you have to hit a couple of Dumpsters. But after you bring the bags out, people leave a bunch of food, and it's still hot and it's not contaminated.

When I mentioned how Dumpster diving could be dangerous in the summer heat when the food would spoil, Dave agreed. He said that was when he had to panhandle the most to buy food.

"Sometimes my friends got food stamps," he continued, "and they let me have them for half price. If I go and get twenty dollars worth of groceries, I pay the guy ten bucks."

Other people in this study mentioned the sale and/or bartering of food stamps. I thought about how well-meaning citizens and government agencies developed those stamps so that poor people could only use them for appropriate food items. I thought of how some poor people then resist that form of control. Poor people, like most everyone, want the freedom to choose what they do with a resource.

Dave also used the local homeless outreach program and community center.

"At the community center you can get bread three times a week, fresh bread. It's right down behind the McDonald's right there—the Cambridge Community Center. They have clothes over there. I found her [Karen] a couple of shirts over there the other day."

Dave explained how he helped out others he saw on the street. This norm of reciprocity is both tenuous among homeless people and essential for those in life-threatening poverty. Researchers Snow and Anderson once summed up this code, which they found shared by many homeless people, as "what goes around, comes around" (1993, 107).

"I found a couple of pairs of Wrangler's, but they were [size] 42s," Dave began. "I took them anyway, and I seen another homeless guy, and I gave them to him and they fit him; that's what I do. I always take things I don't need because then I might run into people that might wear that size, and I just work that way. And people give me things when they find something. Someone gives them certain items of clothing, they give them to me."

Being so marginal to the economy of Las Vegas, Dave and some of his friends seemed to rely on an informal bartering system, hunting and gathering techniques, and the goodwill of others. Dave said, though, that not too many street people share. He also suggested that some homeless people ruined or abused the resources used by others. He said he couldn't depend on other panhandlers keeping the area we now occupied clean, because many homeless people were alcoholics, he thought, who were only interested in feeding their addiction. Selfish individuals within the community of homeless people made life harder for the whole group:

"Mostly guys out here are real bad alcoholics," he said. "I don't drink that much myself. A little bit. I used to, but I cut down. I don't want to be like them anymore. They just trash the place and you can't come to certain spots anymore. Like this spot, I keep clean even though I'm not going to be here sometimes, I keep it clean because the people in the back [of a nearby business] know I'm here, because they have talked to me twice. They said, 'You guys are OK to just sit here, but you can't be partying or trampling all over the place or leaving empty cans.'"

Like other people in this study sleeping outside or flying the sign, Dave and Karen worked to keep their areas clean of trash to avoid complaints from local businesses or attention from the police.

"We've got run out by the cops a couple of times here, but they didn't give me a ticket, [they] just tell you to leave and that's it."

::   ::   ::   "There are a lot of services for homeless people located past Fremont Street and in that area," I mentioned. "Have you ever gone down there?"

"I've been down there and I hate it," Dave replied. "I hate downtown Las Vegas. It's awful, in my opinion. It's not a place I want to be. No. I do a lot better over here. Too much crime down there. Too many cops. It's just a lot of really crazy people, which I try to avoid. I don't hang out much down there.

"This is a whole different homelessness in areas like this and downtown," he continued. "It's a whole different scene down there. You can get the vouchers for monthly rent. You can get a voucher for a couple of months. I think it's [for] three hundred ninety-five dollars, and it's these ratty rooms you can get with a TV. You can stay there. But then, you know, most of those people are homeless because they drink a lot, so they can't get a job, and I don't want—I can't work here, so . . ."

Dave explained that he did not have a permit to work in the United States and thus could not be employed legally. However, he also did not like the area where homeless services were concentrated. In order to avoid downtown Las Vegas and the services in the homeless corridor, Dave, Karen, and their friends need to somehow acquire regular cash, usually by flying the sign.

"How many times a week do you fly the sign?"

"Every day. For maybe an hour, a couple of hours."

I asked how much he made doing it.

"Yesterday I only made five dollars, but some days I can make twenty-five," he said.

I asked Dave about people's responses to his sign. He reinforced what Karen had told me.

" 'Get a job! Will you get a job?' they say. Yeah, rude comments, but most people are real nice. It's not as though I'm asking them for any money. I'm just holding a sign. I don't go out in traffic. I stay on the sidewalk.

"I make enough money to get by," Dave said. "I got a place to go and lay down. I got clean blankets and a nice clean carpet to lay on. It's pretty close to the university here. It's pretty secluded."

"How do you meet hygiene needs, bathroom and showering?" I asked.

"Oh, I've got a friend that lives right over here in those apartments," he said, pointing to a small block of apartments directly across the street. "I go over there twice a week."

Dave also said that when his friend wasn't home, he used public restrooms for hygiene.

"I can wash up in various bathrooms. Well, the library, but there's no mirror. Go to Cambridge Center and inside the stall, the handicapped stall, there's a sink. You lock the door and it's private. [You] strip off and use the washcloth and wash that way."

Dave was describing his use of public sinks for bathing in nearly the same way that Jack had (see chapter 7). Dave reiterated that being homeless in this area of Las Vegas was a very different experience from staying in the homeless corridor. He told me, though, that there were other undesirable areas of Las Vegas in addition to the homeless corridor—that the neighborhood near the intersection of Tropicana and Valley View was very bad, that it was full of homeless people, crack users, and dealers. He said he sometimes visits a friend there who gets a check for $1,600 at the beginning of the month but then spends it within days. Dave avoids his friend's beginning-of-the-month binges, visiting him afterward.

He said the homeless people he knew liked this area near Flamingo Road and Maryland Parkway because they could fly the sign, could sleep in relative privacy and safety, and could use nearby resources like the 99 Cent Store. In addition to the library, Dave said, the Cambridge Community Center (about three blocks away) had showers and discarded things he found useful. Dave did not seem to mind using people's discarded items, even those he did not particularly like.

"I got here and somebody left a beer over here, so I went and picked it up. That's nasty. Still new—I just don't like it. It's too strong, but I'll drink it. It's free."

He described how he, Karen, and their friend usually slept in a single-file line near a building wall.

"It's pretty cool back there. Have to share it with the mice and the rats. As long as I feed them, they don't bother me."

"Really?" I said.

"Yeah. I have to leave food out and then they don't hang around all night. The first time I got bitten, I said, 'Hmm, I got to feed these guys so it keeps them busy all night, some bread or cereal or something.' I tried trapping them, but a bird got sick in one of the traps and that really pissed me off, so I cured the bird. I don't use traps anymore for mice. I don't really want to poison them, so I have to live with them."

Dave lived with mice and rats, conditions most people would describe as inhumane. But he also described techniques he had tried to keep them at a distance. His inventiveness at solving problems, like the alarm he used to protect his bag and his placing food far from his sleeping area to distract the rats, impressed me. Unlike Karen, he did not seem to think as much about how he became homeless or the appalling conditions now he faced. Dave seemed to see his immediate circumstances as facts and was trying to address his situation practically.

He then described the details of his problems with ants in the summertime.

"Feed them and they don't come on your bed. Give them food about ten feet away. Give them an old hamburger. That basically keeps them busy. The same with the roaches. You don't see them in winter."

"In the winter, it gets fairly cold in the desert," I said. "How do you stay warm?"

"More blankets—four or five blankets. Two coats, two sweaters, two pairs of pants, two socks, wear gloves, and a beanie, and the most important thing is a scarf. You need a scarf. I wake up hot because the side of the building [where I sleep] is white, and the sun comes up and it warms everything up. It's been a great winter."

:: :: :: I asked Dave about his family, and if he had communicated with them since becoming homeless.

"I've got a sister, and my dad's still alive. He's eighty-six, eighty-seven years old. About once a year I call them. And I send messages to my sister. She doesn't like me to call her very often, so I send e-mails to my cousin and she sends the message along to her. I got one child. She's twenty-three. She's a nurse. She had a baby last year."

"Does your daughter know you're here in Las Vegas?" I asked.

"No," he said, pausing for a moment before continuing. "She's married to someone I never met. Me and her mom split up when she was about five years old and I've not seen her since then. She lives in England."

Dave again mentioned being from London originally. He noted differences between the experiences homeless people have there and in Las Vegas.

"There's a lot of work [in London]," he said. "I've been homeless there. It's a different situation where you can find an empty apartment and just break in and change the lock. When the police come, if they come, you got the key to the front door. They go away and leave you alone. Most of the squats are owned by the London council. Mainly they leave the places empty because there might be a little damp on the walls, just some really stupid stuff. There's all these empty apartments. They're real nice, [you] just have to fix the plumbing, electrical work, which I can do all that stuff, fix the place up. A lot of times I had two different places, and I'd get the tourists and let them stay there for ten bucks a night. I got mattresses. And that's cheap in London, ten bucks a night."

We talked about the damp climate in England. He showed me his dry skin and the numerous cuts on his hands. He said he washes them regularly and they crack. I asked if he had other health problems.

"I have a bad hip. Sometimes it hurts, but it doesn't really bother me enough to go see a doctor. I had bronchitis last year. I waited nine hours in the emergency room to get a prescription for antibiotics. I took them and it went away. It wasn't any emergency. In England, you don't have to wait that long. But here, there's so many patients and not enough doctors or something."

Soon Karen approached us.

"Here you go, dear," Dave said, returning her backpack. They seemed to be done holding their sign and decided to leave. I gave them a few dollars, and I thanked them for talking with me.

DISCUSSION

Karen and Dave shared important information with me about how they lived far from the homeless corridor in Las Vegas. Their descriptions of their activities and their lives in this area of the city (particularly Dave's descriptions) parallel the findings of other researchers that long-term homeless people frequently avoid or only sporadically use charitable programs, coming up with other ways to survive (Snow and Anderson 1993).

Karen did not talk with me in the same way Dave did. Different interviewees would reveal their lives to me on different levels and at different speeds. I had interrupted her when she was flying the sign, and unlike Dave, she seemed to emphasize her problems and victimization. These might have been stories she kept in her mind while trying to solicit donations—they certainly reaffirmed her "presentation of self" as someone needing help while on the street with her sign.

To some extent, homelessness can become a role that an individual might "perform" for a desired effect (Marcus 2006). Erving Goffman coined the term *impression management* to describe how individuals try to manage the effect they have on a given audience (Goffman 1959; 1961b). Someone like Karen might work at delivering a credible performance, on the street corner with her sign, as a homeless person who needs money. Marcus has also noted how some black homeless men feel they must present themselves in particular ways to access social services. In particular, Marcus notes that one transitional housing interview required such men "to be perfect inmates and perfectly homeless" (2006, 31). For some homeless people, emphasizing disabilities and problems becomes a key to subsistence through charity.

Although such a "presentation of self" can be based in fact, it can also become a dominant filter through which a person sees the world and thus defines him or herself. By emphasizing her loss of several family members, being the victim of theft, being entrapped by the police, and being involuntarily committed to a mental health facility, Karen might now be experiencing role engulfment, which "prevents individuals from distancing themselves from their role" (Snow and Anderson 1993, 297). Ironically, she might feel that she now is her role and that her acceptance of the role is her major strategy for survival. However, Karen also contrasted herself with other people nearby who were flying the sign but who weren't homeless, people who she implied were con artists. She seemed to stress that her poverty and victimization were real and authentic, while others stories or appearances of poverty might not be.

The possibility of role engulfment by homeless people raises disturbing questions about how embodying a role like homelessness reproduces the condition, so much so that the person shifts his or her strategies from trying to end homelessness to simply subsisting. In this manner, Karen seems engaged in behavior that is the opposite of Ricky's and Ron's attempts to pass as having housing or being tourists and eventually trying to escape homelessness (see chapter 1). People like Karen, then, might need not only supportive housing but also help to develop a more positive sense of self.

Dave, on the other hand, seemed less concerned about explaining his homelessness to an audience to gain sympathy. Instead of describing reasons he was unable to work and relating a series of hardships as did Karen, Dave stated rather directly that he didn't much like the type of work he could get. He had been homeless before in England and had currently been homeless in Las Vegas for over a year. Dave suggested that, between troubles getting a work visa, his dislike of repetitive activities, and his age, he was outside the traditional economy in Las Vegas. He seemed to be an alcoholic but said he did not want to "be like them anymore." Although some of his family relations were tenuous, he had other relatives locally whom he visited. He pursued inexpensive leisure at a local casino and the public library between panhandling stints. Homelessness defined him in some ways, but he also defined his lifestyle and the ways he could live more comfortably while homeless.

Dave seemed to indicate that he and Karen were aware of the resources centralized in the homeless corridor but did not like that environment and did not want to be controlled or restricted by homeless shelters. By sharing resources and looking out for each other, Karen and Dave survived through tactics such as using other public resources (the community center and library), scavenging, begging, and sleeping outside. Their survival, though, meant risking health problems (food poisoning, infection, and exposure to the elements), as well as arrest for the city ordinances they violated every day.

It seemed that Karen and Dave were in a conflict primarily with the government of Las Vegas and its laws. They both wanted to avoid the unsavory conditions of the homeless corridor, but to survive while doing so meant engaging in illegal practices such as sleeping on other's property and violating traffic laws. They each seemed a bit too old, too disabled, or simply too uninterested to try to find work that paid a living wage. The city government's laws criminalizing homelessness, though, seemed designed to ultimately force people like them to use the services of and reside in the homeless corridor. Though their plight and survival strategies appeared to be well established, it seemed as though time, the elements, and the law were all against them.

I wondered how long they could continue in such a vulnerable state.

Maintaining Friendships

MARCO AND MANNY

Marco and Manny are friends. Marco is a middle-aged Hispanic male recently separated from his wife in Florida. He works in a fast food restaurant. Manny is an unemployed white male in his sixties. Their story suggests how they support their masculinity while homeless and the challenges homeless people face in maintaining friendships with each other. They also showed me how homeless people can remain friends while pursuing different goals. Homeless friends at various times help and hurt each other through companionship rooted in their vulnerable state, but without being able to offer each other material or emotional stability. Marco and Manny also helped me think about my own role as a researcher and why I felt good hanging out with their small group of homeless friends.

In mid-March 2006 I began regularly visiting Huntridge Circle Park (also known as Circle Park) near the corner of Maryland Parkway and Charleston Boulevard, approximately two miles from the homeless corridor in a residential neighborhood. The park had been attracting many homeless people in the afternoons since Gail Sacco, a retired restaurant owner who had moved to Las Vegas from Massachusetts, began distributing free food there every afternoon.

In early 2006, the *Las Vegas Sun* reported that Las Vegas Marshals watched Sacco distribute the food for weeks, keeping careful track of the number of people she was serving. On February 19, 2006, Sacco was issued a citation for holding a gathering of more than twenty-five people in the park without a permit. The *Sun* also reported that the marshals banned her from returning to the park for six months. When the state American

Civil Liberties Union representatives heard about these written and verbal charges, they became involved. In particular, they said that because Sacco had not yet been convicted of any crime, a ban from the park would be unconstitutional (Pratt 2006).

Sacco still made the food for people in the park that spring, but other volunteers distributed it while she stood and observed from a nearby parking lot. That is where I met Marco on March 17, standing in the free food line. He was a forty-three-year-old married Hispanic male who had come to Las Vegas five months earlier. His wife lived in Orlando, Florida, with his son. He had dark, close-set eyes and curly jet-black hair with traces of gray around his ears.

He was around five foot six and spoke carefully in a gentle voice. He mentioned a friend of his in Las Vegas, an older white man named Manny, with whom he shared resources. "When I have money, I give it to Manny so he can get a bus pass," he told me. "Other than that, I hang out alone."

Marco had a house in Orlando. He left because he had separated from his wife and wanted a fresh start. While in Las Vegas he first worked at a Wendy's. The fast food restaurant chain had employed him once before, as a manager in New York City. The local Wendy's even offered him a manager's job, but he said he turned it down because he just wanted to be on the line crew. He makes $8.50 an hour.

During our first discussion, Marco complains that he often calls his son who has been left alone: Marco's wife isn't properly supervising him. When I ask him what his future plans are, he says his goal is to make sure his son has regular supervision and eventually, once he has a place to stay, to have his son come to Las Vegas. I ask him when he plans to get his son. "I'm going back to Orlando April 26," he replies, or in about five weeks.

On being homeless in Las Vegas, Marco says what so many others have: "You can eat and drink here. You won't starve. When I've been on Fremont, sometimes you don't have to ask. People will just say, 'Are you hungry?' and offer you food."

I ask him about his schedule. "I work from 6 P.M. to 2 A.M.," he tells me. "I get off work at 2 A.M. and sleep on the bus. Then, after seven, I can sleep in Frank Wright Plaza." Working such a late shift means he cannot access most shelters in Las Vegas because of their curfew rules. By the end of our first conversation, he says he would not want to use most of the services in the homeless corridor anyway.

"The Salvation Army up there is very rude, and they used to be [in the same situation] where we were," he tells me, shaking his head. He seems to be wondering how previously homeless people, who often help run such shelters, could so easily mistreat those who are currently homeless.

:: :: :: Two days later I meet Marco's friend, Manny, in Frank Wright Plaza. I felt like I already knew Manny from Marco's description. Manny is in his mid-sixties and has brown eyes. A Boston Red Sox baseball cap covers his white hair. His face is weathered like a fisherman's, and he speaks like a New Englander. Manny is thin but looks tough for his age. After we talk, Manny packs his blanket and other items into his large duffel bag. We travel by bus to meet Marco at the Rescue Mission for their five o'clock dinner.

Marco is in line already, and we all stand together. Marco says he now wants to leave for Orlando on Monday. He quit working at Wendy's, he says initially, because they began questioning him to see if he was homeless—he thinks they grew suspicious because he always carries a backpack and sometimes looks unkempt. He asks me about cities he can go to where being homeless is better—he's heard good things about Seattle, Santa Fe, Santa Monica, and Albuquerque. I tell him my sister in Seattle recently said that they had had forty days of continuous rain. I ask him how he picked these cities. He says they were the ones he could afford one-way tickets to by Greyhound Bus.

The line to enter the soup kitchen moves rapidly, with ten people allowed to enter at a time. Marco and I get in before Manny does, and we become separated. Once inside we quickly shuffle through the line to receive our food and try to find space together at the long, cafeteria-styled tables. Marco and I eat together at one of a few spaces open for two, while I continue to look around for Manny. I watch him enter and then sit with others, but without talking. Eventually there is room beside Manny for all of us.

When Marco and Manny ask me why I'm not eating more, I say that I feel guilty eating food meant for poor people. Manny admonishes me, saying that probably 10 to 20 percent of the people eating with us can afford their own food and aren't homeless. He says some of them live in the neighborhood or perhaps work nearby and come by for a convenient, free meal. I suspect he is right but I still only eat my one bowl of split pea soup without the bread or milk at our table.

Marco says he is going back for more. I think he means he will go back to the kitchen area where they are dispensing the soup, so I am confused when he doesn't return. I realize I must have misunderstood him—he was instead going outside where volunteers were giving away loaves of bread, bananas that are going brown, and past-expiration-date baked goods and sandwiches. Marco has told me to pick up a sandwich and bread for Manny when I leave—they are being distributed outside of the soup kitchen—and I do. "Take as much as you want," a man near the bread says, but other volunteers limit everyone to one sandwich and one bakery item. I get Manny a ham sandwich and four bran muffins. I am not sure he will want them, but I am sure that someone in Frank Wright Plaza will.

As I am getting the baked goods and leaving, I see Marco in line, marching back toward the cafeteria. I hadn't realized that getting an extra helping of soup tonight required him to go through the outside line again. I later guess that this process is not a mean-spirited way of treating poor people but just ensures that everyone who comes from outside has a chance of getting at least one bowl of soup. Otherwise, the first people to arrive might consume several bowls, while those last in line would get nothing. Of course, I could be wrong. Perhaps the rules tonight are simply tradition, or were made up by whoever happened to be on staff that evening. People in shelter positions, like this afternoon's food distribution and security jobs, are often homeless themselves. The people in those jobs come and go. In fact, it really doesn't matter why Marco has to return to the line this early evening for another bowl of soup. What matters is that if he wants one, he has to do it.

:: :: :: I wait for Manny and Marco outside the iron gates. Pigeons feast on the ample bread thrown on the street. Sometimes the pigeons eat bread that people inside the gates seem to have thrown to watch them scurry. A couple of men near me are trying to trade their sandwiches with passersby for nearly anything, including a single cigarette. Nobody wants to trade.

Marco comes through the gate first. We sit and talk on the concrete sidewalk, watching the pigeons and people. He tells me he was not quite honest before. He now says he quit his job because he had been dating three women who worked with him and that the situation had become increasingly impossible. I am suddenly trying to visualize Marco as a Don Juan—I chuckle along with him while this soft-spoken man describes his romantic adventures with each woman, noting the pros and cons of dating each and proclaiming his innocence in this tangled web. He says each woman led him to believe that their relationship was over, which is why he began dating the next. Marco describes one of them as crazy, one as a party girl, and one as an intelligent woman who has a daughter and is waiting patiently for him to come to his senses and decide that she is his best match. I sympathize, saying that workplace romances are easy to start but hellish when they go bad. He nods.

I realize Manny and I are just hanging out, talking guy talk, and it feels good. I feel as though our previous roles, a homeless man and a researcher, are no longer preeminent. I feel in the moment. We are sharing, like friends. I think that Marco is beginning to like me and that I like him.

Manny emerges, stuffed. When I give him my sandwich and muffins, he thanks me, saying someone in the park will be happy tonight.

We walk several blocks back to my bus stop near the depot. We pass homeless camps by an overpass, railroad tracks, and piles of trash, and we discuss how depressing such surroundings are. Manny notes Nevada's high suicide rate. Marco starts talking about the depression he has dealt with for years. He says his doctor has him on medication but at times he still feels depressed and impulsive. He thinks about suicide, sometimes getting sad very quickly, and is afraid because he might kill himself on impulse. He has thought about running into traffic, which echoes the way in which Bruce (from chapter 4) described how he might kill himself. He says if he ever does commit suicide, he knows it will be sudden.

People often consider suicide, not because they truly want to die, but because they want an escape from their pain or problems. When Marco describes his suicidal impulses, I begin seeing a pattern of impulsivity in his behavior. I think about how he seems to have trouble sticking to a plan. He changed his mind within days about moving back to Florida, a major life decision. He can't seem to commit to one woman. But I also wonder if the stress of his situation breeds impulsivity. Great discomfort demands action. A key to mental health is having a feeling of control. I am left wondering how many of his problems are rooted in personal characteristics and how many come from being in a negative, unsupportive environment.

As we part ways at the bus stop, I give Manny and Marco some money for coffee. Marco asks if he will see me before he leaves. I say that I hope so and that I plan to stop by Frank Wright Plaza again before his Monday departure. We shake hands.

On the bus ride home, facing the sun's setting rays, I think about my time bonding with Manny and Marco. Unlike Jessi's friends in the park, Manny and Marco don't want me to steal anything, and I don't have to drink to hang out with them. It's comfortable. I feel happy.

:: :: :: In mid-April I see Marco at Circle Park, which surprises me. He is waiting in line for food. I ask him why he hasn't left town. He said he was planning on it but that his wallet and cell phone were stolen. He really needs his cell phone back to call his son, who says he is "going crazy" because he hasn't heard from him.

Marco says he needs to take a shower at his gym, where he pays fifteen dollars a month for membership—he hasn't showered in two days. Before leaving and while eating two plates of beans and rice, he says he wants to tell me something. The real reason he left his job at Wendy's, he now says, is because he had a seizure. He is bipolar and hasn't kept up with his medication. He said that after he had the seizure, his boss told him to take some time off to get well.

He recently spoke with his former manager at Wendy's when he came to get his check. When he said he was interested in better pay and management opportunities, the manager worked with him, offering him a better job at another branch as an assistant manager. Marco took it.

Marco then pointed out and told me the name of his new friend Eric, who was sleeping on the grass, and another friend named Greg from Frank Wright Plaza, who is still asleep. They have all recently found work together distributing fliers. The advertising company they work for pays eight cents a flier—they want the fliers to be distributed in neighborhood apartment complexes, with each placed on an apartment's front door. Eric and Marco tell me that if each of them can distribute 1,000 fliers in one night from midnight to 7 A.M., each man can make eighty dollars.

Greg begins waking up—he has been sleeping in the park grass in shorts and a T-shirt, and says he is freezing. I have no idea how long he was asleep, but I am surprised he could manage to sleep outside at all: It has been a windy afternoon with occasional slight rain. Eric and Marco are doubtful that Greg can distribute many fliers because of his health problems, but Greg is adamant he can do it.

Greg asks me for money to buy a coat from the nearby Savers thrift store, and I give him five dollars. I also tell him I saw an abandoned sweater on a nearby park table, beside the food being given away. He puts the sweater on, and its sequined pattern and tight fit make everyone laugh. When I suggest that he could wear it inside out, he tries it, and the resulting blue-green and black pattern is deemed acceptable. Greg leaves to get an early start on distributing the fliers.

Marco leaves, and while I wait for his return I interview Eric. Eric is newly homeless and finds many of his new experiences strange. Like many recently homeless people, he seems unnerved at how his new acquaintances live and by much of what he has seen in the last few days (Snow and Anderson 1993). Marco comes back and prepares to take a nap on the grass before his night's work distributing fliers.

As I start to depart, Marco walks me to the bus stop and asks me for $75. He says it's half of the money that he needs for a replacement cell phone. I ask him why he needs a replacement instead of simply getting a new one, and he says that he has signed a contract on the old number and would lose his plan. I sympathize but say I don't have the money. Marco is understanding and apologizes for having to ask. He says that he will have to make sacrifices but that he can get the $150 for the bill by Monday if he works hard.

As I get on the bus, I feel stupid about having just turned Marco down. He wasn't requesting a life-altering amount of money from me, but I rationalized that if I got a reputation for giving out $75 at a time simply when someone asked for it, I could be getting a lot of requests. Before leaving I told him that he could use the five dollars I gave him earlier for a phone card. Thinking about this on the bus, I felt like I was trying to soothe my own conscience instead of helping him.

I felt Marco, Manny, and I were becoming friends. At other times, I realized I was drawing a boundary on the parameters of our friendship, returning to a researcher role. That inconsistency, I later realized, would characterize most of our time together.

:: :: :: The next day at around 4 P.M. I run into Greg on Owens Avenue. His face seems puffy. He is still wearing the same shorts from yesterday, and I see that his legs are swollen and red. He says he paid five dollars to sleep in one of the day beds at the Salvation Army—he's just slept nine hours straight, which must mean he was exhausted, since it is not a particularly quiet place. He feels horrible after having delivered the fliers last night. He shuffles as much as walks.

He was only able to distribute 400 fliers yesterday—he says he just couldn't do the rest.

"There's a reason I'm on disability," he says simply. "I'm disabled."

He is now going to return the other 600 he is carrying in his bag so that he can get some money for his efforts. I tell him I'm going up to the Rescue Mission in hopes of running into Marco and Eric in the soup line.

"You won't see Eric up there," he declares. "He'd rather starve than eat at a place like that."

Before we part he tells me about his experience with what he and his friends usually abbreviate as the Mission.

"I ate up there one time. I had diarrhea for three days," he says. "I spent more money on toilet paper than I would have buying a dinner."

When I arrive at the Mission, no one I know is in line. I had thought about Greg's story on my bus ride here. I decide to go home.

:: :: :: Two days later, I go see Marco, Manny, and Eric at Frank Wright Plaza in the late afternoon. They seem to be hanging out, killing time. Manny is just waking up, rolling off of the cardboard that protects him from the gravel underneath. It takes him a while to get oriented. He has a strong case of sunburn, mainly evident from the red skin around his eyes and on his eyelids. They decide to go the Mission for dinner. Manny calls the group "the boys," and when I ask the boys if I can come along, they say they're delighted to have me. I don't really feel self-conscious around them, maybe because they don't seem self-conscious around me. It feels great hanging out with them—they simply seem like decent, friendly, intelligent guys with some personal difficulties.

I began realizing that much of my time with homeless people over the last year in Las Vegas has been spent in a researcher role. The role constrained me. Because of my conception of that role, I allowed some aspects of my personality to emerge while suppressing others. Thinking I was constrained by the role of researcher at times left me feeling alienated from the very people I was trying to understand.

It takes Manny a good while to get his bags packed. We help him with the zipper of his overfilled duffel bag. Marco and Eric stand patiently for several minutes, saying nothing. They are true friends, I think. They like Manny and realize he isn't intentionally trying to hold them up—he's just older. I don't think they are judging Manny. It also reminds me, though, that being homeless involves a lot of waiting.

:: :: :: On the walk to Bonanza Road, Manny talks homeless politics. He says he wants to start a homeless tour in the city. He is unsure about the rate he wants to charge, at first suggesting $100, then $150 per person, and is wondering how to get started. I mention that he might want to try contacting the Las Vegas Convention and Visitors Bureau, but we agree they might not want to promote a tour that tarnishes the image of the city. We both think, though, that tourists should see this side of Las Vegas. Manny considers all the places he could walk someone through in a day.

I talk with Eric and Marco. They couldn't deliver as many of the fliers as they wanted to the other night because Eric became sick soon after I saw them on Friday. He was throwing up and said he hadn't really eaten for two days. Now his face is sunburned as well. He has mainly been recovering in the park. Marco delivered what he could of the fliers, but the number came nowhere near reaching their goal of 1,000.

We get to the Mission. The line wraps around the building, and even Manny seems surprised. He says the line was half as long two months ago and wonders aloud where all these people have come from.

Eric is suspiciously quiet. I realize that he is now waiting for food at the Mission. Only two days earlier, Greg had said that Eric would starve first before going there. I think that Greg had been partially right: Eric seemed to have starved for two days before going there.

While standing in line, Marco starts to read a book but then puts it away, saying how tired he is. Sometimes people in the line get sick of standing when no one is moving, and they temporarily sit or lie down. Although a brief rest is tempting, I've seen people in this line become very impatient if someone isn't standing up instantly when the line suddenly starts moving. We stand next to a chain-link fence, and Marco grabs a piece of it where he stands, first with one hand, and then with the other. His eyes start to open and close, fighting back the throes of sleep. I watch casually, but in mild disbelief. He finally succumbs, leaning against the fence slightly, steadied by his hands wrapped like claws through the fence holes. His head hangs slightly as he sleeps while standing for a minute at a time.

:: :: :: As the line moves forward around the corner, an attractive woman, braless and wearing a white T-shirt, walks by. The men in line turn around one after another, like a line of dominoes falling, as she passes. The four of us wait for her to go by, then look back at her with a smile or raised eyebrow. Manny then looks at our group, nods slightly, and slowly says, "Nice," in his Maine accent. We all smile and laugh. I feel good having heard this from a sixty-plus-year-old man. It's the same feeling I had with Marco when he spoke about his girlfriends. We are men acknowledging an attractive woman after she passes. We are establishing a shared interest and appreciating one another's good taste, just as I did with Ron and Ricky. I realize these are moments defined, not by homelessness, but by hetero-sexual male friendship—men defined as a status in relation to another group, women. I find in those moments I completely lose my self-aware-ness of being a researcher, of being the only person in this group who has a home. I feel included. Being with the boys feels normal.

This incident was important because our shared, pleasurable reaction to the woman passing by seemed to suggest a key aspect of homelessness for men: It is emasculating. Homeless men have failed at their traditional role as breadwinners (Snow and Anderson 1993). They are not independent and self-sufficient; they are seen (and might see themselves) as having nothing to offer a woman; they are often forced to live in sex-segregated quarters within shelters; and they might have difficulty maintaining personal hygiene. Hanging out together, though, can allow homeless men to forget all these troubles for a while, reaffirming one another's masculinity. It gave us all a chance to share a fun moment and to feel good. Even the most marginal homeless man can, without any cost, describe the things he likes about women or how a woman hurt him and will immediately have a shared point of reference with many other men. Together, homeless male friends can reaffirm one another's status as sexual, capable, and desirable, against the dominant image of homeless men as incapable, undesirable, or asexual.

:: :: :: Inside the Mission, we sit apart again because there are so few spaces. I see Marco can get two bowls of soup today, and Manny does the same. Eric seems to be eating slowly. Outside at the free food table I collect a Hostess pastry, an orange, a mango, and bread. I then wait with Eric for the others.

On the walk back to the bus depot, Eric says he doesn't feel well. We all agree that he looks a little ill. He says he wants to go to the University Medical Center of Southern Nevada for antibiotics and asks what bus will get him closest. I tell him which bus line should take him within a few blocks, and he asks me for fifty cents for the fare. I give him five dollars, and he thanks me profusely, saying, "I'll pay you back for this." I tell him not to worry about it. He thinks he will have to wait there all night to be seen and get the medicine. Because he thinks that he won't get back to camp before daybreak, Eric tells us all good night.

When we return to the downtown, I give Manny and Marco five dollars each, and they are thrilled. They wanted to just get a coffee but now want to go to a convenience store just off of the Fremont Street Experience to get cigarettes. At the shop Manny buys a very cheap pack for a $1.18. When I tell him I didn't realize a pack of cigarettes could be so inexpensive, he explains that they are actually several cigars that "you can still smoke like cigarettes."

We walk to the Plaza Hotel. Manny and Marco get a coffee at the McDonald's inside. They explain that the senior discount price for coffee, which Manny can order, is 53 cents and that, if they're lucky, Manny can order for both men, making their total bill $1.06. When Marco shows me their receipt, I notice that it lists the condiments and the amounts of each that was requested ("four cream," "four sugar"). Marco tells me they track the condiments and keep them behind the counter to control their distribution. "If you order more than four of either condiment," Marco says, "you have to pay a dime extra." The printed receipt also notes the time when the order was placed. Manny and Marco are each entitled to one free refill, but only within a half-hour of their first order. We talk while they occasionally note the time. Manny has to hurry to finish his coffee within the allotted period to get his second cup.

It strikes me that we had just come from a charity where past-date food was being given away. Having now walked twenty minutes to a McDonald's on the Fremont Street Experience, there are buffets all around us where food will likely go to waste. The McDonald's managers want the store to make a profit, but it seemed petty to me that they would track the condiment use of paying customers. The McDonald's would also likely be throwing away food that night. Marco and Manny are literally trying to save pennies on small purchases like coffee. The poverty and excess around us, and the value of things such as food, began to appear oddly arbitrary to me.

Manny and Marco also ask me to help them pick up all their trash. They both believe that they are allowed to come in and sit at this McDonald's because they pick up their trash after they are done—they leave their area the same as they found it. Here Manny and Marco indicate a self-consciousness about needing to keep their surroundings clean, one similar to that shown by Melissa, Cory, Karen, and Dave, whom I met at the intersection of Maryland Parkway and Flamingo Road (see chapters 5 and 9).

It strikes me as important that neither Manny nor Marco feels they should be allowed to come in and sit at McDonald's, even though they are paying customers. They are concerned about being refused service. I think about how, at McDonald's restaurants around the nation, millions of customers buy food and leave trash at their tables without worrying about whether they could ever return. Observing Manny, Marco, and Eric also suggested to me how little each man had—that receiving five dollars made their night and that they used the money for simple things like paying for a bus ride, cigarettes, and coffee.

:: :: :: I see Manny again, along with his friend Scott, on April 24 at Frank Wright Plaza. A few days earlier an article on my research had been published in the *Las Vegas Sun*, and Scott, one of the guys in the park, says it was pretty good. Scott gives Manny a loaf of bread so Manny can make Spam sandwiches. Scott says that he tried begging various storeowners for a loaf but that nobody would give him one, so he bought it.

They eat several sandwiches while Scott shows me a recent article in the paper that carries the claims by Mayor Oscar Goodman that he has done more for the homeless than anyone and that if homeless people were asked who had done the most to help them, they would point to the mayor and say, "Him." Scott calls this a lie. In response, Scott wants to stage a protest on the Strip by having several homeless people block traffic, showing the mayor how wrong he is. He says that the time is coming for some type of action, that homeless people are tired of being mistreated here.

:: :: :: In late April 2006, I ask Marco if he would be willing to try an experiment. I give him a disposable camera and ask him to take photos of his everyday life and experiences as a homeless person. I say that afterward, I would like to interview him about the photos. I promise to give him a copy of the photographs. He agrees to take the pictures.

A few days later, we discuss several of the photographs. He took one of Manny and me posing in front of the Walgreen's store by the Fremont Street Experience where we bought the disposable camera.

KURT: What does this photo have to do with homelessness or your life right now?
MARCO: It reminds me of, where I'm at right now. Looking at Manny, he's a typical guy, like us, like me.
KURT: He's typical . . .
MARCO: Homeless . . . like what I'm going through right now.
KURT: What do you feel when you look at the photo?
MARCO: I'd like to be in a better position. But when I look at the picture, when I look at Manny, reality hits me in the face. Reminds me of where I'm at.
KURT: Reality hits you?
MARCO: Yeah. You know you think of taking a picture, and being on the Fremont Experience is like, an experience. You want it to be with your family and your

friends, you want a place to stay. You go home, you get to go home [Manny says while looking right at me]. We don't. That's the reality of it, the difference.

Another photo was of Marco and Manny. Marco had asked me to take that one, from the opposite direction. I asked him why he wanted me to take this photo.

MARCO: It reminds me of being with him. We share a lot of things, we do a lot of things together. He's the only guy that really, [I] can't have no complaints about. He's just straight up. He don't look at my situation and make judgment about me.

KURT: You don't judge each other?

MARCO: No. In my mind, it captures the whole Fremont Experience. I guess it kind of takes me to where I wanna be one day. Like, you take the two pictures here.

KURT: Um hum . . .

MARCO: You take another set of pictures when I have a place already. . . . You'll see that I'll be smiling more in the pictures than now.

KURT: What do you feel when you look at the photo?

MARCO: Sad.

KURT: Really?

MARCO: Because I can't, I cannot picture this, other than what my life is already. I would like to picture, like, friends, having a good time outside, and we are. But then reality hits us. And I don't know whether Manny talks about it, or whether he expresses it to you or whether he expresses it aloud, what he feels about homelessness. But I don't like it. Not my personal thing. Manny never, never expresses how he feels. Sometimes it's just like [homelessness is] normal or something.

We look at another photo, one of Marco, Manny, and me on the Fremont Street Experience. He looks at me and says it's a picture "with a good friend." I smile and thank him. Then he discusses other thoughts.

MARCO: It's a constant reminder. When I look at these pictures tonight when I'm alone, like, a lot of things will go through my mind. I just now concentrate on the pictures and say "Whoa, I wish I was better. I wish I was somebody who I want to be." One day when I get on my feet and I look at these pictures I'll say, "Wow, I remember when I used to be there."

KURT: So the photo is like documenting a part of your life now?

MARCO: Yeah, yeah. It's like, I could look back and say, "That was when I was homeless." I mean, reality, if you showed these pictures to anybody, I don't think they would notice that I'm homeless.

KURT: Oh, you mean by how you're dressed?

MARCO: Yeah. Or even Manny for that matter. Apart from that . . . [pointing]

KURT: Apart from the bag that he's carrying . . .

MARCO: Yeah.

Another photo we discussed was of Neonopolis, a small courtyard with a movie theater, restaurants, and a bowling alley adjoining the FSE.

MARCO: I go in there and watch the movies they have, for like, five dollars. So I have seen a lot of good movies in there, and also they have a church there on Sunday. Sometimes I go there for the service, and they give you coffee or doughnuts. It's in the theater. So I wanted to capture it, because it reminded me of good moments.

I ask him what the photo has to do with his homelessness.

MARCO: I can remember going in there. They never know if I'm homeless. I can go in and enjoy myself, just be part of society, watch a movie, with nobody bothering me. Just being like a normal person in there, nobody knows that you're homeless watching a movie. It makes you forget your problems for a while, for like two hours and a half.

KURT: How do you feel when you see this photo?

MARCO: Happy. Content with like, what I see. I knew I wanted to take a picture. And not because you were going to interview me or anything, I just saw it.

At several points in this interview Marco expresses feelings that he is judged negatively for being homeless, and in particular that he judges himself negatively. He seems to say that he enjoys escaping the judgment for a while by seeing a movie or attending church, when he can briefly return to being a "normal person." He says he looks forward to a time when he will feel "better" because he will "have a place," a time when he will "be smiling more." He has internalized negative judgments of homelessness so much that when Manny does not seem to share his view, Marco cannot understand. At one point Marco said that Manny does not judge him. Yet because Manny does not seem to consistently judge himself negatively for his homelessness, Marco seems to be judging Manny.

Marco then describes a few photos he took on Fremont Street, pictures of the lights and the people. He said he wanted to capture images of pretty girls in costumes and street performers. Like Ricky and Ron, Marco wanted to enjoy Las Vegas as tourists do on Fremont Street.

The final photo we discuss is of the Plaza, or as Marco says, "where we go for coffee, at the McDonald's."

KURT: What do you feel when you see the photo?

MARCO: It reminds me that, that's our life routine right now. After the Mission, we go there, when I'm not working. It reminds me that, I'm not on my feet right now, but after . . . don't forget, I get on my feet, you know, I'm gonna get my life back. Maybe even [be with] a woman, maybe Martha for that matter. You know, Manny, I don't know what's gonna happen with him. I mean I will always like to come back and see him, see that he's doing all right, that he's got something or whatever. That's exactly—I'm not sure what I think about that, Manny. Cause he doesn't want to, he doesn't like sharing or anything. And I just wonder about, what's gonna be . . . You know, things change.

Marco seemed to be emphasizing the shame he feels about his homelessness. He even indicates that he is going to "get my life back." He kept comparing how he looked now to how he would look in the future, when he would have housing. He wanted to go to a theater where he would be anonymous, where he would blend in. Marco also emphasized distinctions to me between himself and Manny. Marco seemed to be visualizing an end to his homelessness. But he seemed concerned with or perhaps annoyed about Manny, who he thought might not end his homelessness, who didn't share his feelings or seem to consistently judge himself by his homelessness in the same way Marco did. Because Manny did not seem to embody shame at his condition, Marco might have been implicitly justifying leaving his friend behind, on the street.

:: :: :: On May 4 I meet Manny, who is by himself at Frank Wright Plaza. We walk over to the McDonald's in the Plaza hotel for a coffee. Manny is a private person—he has told me he will talk to me about local homelessness, but in general terms, to give me his insights into the condition.

He is thinking about something that a former homeless person told him: "You've got to get to these people within the first three months. Otherwise, you've lost them to the streets." Manny thinks that his friend was right—that many of the long-term homeless people he now knows would probably be unable to function in "normal society" again. I tell him about a homeless services provider I knew who ran a program finding apartments for people who had been homeless for years. She was frustrated because some of the people she served still engaged in practices they learned while homeless, such as Dumpster diving. She said that when they brought items they found in Dumpsters into their apartments, they also carried lice and other bugs inside.

Manny responds that there are "freedoms of the street" and says that once you are homeless, you can do exactly what you want. He says that is what also makes Las Vegas so compelling for some people. "You can be an oddball," he says. "People with problems come to Las Vegas—'Come on over, you've got friends here.' Here you've got a whole bunch of crazies you can hang out with. And they begin to like it.

"The paradox is that Las Vegas advertises itself as a party town," Manny says, "and then punishes those people who come here with problems. You cannot hold out gambling, drinking, partying all the time and not expect people to be attracted to it. They say, 'Come here, do what you want, raise hell, but then leave.' Las Vegas holds out the carrot but then blames the rabbit for going after it."

I smile and think he's absolutely right. Manny and I have good conversations, ones that often remind me of other late-night talks I have had with intellectual friends and colleagues. Manny is an introvert who enjoys analytical thinking. It doesn't hurt that he looks like a thin Ernest Hemingway. His homelessness is a puzzle to me. He often refers to it as an "experiment." He sometimes mentions Eastern philosophy and meditation techniques, discussing the importance of being mindful of the present moment, of "paying attention." He says it's something most people don't do—that most people are so caught up in the past or the future that they don't pay attention to what is happening *right now*. He doesn't seem to drink or gamble, and he doesn't complain much about the deprivations or inconveniences of being homeless, or of the discomfort he must experience sleeping outside or carrying all his belongings everywhere.

He then tells me a quote he attributes to Oliver Wendell Holmes: "The average person will go to his death with his music still in him." He says

Holmes meant that the average person is oppressed by the daily grind, but has secret longings and passions. Manny says this is the appeal of Las Vegas: "The average person wants to get away from the world he or she knows—'I want to see things, find my music. I've got five kids and responsibilities, but I want to experience life.'"

Manny thinks the quote reveals why some people become homeless: They would rather not be employed for so little pay that they have no freedom. He says he could get a job within six hours that would pay him five to six dollars an hour. "But I'm still stubborn enough that I want to play *my* music, *my* violin. I want to find out what music is in me." I mention that his quote reminds me of what I think is a line from Thoreau, that "most men lead lives of quiet desperation." He confirms that it is Thoreau, and he begins describing transcendentalism, a philosophy paralleling some of the ideas he expressed earlier.

Manny says that the street has taught him that to survive, you have to give. "If you're selfish, you won't survive. People share with others because others have shared with them." When I point out the fallacy of this reasoning—that people wouldn't be able to accumulate enough resources to leave the street—he agrees. Talking about homeless people, Manny says, "It becomes a community. No man is an island. It simply could be a congregation of lonely people who met along the way through circumstances. Because of the sharing and the camaraderie, people begin to like this lifestyle."

Manny's comments caused me to wonder if some people become homeless after abandoning their previously dissatisfying lives. I thought about how contemporary life, even with its interconnectivity, can feel superficial and lonely. Putnam and Feldstein's study, *Bowling Alone*, notes that fewer Americans today engage in social and civic participation. The researchers note decades-long declines in everything from PTA membership to civic organizations to league-based sports (2000). The everyday friendship circles in contemporary life appear to be contracting as our society grows more electronically mediated and individualistic. In contrast, there was, as Manny said, camaraderie in street life. It was face-to-face, simpler, and more communal.

:: :: :: Other aspects of homelessness, Manny said, took longer to adjust to.

"When you first hit the streets, things are *so* tough. You have to carry forty-five pounds everywhere you go," he says, motioning to his bags. "You try that sometime. It's terrible at first. But now I wouldn't think, 'This is rough.' I don't even think about it. You don't think about how you can't take a shower every day, or 'my feet hurt.' Now, it's just a part of what I do. You get used to it. It becomes normal.

"When we grow up, we're so programmed," Manny says. "We grow up thinking, 'what will I be? A doctor? A fireman?' And I guarantee you, every single one of these people in the park were programmed that way. Now, some will go on to adjust the dream. I don't know what some of them will do. I will go on—I will be successful, in a better way, in another way. The experience will improve me as a human being.

"Vegas is tough because you have to break through so many barriers. You have to put up with so much degradation, humiliation. When you're homeless here you're like the wandering Jew."

Although Manny wanted to speak about homelessness in general terms, he began using personal examples.

"I was sleeping on the chairs in the DTC. I didn't know I couldn't do that. The marshals came through—they told me to stand and put my hands behind my back. They eighty-sixed me for six months. They said you cannot be inside here for more than fifteen minutes before you're catching a bus. So I asked, 'Where can I go to sleep?' And he said, 'You can go sleep over there [pointing to the park], with the rest of the bums.' That made me want to get even with these people. This constant pushing, the way they browbeat people. They're pushing people who are mentally unstable and who are hurt. And they're gonna want to get back at them. That's why I want to have a homeless convention here, where people all over the country converge here in October. It would paralyze this place. That's what I want to do. We could shut down the Strip. First, you would get some media coverage, get some leaflets. Homeless people would spread them. It's very possible that it would work."

Manny seems to be suggesting that treating people badly "who are mentally unstable and who are hurt" is heartless. His complaints are not about material deprivation as much as mistreatment by authority figures.

He seems to say that it's enough that some people are homeless; further degrading those people, especially those who are mentally unstable and hurt, will only hurt them more. He is also angry and thinking of ways to communicate his hurt to others so they will take notice and enact changes.

"Now, where does this idea come from?" Manny says about his plan. "It comes from anger, from being called a bum when you don't even know me. I have no argument with the practical ordinances and laws here. The reason you can't stretch out on a bench is that this is a public park—everyone should be able to use it. These laws are practical. When guys leave a mess behind, they're ruining it for everybody. But the guy who says, 'You have no rights. Go sleep with the rest of the bums,' that is wrong."

Manny makes a strong case that the civil rights of homeless people are regularly violated and that authorities do so because they know they can get away with it.

::   ::   ::   I ask him about his everyday life and activities.

"I'm not as concerned with long-term goals now," Manny says. "I don't think about that programming, having 2.6 kids and all that. [When you're homeless] you're always thinking of immediate needs—'I need $1.25 for a bus pass, I need a new pair of shoes.' You need to see yourself clear of want."

I think about how Manny constantly fights off immediate wants. Homeless people are an entire category of humans who never get ahead of their wants, for whom real comfort is perpetually out of reach.

"People are always thinking, 'These homeless people are so depressed, they always have their heads down,'" he tells me. "They don't know that we're *working*, looking for quarters."

Manny also expresses a Zen-like attitude toward his homelessness. At times he argues for worldly asceticism and transcendence as keys to personal enlightenment.

"I'm always thinking about bringing the mind back, working on positive imagery. I call it practicing. You have to spend time every day practicing, working on mental concentration. If you *practice* a great deal, you can be above the fray. There is very little in this life to be upset about. I try to be cool, like Cool Hand Luke. You hear about road rage and all these things these days. People just have to cool out. The mind should be practical. That way, you can stop focusing on the garbage."

Manny says that most homeless people have personal problems that have landed them in trouble.

"When somebody in the park tells you, 'I got two weeks in jail for jay-walking,' you're getting about one-third of the story. They probably jay-walked, had an open container or were drunk, and mouthed off to the officer. If you say 'yes sir, no sir,' you'll get some leniency. You really have to beg for the truth of the matter and the whole story.

"On Fremont Street, they call me 'Move On.' I'm Mr. Move On. Security is able to use a valid law, impeding pedestrian flow, to sanitize the area and get their way. They're able to use valid ordinances, you end up in court, and you get time served. No one [who is homeless] has the money to fight it.

"Homelessness should make you braver, should make you say, 'Why not give it a try?' But people don't become free because people don't get down to the issue of what they're thinking. People who come to Las Vegas think they're going to be free, but the minute they get here the doors are shut. [If you're homeless] your freedom is gone when you hit Las Vegas. The tourist is free, but [for homeless people here] for the first time there's no 'God Bless America' or 'Life, Liberty, and the Pursuit of Happiness' for you."

In a later conversation, Manny challenged those who have said to him that if he doesn't like the way homeless people are treated in Las Vegas, he should leave.

"Why is it that everyone else in the U.S. is entitled to freedom of movement and relocation except for homeless people?" he asked. "And why is it that once homeless people are here, they are told accept it or leave it, rather than possibly trying to help them become part of the community and trying to change it?"

:: :: :: A few days later in the first week of May I visit Manny and his friend Ed at Frank Wright Plaza. They want to get coffee at the Plaza, but first Manny hides his blanket at the bottom of a metal trash barrel in the park, between the barrel and the plastic bag. Manny and Scott have told me that one of the biggest problems homeless people have is storing their stuff; sometimes when it is stashed in public places, it gets found and stolen or thrown out.

During our conversation at the Plaza, Manny says the corporate culture around us emphasizes *protection*—the need for insurance for health and safety, protection from crime, from weather, and from other problems.

The logic of protection says save money and be careful. "Money is your safety—we're all taught this. You're raised on a diet of investment plans, insurance plans, warnings, [teaching you to] 'be careful.' Homeless people have no protection," he says, smiling.

I point out that this idea plays into the logic of conservatives who could say that homeless people then represent a lesson—that they embody a warning about what can happen to you if you don't work hard and acquire material protection. Manny counters by pointing out how homelessness can happen to anyone.

"Irrespective of how much stock, insurance, or investments you have, what happens if something happens to the mind, to the body?" he says. "The mind can be very fragile. The right group of setbacks can bring you down."

He returns to the Oliver Wendell Holmes quote.

"It makes a person ask, Is there something else I could have done? Are there different things I would have liked to do, another path I would have enjoyed? Coming to Las Vegas allows people to hear the music inside them—they can do what they really want to do. The *warnings* don't apply in Las Vegas—that's the music, a reprieve from the warnings."

I realize that a few days earlier, Marco was telling me that even though he and Manny are both homeless, I shouldn't think they are the same. Marco, ashamed of his homelessness and wanting to end it, sees it as oppressive. Manny seems to be suggesting that his homelessness is a form of freedom.

He talks more about what draws people to Las Vegas.

"This is the city of final release—this is heaven," Manny tells me. "'I can let it all go, let it all hang out.'"

"There's a lot of hell here, too," I reply.

"They're very close," he adds. "There's a lot of heaven in hell and a lot of hell in heaven," he says, smiling. "There's a constant pushing of images designed to lead a person to excess. They come here to experience this, to gain that elusive, brief sense of hope."

I think about Manny's idea that Las Vegas represents heaven and promise, optimism and paradise: how there are so many blue, heavenlike skies painted in the interiors of shopping malls and resort casinos on the Las Vegas Strip. It seems like you can always find blue skies in Las Vegas, but many of them are indoors and illusory. And therein lies the deception, the hell.

:: :: :: Ed has quietly sat through our discussion. When Ed goes off to use the bathroom, Manny tells me more about him. Ed had a normal life until he took too many drugs and had a bad trip. Ed told Manny that one night he got into a huge fight with his former girlfriend and then overdosed. Now Ed has very little short-term memory. Manny says, "You look at a lot of the homeless, and there's a lot of damage there—physical, emotional. It's not all irreparable damage, but many people are damaged."

"Homelessness is the little cancer that Las Vegas has," he continues. "The vast majority of people here don't know how badly homeless people here are treated."

He makes one napkin descend onto another to illustrate his next point about changing class distinctions within a range of income.

"This one represents the lower class, and this one represents the homeless. As the lower class has less and less, more and more will become homeless." He says that more and more people will be fighting for fewer and fewer material resources and that the measures people will have to take to survive will become more and more extreme.

We talk about how rich this country is compared to most and that millions of people would love to come here. Even if you face dire poverty here, Manny says, it is so much easier than in so many immigrant's home countries:

"Most Americans have no idea how poor much of the world is," he says. "They travel to Paris and they see the Eiffel Tower, or they go to London and see the changing of the guard. They don't see how people live in Africa. For people coming here from the poorest countries in the world, being homeless here would be the equivalent of you staying at the Wynn," he says, referring to an expensive resort casino on the Strip. "It would be unbelievable—'You mean, I get to eat food every day, for free?'" he says, indicating how someone from a developing country would react to free food offered by the soup kitchens in the homeless corridor.

He mentions wanting to have a homeless convention in Las Vegas, that a homeless convention would draw people here and that the repressive police response would shed light on how homeless people are treated here. "It would cause the bureaucracy to respond, and it only knows how to respond in one way—repressively."

When I mention that a nationwide protest by homeless people in Las Vegas, especially something like a mass sit-in on the Strip, might draw a repressive response similar to Selma's reaction to civil rights protesters, Manny agrees. I also mention that although he's arguing for the necessity of a revolution, there's a possibility that the system that created such an ongoing contradiction might simply continue indefinitely—poorer and poorer people might simply fight harder and harder and be forced to become more and more resourceful in order to just survive. I mention the idea that the repression might simply continue indefinitely, and Manny reacts strongly.

"The purpose would not be to ruin the economy of Las Vegas or harm its citizens," he says. "The purpose is to call to light the heavy-handedness [of police treatment of homeless people]. There is no check on the heavy-handedness now."

Later I consider Manny's idea for a massive, nationwide call to homeless people to converge in Las Vegas and protest. I wonder if it was kindled by that one slight he endured from the marshal who told him to "sleep out there with the rest of the bums." I think that Manny tends to be prone toward politeness but seems to rage against injustice. In his search for freedom, in his search to find his music, he does not want for much. He simply wants to be treated with dignity.

:: :: :: On May 10 I visit Manny and Marco again at Frank Wright Plaza. Marco asks to speak to me in private. We go into the nearby bus depot. Marco tells me he needs ten dollars for medicine to control his seizures. I ask him if he has insurance, thinking it's a co-pay. He says he doesn't. Although his story doesn't add up, I give him the ten.

It seems odd that he would need money today, Wednesday, since he tells me he got paid $191 on Monday. He says he needs to tell me something— he has been seeing a girl at work, Valerie. He says he that was sexually molested when he was eight and that whenever he has sex with a woman, he has flashbacks to his molestation. In order to overcome them, he says he, and Valerie, have been smoking heroin.

He tells me that he made a mistake with her and that he doesn't want to become a drug addict. He reminds me he has a seven-year-old son and says that he wants to be a good role model for him. The more I think about his story later that night, the more it bothers me. Though I said that I believed him when he said he made a mistake, I also mentioned that heroin is a serious drug. He says he will never use it intravenously, because he can't stand needles. He says Valerie is a bad influence on him and that he's even thought of quitting his job to get away from her. He's hoping that in a week she will be transferred to another restaurant, because she's not a good employee.

He also asks if I can give him ten more dollars on Friday, because he needs money for his bus pass next week. I say I will give it to him Friday. I begin to wonder if I'm being played for an easy mark—I wonder if Marco thinks he can get money out of me if only he says the right things.

When I see Manny in the park before I go home, he asks me in a vague way what I think about Marco and his situation. I tell Manny in general terms that I found it disturbing. I'm wondering if Manny is being intentionally vague with me because he doesn't want to betray Marco's trust; but I'm also wondering if this indicates a new bond of trust between Manny and me, because he has always emphasized to me that Marco is different from many of the others in the park who drink and/or use drugs.

:: :: :: Two days later, I go back to the park to give Marco the money he wanted, but he's not there. Manny says he's working a double shift, then adds that he *hopes* he's working a double shift. Manny then asks me again about what I know of Marco's situation. I say that Marco told me about his heroin use. I also tell Manny that Marco asked me for money and that I was now beginning to wonder if it was for drugs. I said I didn't know why Marco would need money on Wednesday since he got paid Monday.

At the Plaza over coffee, Manny says Marco told him that a bag of heroin costs twenty dollars. He says that on Monday, the night that Marco didn't come for coffee at the Plaza, he was with Valerie. Manny says Marco and Valerie smoked four bags each that night. He then says they smoked it all night and Marco said it felt great. The story accounts for Marco's money being gone. I grow depressed at the explanation.

I tell Manny that I really had hopes for Marco. Manny reminds me that Marco is in a very depressing situation, being homeless. Even Manny can understand the appeal of a ready escape for a night.

Manny also surprises me—he begins to talk about how he can get out of his situation. He refers to the article in a February issue of the *New Yorker* about new, more cost-effective ways to help some chronic homeless alcoholics through housing and harm reduction programs rather than their continuing, frequent use of social services and expensive emergency room visits (Gladwell 2006). He says he wishes a social worker would simply ask him what he needed. I take this as a cue and ask him. Strangely, he hedges. He says he wants to start a tour business or other self-employment, repeating that if he really wanted to, he could find work for five to six dollars an hour with just a half-hour of knocking on doors. He also confuses me, saying that he's not like other homeless people out here, again telling me that for him this is more like "an experiment." He then tells me he's been living for months on virtually nothing, which I always assumed was because the homeless people I spoke to *had* nothing. I ask him about when he can begin collecting Social Security. He says in a couple of years.

:: :: :: On May 19 I go to the McDonald's in the Plaza to see if Manny is there; I should have seen him yesterday but couldn't make it. It's 8:30 P.M., and I see Manny, Marco, and Ed all having food. I haven't seen Marco in weeks. We shake hands and he is very happy to see me.

Marco says "I have a surprise for you," and hands me something. It's a ticket, in his name, for a Greyhound bus leaving at 1 A.M. for Ft. Lauderdale, Florida. He bought it this morning for $186.

Marco decided to go back to live with his brother and son. Marco explains that his brother owns an air duct business, so he will work for him. He's very happy tonight, buying everybody food. He buys me a McDonald's apple pie and soda, despite my protests.

For the last ten days he has been in a halfway house called TLC. The managers took part of his check, and he lived in a room with three other men. The room had bunk beds and a television—he said it was the first television he had watched consistently in a long time. He regularly had to attend Alcoholics Anonymous and Narcotics Anonymous meetings. He felt like he could now go back to Florida and get the same level of support there through AA and NA. He thought his brother, who is older, would help him.

Marco goes to the bathroom, and Ed leaves. When Marco returns, he says he wants to keep in contact with Manny and asks me if he can do that by sending e-mails to me. I tell him sure and write down my e-mail address again. We begin walking to the Greyhound terminal. At the terminal Marco realizes he has two library books he needs to return. I offer to return them for him.

I ask Marco what his favorite memory was from the last ten months he's spent in Las Vegas. "Having coffee at the Plaza," he says, smiling. He liked the camaraderie. He also says he enjoyed time in the park with Manny. I asked him what his worst memory was from Las Vegas. "The drugs," he says.

He then asks me what the best part of my time in Las Vegas has been. I tell them both that I enjoyed conversation at the Plaza, too. I say that when I was hanging out with him and Manny I stopped feeling like a researcher and that I have made good friends. I tell them that I never felt like anyone whom I researched before had accepted me into their group, had confided in me, and had made me feel so welcome. I realized I had been missing a feeling of being liked just as I am, just for being me. Hanging out with them was one of the best experiences I had in the city.

My time with Manny and Marco reminded me of how important social connections are for people. We all long for warm social connections with people we care about. Despite Manny's idea that homelessness promotes a sense of camaraderie, many homeless people I have spoken to feel lonely, distrustful of others, and isolated. A problem for homeless people is that at times their material conditions work against their having good social connections with others. Not having friends or people to talk to is depressing, making it difficult for a homeless person to do all that is necessary to gain housing. At the same time, homeless people are encouraged to feel shame, to hate themselves for their homelessness. The nonjudgmental social support of homeless friends, however tentative it may be, is crucial for most homeless people to survive. Acceptance by and companionship with others is a key source of human happiness.

:: :: :: We wait in the long lines at the Greyhound Bus depot that snake in front of doors numbered one to five, which list different destinations. Marco's ticket is for 3,300 miles of travel. It will take him through Utah, Colorado, Kansas, Missouri, Illinois, Tennessee, Georgia, and Florida. He will spend the next fifty-eight hours either waiting for or riding on a bus.

As the driver announces that he is now taking tickets and the line prepares to move, Marco reaches out and surprises me with a hug. He also has a warm embrace for Manny, who razzes him about his love of baseball and the Mets. "Oh God, it's happening," he says, exhaling, his eyes welling up as the line begins moving forward.

Manny immediately says his final goodbye and begins walking away before Marco reaches the head of the line. Though I felt it was a premature exit, I follow him.

We leave the terminal, but I ask Manny to wait for a second so I can look back through the windows at Marco. I want to make sure he gives the driver the ticket and gets on the bus. I want to experience the moment, to see him leaving the city and to feel his hope.

DISCUSSION

What makes people happy? Quality of life surveys in the United States reveal that social values such as love and romance, warm family and friend relationships, feelings of autonomy and control, and good self-esteem outrank material values like economic security and success (Jhally 2000). While basic material comfort is important, these surveys indicate that, after a certain point, material wealth does not contribute substantially to individual happiness.

Marco wanted to be happy. He enjoyed communicating and spending time with his friends. He wanted to have good romantic relationships. His bipolar disorder, suicidal thoughts, intermittent drug use, and childhood sexual abuse were factors that worked against his self-esteem, relationships, and, in particular, feeling a sense of autonomy and control. He also seemed to feel a strong sense of shame because of his homelessness, feelings that likely undermined his ability to address his other problems. I thought that his returning to Florida to work with his brother was a great plan. His son's presence might well encourage him to attain greater personal stability through steady work and by treating his bipolar disorder with medication. A strong, supportive social environment also seemed his best hope for addressing and/or managing deeply rooted personal problems like his childhood sexual abuse, illegal drug use, depression, and impulsivity.

Manny also seemed to want happiness through individual freedom, autonomy, and control. Because he was in his sixties, his personality and sense of self seemed more stable than Marco's. His knowledge of existential and Eastern philosophies suggested that he knew happiness did not come from material wealth. He called homelessness his "experiment," and because he asked me not to specify details of his personal history, he rarely discussed with me his background or the circumstances leading to his homelessness. I do not think he thought less of himself because of his homelessness, as Marco did. I knew he relished the freedom to think and make plans to start small businesses or create social movements to improve the lives of local homeless people. I also know Manny despised the "heavy-handedness" of local police and government officials, whose procedures and policies ultimately led to his harassment for homeless practices when, as he pointed out, he harmed no one.

Manny, Marco, and their friend's stories showed men who were on the fringes of Las Vegas's economy but who still had to live. Their lives centered on dealing with their individual demons and acquiring food and small comforts. Though the men I met in Circle Park and Frank Wright Plaza had many personal problems, I strongly felt these were not bad people. They were people with problems in a bad situation.

I also felt happiest during this period of my research in Las Vegas. I enjoyed the companionship of these fellows in the park, men who talked to me about their days, who liked thoughtful discussion, and who didn't drink, at least around me. Toward the end of my research I began to feel awkward about the small amount of money I regularly gave them and wondered at times about the effect it had on my research and on our relationship. Five dollars seemed such an inconsequential amount to me, but the men in Circle Park and in Frank Wright Plaza would look at the bill in their hands with awe. When Marco asked for more money than I wanted to give him, I said no, setting a boundary. Such boundaries are key to healthy friendships, but they could perhaps reinforce a sense of hopelessness and worthlessness in someone grasping at straws out of desperation because he or she cannot get sustained help and social support in the community.

I hope Marco and Manny still think of me as a friend today.

ELEVEN

Updates

In this book I describe encounters with some people, like Ricky, Ron, Jessi, Kevin, Manny, and Marco, whom I was able to see on several occasions and over several weeks. Additionally, I was able to catch up with three of these people (Ricky from chapter 1, Jessi from chapter 2, and Manny from chapter 10) several months after our last encounter.

:: :: :: On April 17, 2006, I am exiting the Rescue Mission with a homeless friend when I see Ricky standing outside the gate. We greet each other and shake hands. It had been five months since I had last seen him or attempted to contact him and Ron at the Budget Motel.

He said he and Ron had a falling-out several months ago. He stopped living with Ron in November.

"He was a slob. I couldn't stand always having to pick up after his lazy ass. I was getting so tired of him sitting around, not doing anything for himself. He would just work two days a week, and sit around the room."

When I ask Ricky if Ron still works at the bar on Fremont where we partied, Ricky says he doesn't care. He hasn't seen him in months.

"Once he started complaining about the way I was chewing my *gum*," he said, exasperated. "I told him, 'Just keep playing your damn video game.' I was so angry, I thought we were gonna fight, so I knew that was it. I packed up my things when he was gone the next day and I left."

I asked him about his security job on Fremont Street. He said he left that too, around the same time. He said he tried various jobs and moved in with a roommate who ended up being a drug user. He railed against room-mates in Las Vegas.

"You can't find people who will just work a job and pay the rent. There's always some other issue. Next thing you know, they're drinking too much, or they're doing drugs, and it's like, 'Oh no, I know he's gonna stop going to work.' The writing's on the wall."

He said he had been staying at a hotel for a few days with a friend, a young Caucasian man who stood nearby but who didn't introduce himself. They finally ran out of money, and Ricky was given a bed at the Mission for one week, which was what he was now waiting for.

"I never come down here to this part of town," he said.

He said his girlfriend, whom I met briefly at the DTC when they were heading to the airport, had successfully delivered their child, a girl, back home in Ohio. His daughter was now four months old.

His girlfriend had come back to Las Vegas to live with him, but his lack of money complicated things. While he was staying at the Rescue Mission, she was staying with his daughter at the Shade Tree.

"We're all gonna get a place," he said. I remembered him using nearly the same phrase when he wanted to get housing with Ron. "I got a new job starting next week. It's a division of Sony."

He says he's not much into partying anymore, but he still likes to gam-ble once in a while.

He talks for several minutes about how he's still working hard to make it here, and says that he refuses to give up. He says this situation is tempo-rary, maybe only for a few weeks.

"The most important thing was for [my girlfriend] to get shelter, because otherwise she's outside during the daytime trying to nurse a four-month-old."

He says he wants to eventually get enough money together to start a Laundromat. He says that most of the Laundromats in this city are run-down and filthy. He says a nice Laundromat, maybe with a pool table and some video games in it, would be something people would like and would be profitable.

Ricky takes down my phone number and says we should all go get something to eat next week, at Main Street Station near the Fremont

Street Experience. The guards call all the men who were assigned a bed number that night, and he pulls his rolling suitcase inside the gate.

That was the last time I saw Ricky.

:: :: :: Earlier that same April morning, my phone rings. It's Jessi. She is calling from Albuquerque, New Mexico. She has just moved into her new apartment, which she is in the process of furnishing. She had been looking through her old papers and had found my contact information. She said she remembered me and thought she would call. I tell her I'm glad to hear from her and that I've thought of her many times when I've been to Frank Wright Plaza.

"I'm getting healthy again, exercising, going for walks. I live by the mountains. It's beautiful here."

She remembers the day she left Las Vegas—December 7. I told her that I thought I saw her around the courthouse in late November with the last guy she was dating. "Yeah, he was bad news," she said. "I had to get away from that.

"It was a period of my life where I had to learn some things."

I say that sometimes Las Vegas is a good place for people to get away from. I also said that I remembered something a police officer in Las Vegas once told me: One of the first things that happens to homeless people there is that they become victims.

"Yeah, that happened to me. I was victimized. Bad things happened to me. But I was a victim of my own self."

I think about how our sense of self changes over time. Others hurt us, but we also hurt ourselves. We change our minds about who we are, about what we want to be, and about what we can be.

"I can't believe I was asking people for money," she says at one point, laughing.

:: :: :: "I'm going back to school again in May," Jessi says. "I'm going to be a med tech here. Right now I'm doing telephone sales. The pay sucks. I tried to get on assistance here, but because of [my] lawsuit I have to work. It's OK, but the pay is bad. But work keeps my mind off things."

I ask her how she chose Albuquerque. She says, "That's what I could afford a bus ticket to." I ask about her daughter in California. She says that her daughter is doing great and that she's coming out for a visit.

I mention her old friends, saying that I saw S.P.

"He's out of jail?" she said, surprised.

I told her he was and that he looked healthy. He seemed to be moving quite well, probably because he had to sober up in jail.

"I bought him that cane, you know," she reminded me.

I mention that I had seen Ebony in January and that his eyes were bloodshot.

"He was doing drugs, using a needle," she said.

She asks how long I am staying in Las Vegas. Late June, I answer.

She invites me to come visit her. She says the Native Americans are going to have a powwow there this summer and that I should see it. I take down her address and tell her I will send her some things, including a clipping from the local newspaper about my research.

I ask about her leg. She said it's good, healthy. She's waiting for the settlement from the accident to get a new one. She says it seems like the defense lawyers are delaying the process so they won't have to pay.

"I need my leg. I just want my leg," she says.

After we hang up, I realize the sound of her voice is reminding me of her face. I was picturing her smile.

:: :: :: On July 1, 2006, on my drive back from Las Vegas to Nebraska I visit Jessi in Albuquerque. Her sparsely furnished apartment is a large one-bedroom unit near the old town area. She pays around four hundred dollars a month. She's working as a dispatcher for a cab company.

She says she had a plan to leave Las Vegas, and she had resources that most homeless people don't have. She got on the Internet and found a job before she left Las Vegas, and she also found her apartment. She had arrived in Albuquerque before her lease was set to start. She had to temporarily stay in what she called a "crack hotel." She begged her landlord to move in early, and he gave her the key. She had no electricity, heat, or television for four days. She says she felt suicidal. The people at work warmed to her, though, and they checked in on her. The cabbies now regularly give her free rides to and from work—she says she tries to pay them, but they refuse the money. Jessi recently failed her driver's test but wants to take it again. She walks to a 7-Eleven several blocks away for her groceries. She says she would have to take three buses to get to work.

She tells me several times, "I had to get out of Las Vegas or I was gonna die."

:: :: :: During my visit she clarifies several things for me. When she traveled to surf, she went to Australia, Brazil, and Hawaii. Her parents would pay for the trips. She was an avid cross-country skier, and she was learning to skydive when she had her accident, which was in 2002. She says she still dreams about surfing.

Her accident involved a moving company. A well-known legal firm in New York is representing her. She said that she wants $15 million but that they are going to wait until the last minute in 2009, seven years after the initial suit, to settle or go to trial. She also said she is interested in a bionic leg, but that would cost so much now that it would leave her very little to pay for the medical bills for the rest of her life.

"Once they see the pictures of how I was back then, and hear about my life compared to now—I have artificial arteries made of Gortex. I have clotting and am supposed to take blood thinner. When they see me then and now, they'll have to rule for me."

She says she and her former boyfriend Terrence had drug and gambling problems. When she was attacked, she says it was because Terrence had left her alone. He still calls her sometimes from Las Vegas, and she says he's doing well, working at Goodwill and now renting a place.

She plans on staying in Albuquerque a year. Her daughter is doing well in San Diego. She has started dating a young man, and she and Jessi talk about that. Jessi gives her advice on making decisions and says there are consequences for every decision. She feels good, though, because she gave her daughter "her center." She recently asked her daughter what she would think if she had a baby brother or sister, and Melissa said, "Mom, what are you doing?" making Jessi laugh. Melissa plans to visit Jessi in Albuquerque in October for the local hot air balloon festival.

Jessi seems more nervous talking to me in person then on the phone or when she was in Frank Wright Plaza. When I called her from the road she couldn't remember who I was, reminding me of her blackouts. She still drinks occasionally and still smokes. She also says she is in constant pain and is having a hard time walking any distance lately. Before we go out to dinner, she tries to think of something to give her leg extra padding for the walk, even though I assure her we won't need to go far.

While driving and at dinner, she takes a cell phone call from a woman friend from work. Jessi thinks the woman has a crush on her, but says they are good friends. She says the woman is very abrasive, but they tell each other the truth and respect each other.

She says, though, that she mostly just works and stays home. She rarely goes out on the weekends. "I'm a hermit now," she says, smiling. She says she doesn't want to introduce people into her life right now, because "people love drama. I don't need drama. I create enough of my own." She's afraid having close friends would bring her down and get her back into bad habits she does not want.

:: :: ::   I tell her that when I knew her in Las Vegas, it seemed that she was having an identity crisis. She says she had to come to terms with losing her leg, and that she has now accepted it. She'll never be the person she was, but she says she has found peace.

After dinner as I drive her home, she points out a house that is condemned that she'd like to buy and fix up. She is proud to show me her neighborhood and her garden, where she grows tomatoes. Her next step, she says, is to buy a car.

I have to begin driving back to Nebraska. I say I was glad to see her as I give her a big hug. I take a picture of her. She is smiling, in front of her house.

:: :: ::   After I left Las Vegas in June 2006, Manny and I kept in touch through Amanda Haymond. Amanda was the editor of *Forgotten Voice*, a newspaper for homeless people and homeless advocates in Las Vegas.[1] Amanda would run into Manny in Frank Wright Plaza every few weeks, and sometimes Amanda would surprise me by putting Manny on her cell phone to talk to me. Eventually, Amanda saw less of Manny.

In August 2006, the *Las Vegas Review-Journal* ran an article about the Las Vegas City Council having recently passed a provision in an ordinance that "made it illegal to sleep within 500 feet of human urine or feces" (Curtis 2006). Although the ordinance was first passed unanimously by the Las Vegas City Council in August 2006, it was revised on September 20 and the provision mentioned above was deleted. Despite that change, Las Vegas Police Department officers arrested three homeless men later that year for violating the deleted portion of the ordinance. One of those men turned out to be Manny.

Local homeless activists, along with local American Civil Liberties Union (ACLU) Executive Director Gary Peck, became involved. Attorney E. Brent Bryson and the Las Vegas ACLU filed a lawsuit in federal court in December 2006 on behalf of the three men who had been arrested and had spent a night in jail.

On March 29, 2007, the *Las Vegas Review-Journal* reported that a $45,000 settlement had been reached on behalf of the men. Each plaintiff would receive $10,000, while their lawyer Bryson received $15,000 (Curtis 2007b). Amanda said she had not seen Manny in the park since the ruling.

:: :: :: In early November 2007, I returned briefly to Las Vegas to speak about my first book on local homelessness at the annual Vegas Valley Book Festival. I presented my work in a panel discussion with Matthew O'Brien, a local journalist who had written about homeless people living in the underground tunnels in the city. While I gave my presentation, a man in the back of the room, collecting complimentary food, drew my attention. It was Manny.

I waited until after our panel finished and then ran over to say hello. He looked nearly the same—he still had the gray beard, the baseball cap, the jeans, and the large duffel bag that held his belongings. Amanda joined us as we left the meeting room so we could all talk and Manny could sit and eat.

Manny told us that his money from the settlement was spent. He was still sleeping at Frank Wright Plaza and still eating at the Rescue Mission. I was in disbelief. I later did the math and realized that the $10,000 settlement, which sounded like a windfall at the time, is not necessarily a life-altering amount for someone who is destitute. He had to pay taxes on the settlement. It had also been eight months since the settlement, and many people in the United States could spend $1,000 a month on basic expenses like housing, food, transportation, and health care. I also did not know what debts Manny had incurred before the settlement.

Although the three plaintiffs' initial lawsuit sought damages of $2 million, they had settled for far less. Their attorney at the time pointed out that "these individuals are not capable of maintaining and sustaining an ongoing litigation. This quick money to them represents an ability for them to get back on their feet" (Curtis 2007b). Manny said he was able to live off of the streets for a while; but without a steady income after the settlement, he could not rent an apartment long term.

Manny, Amanda, and I chatted for a half-hour, reminiscing about old times and discussing the current difficulties homeless people faced in the city. Before we parted, Manny asked me for a copy of my first book. As I signed it for him, I grew emotional, realizing that not much was changing in Las Vegas and that Manny, someone I had spent so much time talking to, was still sleeping in the park.

I thought about Marco's idea that Manny didn't seem as ashamed of his homelessness as are most homeless people, that Manny seemed to either be resigned to it or that he didn't seem to mind it. I watched Manny push the book into his overstuffed duffel bag along with a few sandwiches. After he said goodbye, shuffling slightly under the bag and its additional weight, I wondered how long he could afford to keep carrying it.

Epilogue

The people I interviewed in this work often expressed an identity rooted in both freedom and poverty. They were poor, but in a wealthy environment. Homeless people I met in Las Vegas were frequently destitute but were also trying to partake of the city, deciding to purchase nonessential items and engaging in leisure pursuits for the sake of enjoyment or simply distraction from their problems. The rhetoric of homelessness as a "lifestyle" reflects the belief that homeless people are "choosing" poverty. Such rhetoric often reinforces stereotypes about homeless individuals that emphasize their character flaws, leading to misunderstandings about homelessness and often ill-conceived public policy rooted in blaming the victim.

The lifestyle choices of the homeless people I interviewed must be understood in context. I hope their stories help us collectively rethink judgments about the morality and/or appropriateness of their choices. Instead, their stories might lead us to ask more ominous questions: To what extent have we created a permanent category of people marginal to "our" competitive, capitalist economy? In the postmodern era, to what extent does that economy include and reward people based on *their* image, and what groups are likely excluded from this economy? Remembering that every human life involves long periods where that person does not or cannot work, to what extent does our society provide healthy and supportive environments for those citizens who, for whatever reasons, are outside the traditional economy? To what extent should such supportive environments be considered rights? Have we created a group of superfluous, permanently marginalized people, and if so, *what should they do with themselves?*

:: :: ::   I have argued that we need to listen to what homeless people are telling us—that they have valuable insights into what led to their homelessness, the troubles they face, and what would help them now. First and foremost, they are strongly suggesting that they *want and/or need housing*. The streets are a painful place. Their lack of housing exacerbates their problems and/or interferes with their facing and addressing them. Their stories suggest that they frequently encounter harassment and disrespect from members of the larger housed community and even by those charged with helping them.

They seem also to suggest that *they need a sense of community and connection to others*. If they cannot participate in a healthy community, they will join or create unhealthy communities and/or relationships, because the worst thing for most people is having no connection to others at all. Their stories and actions suggest that they have needs and wants and that they will try and find ways to get their needs and wants met. If it is through trying to work, scavenging for goods, prostitution, stealing, using new technologies, asking people for help, or other means, they will be resourceful enough to keep alive. They also seem to be saying and showing that if the conditions leading to social problems like homelessness go unaddressed, those problems will invariably grow worse. It also seems that, in the long run, *the problems that stem from homeless people's lack of housing could well cost taxpayers more than it would have cost to provide them with housing and substantial help in the first place.*

If we take what homeless people say seriously, they suggest that *housing should be considered a basic human right.* The United States is the wealthiest country on Earth. If we care so much about the value of human life, as so many polls and politicians suggest, then we should care about all people, even those (perhaps especially those) who are marginal and hurt. By discussing many of the troubles they faced as children and adults, they suggest that they would likely benefit from compassion rather than judgment.

Listening to homeless people reveals that some people at some points in their life simply cannot find a place in the "productive" world (Marin 1987). Not being employed, or not having access to appropriate care for personal problems, should not result in a stigmatized identity at best or a death sentence at worst. We all have troubles at times, we all are dependent on others at times, and at some point each of us needs help. Constructively addressing homelessness then requires that we first recognize our shared humanity.

Notes

INTRODUCTION

1. Housing first programs, as the name implies, are social service programs that provide housing to a homeless person before he or she is asked about making behavioral changes. The housing first model was first developed by the Pathways to Housing agency in New York City in 1992. The model stresses that housing is a basic human right and that homeless people are consumers who make choices based on their needs and goals. For studies on the effectiveness of housing first programs, see Padgett, Gulcur, and Tsemberis (2006), Tsemberis and Eisenberg (2000), and Tsemberis, Gulcur and Nakae (2004). Harm reduction programs are frequently used with populations engaged in self-harming behavior such as drug users, alcoholics, and prostitutes. Their core principle is to try to reduce the harm that people engaged in such behaviors might be doing to themselves by providing them with some social services (such as clean needles and condoms) rather than trying to deny help until they change. Harm reduction programs assume that people engaged in self-harming behavior might not be able to change their behaviors immediately because of addiction or, in the case of prostitution, a need to make money. See Ending Community Homeless Coalition (2009) and the Wellesley Institute (2009) for studies on the development and effectiveness of harm reduction programs.

5 : THE DISCONNECT OF MENTAL ILLNESS

1. The Moulin Rouge was Las Vegas's first desegregated resort and casino, famous for housing and entertaining celebrities such as Sammy Davis Jr. and Pearl Bailey. It is in the homeless corridor. The majority of the building sat in seeming disuse for several years in the early 2000s, while some old rooms were rented as apartments. The structure has since had several fires, and in 2009 a large fire consumed the building (Mower 2009).

11 : UPDATES

1. The development of the paper toward the end of my study was an important step toward self-organizing among local homeless people. Forgotten Voice also augmented street networks by providing homeless people with up-to-date information about services and the requirements they would need to meet for some services and for employment. The paper also helped homeless people share stories, reminding them that whatever problems they faced, they were not alone.

Bibliography

Anderson, N. 1961. *The hobo: The sociology of the homeless man.* Chicago: University of Chicago Press. (Orig. pub. 1923).

Anderton, F., and J. Chase. 1997. *Las Vegas: The success of excess.* London: Ellipsis London.

Anucha, U. 2003. *A study of tenant exits from housing for homeless people.* Canadian Mortgage and Housing Corporation report.

Archibold, R. C. 2006. Las Vegas makes it illegal to feed homeless in parks. *New York Times,* July 28. http://www.nytimes.com/2006/07/28/us/28homeless.html.

Babula, J. 2003. Flooding leaves mold worries: Quick cleanups urged to avoid respiratory problems in homes. *Las Vegas Review-Journal,* August 27. http://www.reviewjournal.com/lvrj_home/2003/Aug-27-Wed-2003/news/22027333.htm.

Bahr, H. 1973. *Skid row: An introduction to disaffiliation.* New York: Oxford University Press.

Bahr, H., and T. Caplow. 1973. *Old men drunk and sober.* New York: New York University Press.

Bauman, Z. 1995. *Life in fragments.* London: Blackwell.

———. 2007. *Consuming life.* London: Polity.

BBC News. 2002. Swiss help for heroin addicts. February 9. http://news.bbc.co.uk/1/hi/programmes/from_our_own_correspondent/1810039.stm.

BBC News. 2007. A fix on the state. November 19. http://news.bbc.co.uk/2/hi/uk_news/magazine/7099138.stm.

Blumberg, L., T. Shipley, and J. Moor. 1971. The skid row man and the skid row status community. *Quarterly Journal of Studies on Alcohol* 32:912.

Bogue, D. 1963. *Skid row in American cities.* Chicago: University of Chicago Press.

Bocchino, R. 1999. *Emotional literacy: To be a different kind of smart.* Thousand Oaks, CA: Corwin Press.

Borchard, K. 2000. Fear of and sympathy toward homeless men in Las Vegas. *Humanity and Society* 24 (1): 3–18.

———. 2005. *The word on the street: Homeless men in Las Vegas.* Reno: University of Nevada.

Bristol, E. 2006. Bigmouth strikes again: Mayor Oscar Goodman opens up a six-pack of hate on the homeless. *Las Vegas City Life,* June 29. http://www.lasvegascitylife.com/articles/2006/06/29/local_news/news03.txt.

Casey, J. V. 2005. Shift seen in homeless count. *Las Vegas Review-Journal,* February 24.

———. 2002a. 'Bumfights': Cause for concern: Homeless fighter regrets role. *Las Vegas Review-Journal,* December 27, 1B.

———. 2002b. 'Bumfights' video leads to charges. *Las Vegas Review-Journal,* September 26,: 1B.

———. 2001. Leaders gather to discuss valley's homeless problem. *Las Vegas Review-Journal,* October 25. http://www.lvrj.com/lvrj_home/2001/Oct-25-Thu-2001/news/17301896.html.

Casey, J. V., and M. Squires. 2002. 'Bumfights' video prompts call for investigation from congressman. *Las Vegas Review-Journal,* June 24, 2B.

CBS News. 2006. 'Bumfight' videos inspired joy-killing: Florida teen tells Ed Bradley he killed homeless man 'for fun.' *60 Minutes,* September 28. http://www.cbsnews.com/stories/2006/09/28/60minutes/main2049967_page3.shtml (accessed December 12, 2006).

Clotfelter, C., and P. Cook. 1991. *Selling hope: State lotteries in America.* Cambridge, MA: Harvard University Press.

Curtis, L. 2006. Don't sleep near feces or urine: That's what new Las Vegas ordinance aimed at homeless mandates. *Las Vegas Review-Journal,* August 18. http://www.reviewjournal.com/lvrj_home/2006/Aug-18-Fri-2006/news/9130007.html.

———. 2007a. Crisis chronicled: Veteran homelessness increasing. *Las Vegas Review-Journal,* November 8. http://www.lvrj.com/news/11105406.html.

———. 2007b. Three scoop up cash after false arrest: Homeless men settle in sleeping-near-feces case. *Las Vegas Review-Journal,* March 29. http://www.reviewjournal.com/lvrj_home/2007/Mar-29-Thu-2007/news/13450918.html.

Davidson, L. 2003. *Living outside mental illness: Qualitative studies of recovery in schizophrenia.* New York: NYU Press.

Davis, A. 2000. *The prison industrial complex.* Oakland, CA: AK Press. Compact disc.

de Botton, A. 2004. *Status anxiety.* New York: Pantheon.

Donzinger, S. 1996. *The real war on crime: Report of the national criminal justice commission.* New York: Harper Perennial.

Duneier, M. 1999. *Sidewalk.* New York: Farrar, Straus and Giroux.

Dyer, J. 2000. *Perpetual prisoner machine: How America profits from crime.* New York: Basic Books.

Eighner, L. 1994. *Travels with Lizbeth: Three years on the road and on the streets.* New York: Ballantine Books.

Ending Community Homelessness Coalition. 2009. *Solutions for homeless chronic alcoholics in Austin.* September. www.frontsteps.org/ (accessed November 21, 2009).

Esping-Andersen, G. 1990. *The three worlds of welfare capitalism.* Princeton: Princeton University Press.

———. 2002. *Why we need a new welfare state.* Oxford: Oxford University Press.

Findlay, J. M. 1986. *People of chance: Gambling in American society from Jamestown to Las Vegas.* Oxford: Oxford University Press.

Fox Piven, F., and R. Cloward. 1971. *Regulating the poor: The functions of public welfare.* New York: Vintage.

Gabler, N. 1998. *Life, the movie.* New York: Knopf.

Gergen, K. 2000. *The saturated self.* New York: Basic Books. (Orig. pub. 1991).

Gladwell, M. 2006. Dept. of social services: Million-dollar Murray. *New Yorker,* February 13.

———. 2009. *What the dog saw: And other adventures.* New York: Little, Brown, and Company.

Goffman, E. 1959. *The presentation of self in everyday life.* New York: Anchor.

———. 1961a. *Asylums.* New York: Doubleday.

———. 1961b. *Encounters: Two studies in the sociology of interaction.* Indianapolis: Bobbs-Merrill.

Goleman, D. 1995. *Emotional intelligence: Why it can matter more than IQ.* New York: Bantam.

Gottdiener, M., C. Collins, and D. R. Dickens. 1999. *Las Vegas: The social production of an all-American city.* London: Wiley-Blackwell.

Hess, A. 1993. *Viva Las Vegas: After-hours architecture.* New York: Chronicle Books.

Hoffman, L., and B. Coffey. 2008. Dignity and indignation: How people experiencing homelessness view services and providers. *Social Science Journal* 45 (2): 207–22.

Hopper, K. 2003. *Reckoning with homelessness.* Ithaca: Cornell University Press.

Hopper, K., and J. Baumohl. 1994. Held in abeyance: Rethinking homelessness and advocacy. *American Behavioral Scientist* 37:522–52.

Huard, R. 2005. 'Bumfights' producers may face jail time. *San Diego Union-Tribune,* January 20, B-1.

Jhally, S. 2000. Advertising at the edge of the apocalypse. In *Critical studies in media commercialism,* ed. R. Anderson and L. Strate, 27–39. Oxford: Oxford University Press.

Lachenmeyer, N. 2000. *The outsider: A journey into my father's struggle with madness.* New York: Broadway Books.

Landreth, K., C. Brandenburg, and S. Gottschalk. 2005. Mental health problems and needs in Nevada. *Social health of Nevada report.* http://www.unlv.edu/centers/cdclv/healthnv/mentalhealth.html.

Langan, P., and D. Levin. 2002. Recidivism of prisoners released in 1994. Bureau of Justice Statistics. http://bjs.ojp.usdoj.gov/index.cfm?ty=pbdetail&iid=1134.

Lardner, J., and D. A. Smith, eds. 2007. *Inequality matters: The growing economic divide in America and its poisonous consequences.* Foreword by Bill Moyers. New York: New Press.

Laurance, J. 2006. Heroin: The solution? *Independent* (London), June 2.

Lopez, S. 2008. *The soloist: A lost dream, an unlikely friendship, and the redemptive power of music.* New York: Putnam.

Marcus, A. 2006. *Where have all the homeless gone? The making and unmaking of a crisis.* New York: Berghahn Books.

Marin, P. 1987. Helping and hating the homeless. *Harper's Magazine.* January, 39–49.

Maslow, A. 1943. A theory of human motivation. *Psychological Review* 50 (4): 370–96.

Miller, A. 1997. *The drama of the gifted child: The search for the true self.* New York: Basic Books.

Mills, C. W. 1959. *The sociological imagination.* New York: Oxford University Press.

Mitzman, A. 1985. *The iron cage: An historical interpretation of Max Weber.* New Brunswick, NJ: Transaction Books.

Mizruchi, E. H. 1987. *Regulating society.* 2nd ed. Chicago: University of Chicago Press.

Moehring, E. P., and M. S. Green. 2005. *Las Vegas: A centennial history.* Reno: University of Nevada Press.

Moller, J. 2001. Police look for homeless link to crime. *Las Vegas Review-Journal,* July 1.

———. 2002. LV officials study charges against makers of video. *Las Vegas Review-Journal,* June 28, 3B.

Mower, L. 2009. Moulin Rouge site goes up in smoke: Fire sweeps through apartments at historic casino. *Las Vegas Review-Journal,* May 7. http://www.lvrj.com /news/44517007.html.

Nadelmann, E. 1995. Europe's drug prescription: Innovative approaches to the drug problem from over there. *Rolling Stone,* January 25.

National Coalition for Homeless Veterans. 2010. Facts and media. http://www.nchv. org/background.cfm.

National Coalition for the Homeless. 2004. *Illegal to be homeless.* http://www.national homeless.org/publications/crimreport2004/problem.html.

———. 2007. *Hate, violence, and death on main street USA, 2007.* http://www.national homeless.org/getinvolved/projects/hatecrimes/video.html.

———. 2008. *A dream denied: The criminalization of homelessness in U.S. cities.* http:// www.nationalhomeless.org/factsheets/criminalization.html.

National Institute of Corrections. 2010. *Statistics for the state of Nevada.* http://www .nicic.org/features/statestats/?State=NV (accessed January 20, 2010).

Nibert, D. 1999. *Hitting the lottery jackpot: State governments and the taxing of dreams.* New York: Monthly Review Press.

O'Hara, Brett. 2004. Do medical out-of-pocket expenses thrust families into poverty? *Journal of Health Care for the Poor and Underserved* 15 (1) : 63–75.

Padgett, D., L. Gulcur, and S. Tsemberis. 2006. Housing first services for people who are homeless with co-occurring serious mental illness and substance abuse. *Research on Social Work Practice* 16 (1): 74–83.

Parenti, C. 2000. *Lockdown America: Police and prisons in the age of crisis.* London: Verso.

Parker, R. 1994. *Flesh peddlers and warm bodies: The temporary help industry and its workers.* New Brunswick, NJ: Rutgers University Press.

Postman, N. 1985. *Amusing ourselves to death.* New York: Penguin.

Pratt, T. 2006. No picnic this time. *Las Vegas Sun,* March 7. http://www.lasvegassun.com/news/2006/mar/07/no-picnic-this-time/.

Putnam, R., and L. Feldstein. 2000. *Bowling alone: The collapse and revival of American community.* New York: Simon and Schuster.

Raphael, S., and M. Stoll. 2009. *Do prisons make us safer? The benefits and costs of the prison boom.* New York: Russell Sage Foundation.

Ropers, R. 1988. *The invisible homeless: A new urban ecology.* New York: Human Sciences Press.

Rothman, H. 2003. *Neon metropolis: How Las Vegas started the twenty-first century.* New York: Routledge.

Schumacher, G. 2004. *Sun, sin & suburbia: An essential history of modern Las Vegas.* Las Vegas: Stephens Press.

Shinn, M., and S. Tsemberis. 1999. Is housing the cure for homelessness? In *Addressing community problems: Research and intervention,* ed. X. Arriaga and S. Oskamp, 52–77. Thousand Oaks, CA: Sage.

Shlay, A., and P. Rossi. 1992. Social science research and contemporary studies of homelessness. *Annual Review of Sociology* 18:129–60.

Silver, K. 2001. Goodman's solution hits a snag. *Las Vegas Weekly* 11 (31): 7.

Snow, D., and L. Anderson. 1993. *Down on their luck: A study of homeless street people.* Berkeley: University of California Press.

Snow, D., S. Baker, and L. Anderson. 1988. On the precariousness of measuring insanity in insane contexts. *Social Problems* 35:92–96.

Snow, D., S. Baker, L. Anderson, and M. Martin. 1986. The myth of pervasive mental illness among the homeless. *Social Problems* 33 (5): 407–23.

Spradley, J. 1970. *You owe yourself a drunk: An ethnography of urban nomads.* Boston: Little, Brown and Company.

Squires, M., and J. V. Casey. 2002. Film cashes in on street scenes. *Las Vegas Review-Journal,* May 5. http://www.reviewjournal.com/lvrj_home/2002/May-05-Sun-2002/news/18662641.html.

Tough, P. 2008. *Whatever it takes: Geoffrey Canada's quest to change Harlem and America.* New York: Houghton Mifflin Harcourt.

Tremblay, J. 2009. *Keeping the homeless housed: An exploratory study of determinants of homelessness in the Toronto community.* Toronto: Wellesley Institute.

Tsemberis, S., and C. Elfenbein. 1999. A perspective on voluntary and involuntary outreach services for the homeless mentally ill. *New Directions for Mental Health Services* 82:9–19.

Tsemberis, S., and R. Eisenberg. 2000. Pathways to housing: Supported housing for street-dwelling homeless individuals with psychiatric disabilities. *Psychiatric Services* 51 (4): 487–93.

Tsemberis, S., N. Gulcur, and M. Nakae. 2004. Housing first, consumer choice, and harm reduction for homeless individuals with a dual diagnosis. *American Journal of Public Health* 94 (4): 651–56.

Twitchell, J. 1991. *Carnival culture.* New York: Columbia University Press.

Wacquant, L. 2001. Deadly symbiosis. *Punishment & Society* 3 (1): 95–133.

Walters, H. 2001. The other strip. *City Life* 9 (35): 18–22.

Wellesley Institute. 2009. *Towards effective strategies for harm reduction housing.* Final Report. August. www.wellesleyinstitute.com.

Index